Back On The Streets

The Gary Moore Story

Brian Ireland

Back On The Streets

The Gary Moore Story

Brian Ireland

WP
WYMER
PUBLISHING
Bedford, England

First published in Great Britain in 2024
by Wymer Publishing
www.wymerpublishing.co.uk
Tel: 01234 326691
Wymer Publishing is a trading name of Wymer (UK) Ltd

ISBN: 978-1-915246-46-2
(also available in eBook)

Edited by Jerry Bloom

Typeset by Andy Bishop / Tusseheia Creative.
Printed by Halstan, Amersham, England.

A catalogue record for this book is available from the British Library.

Cover design: Tusseheia Creative
Front cover image © Alastair Thain / Pictorial Press Ltd / Alamy Stock Photo

Contents

Preface

Over a decade after his untimely death, Northern Irish musician Gary Moore remains something of an enigma. A private, sometimes troubled man, he nevertheless chose a profession that exposed him to public scrutiny. He coped with that contradiction by channelling his energies into his songwriting and guitar playing, expressing himself almost entirely through his music. This became the public-facing side of his life, with his private life only occasionally garnering media attention. Moore let his body of work speak for him, and on those occasions when he opted to give interviews, they were usually timed to promote music releases rather than provide reveal details of his private life, something which even now remains largely hidden from view. For those writing about Moore, this poses a conundrum: to what extent is it necessary to probe Moore's non-public life to understand and appreciate his music?

Aside from some insightful music journalism, very little has been written about Moore. An official biography by Harry Shapiro was included in the vinyl boxset *Blues and Beyond* (BMG 2017). This relatively short biography, entitled *I Can't Wait Until Tomorrow*, proved something of a disappointment for the Moore fanbase: despite the author having exclusive access to Moore's family, friends and fellow musicians, the finished work was somewhat disjointed and anecdotal, and fans were left awaiting a comprehensive, in-depth study.

When I first had the notion about three years ago to write my own biography of Moore, Shapiro's work was the sole competition; by the end of 2023, however, two further biographies of Moore had been published. One is by Shapiro (*Gary Moore The Official Biography*, Jawbone 2022) and is a more fleshed out version of his earlier work. The second is Martin Power's *White Knuckles: The Life of Gary Moore* (Omnibus Press, 2023), which is, at least in part, the product of interviews with friends, acquaintances, and fellow musicians. Power's work should therefore reveal more behind-the-scenes information than has thus far been unearthed.

In a 1987 interview with *Guitar World* magazine Moore explained that he preferred to keep his private life separate from the music business: 'When the two realms mix too much, sometimes it goes downhill', he said, somewhat enigmatically. Yet when asked if his lyrics had personal background, he responded: 'most of them do'.[1] In a separate interview that same year, Moore gave a specific example, explaining that the track 'Take A Little Time', from his *Wild Frontier* album, was based on a personal experience about someone he knew who had taken him for granted. He explained, however, that the lyrics might be interpreted in multiple ways, and could be about any kind of relationship.[2] It is notable that Moore chose not to use personal pronouns in the lyrics, so that the gender, and by extension the identity of the protagonists remained open to question.

A certain level of obfuscation such as this is typical of Moore: some of his lyrics are autobiographical, and on occasion he was willing to discuss that with music journalists if he believed it would generate interest in his music. Conversely, other lyrics pertain to more universal feelings and experiences that are easily accessible to a wider audience, yet Moore knew music journalists would find those songs of less interest.

His approach wasn't always consistent yet was guided by years of experience in the music industry, getting to know individual music journalists and news outlets, developing a stage persona, and learning how to balance public and private knowledge of his life. Over time, he became more media savvy and acquired increasing awareness of the value of a good soundbite or narrative hook that might generate interest in his music. For example, he often adopted an iconoclastic approach towards other musicians, speaking honestly about their real and perceived flaws, while knowing these comments would generate publicity and set tongues wagging.

Yet Moore remained secretive about most aspects of his private life, especially his relationships, his family, and his children. Furthermore, he seldom spoke about an event that undoubtedly affected him greatly, the incident that caused his facial scarring.

Initially, his record company claimed the injury happened in an automobile accident but over time stories emerged of an incident in a bar when Moore allegedly had a bottle or glass smashed against his face while protecting his girlfriend from some abuse. Because only those involved know what transpired, and Moore never revealed if or how it influenced his music, that story won't appear in these pages, except to note that Moore was clearly self-conscious of his disfigurement to the extent that in future publicity photos and on album and single cover designs, he often posed with the scarred side of his face looking away from the camera.

If Moore wished to keep his personal life and professional career separate, but also drew on personal experiences in his song writing, to what extent then is it necessary to discuss Moore's private life to understand his music? Surely some knowledge of Moore's character and private life can help illuminate his art.

Indeed, even on those occasions when he did not openly express in his music and lyrics his personality, his political and social views, or his internal demons, he likely drew on these experiences in the creative process. For instance, Moore disclosed how he drew on real-life events as inspiration for his 1983 song 'Empty Rooms', which was co-written with Neil Carter. Calling the song 'very personal', Moore said it was based at least in part on 'something I went through at one time — something that everyone goes through at one stage or another'.[3]

Foremost, then, this biography offers a different approach to that of Shapiro and Power in that it focuses mainly on Moore's public life, and it is for that reason that I have avoided making any more than passing reference to their work: after all, music was Moore's chosen mode of expression as well as his main interaction with the public sphere, albeit mediated as always by the commercial demands of the music industry. His attitude to life was articulated through his lyrics, guitar playing, promotional videos, stage costumes, and interviews, and exploring the critical response to his music is a useful way to measure how successful he was in expressing his emotions, concerns, and viewpoints.

Yet, it seems clear that at least some consideration of his private life is required when that approach leads to deeper and broader understanding of his music. This dual, balanced approach will provide relevant narrative context, as well as uncover motivations and meaning.

The second major concern for biographers is that of genre expectations. An axiom familiar to fiction writers is that the entire scope of literature has only seven basic plots.[4] In contrast, biographies of rock stars who died before their time usually have just one plot: someone exceptionally talented, often from an unlikely background, achieves fame and fortune, before being destroyed either by their own tragic failings, usually addiction to drink or drugs, or by the circumstances of their fame.

Certain elements of this story apply to Moore's life. For example, as Moore himself admitted, a white kid from Belfast likely wouldn't necessarily be most people's primary candidate to become a blues legend. However, this one-size-fits-all approach won't work for Moore as it cannot account for the passion of his music or its artistry and meaning.

Moreover, if Moore's music is considered in broader context, his story might begin not with the basic facts of his birth in Belfast in 1952, but instead maybe it originates a few decades earlier, in America, with the birth of the blues.

Whereas Moore's musical output included jazz, progressive rock, and heavy metal, it was in fact the blues that shaped his musical career. It is his journey from playing the blues in anonymous Belfast clubs, to his triumphant return to the blues later in life, that bookends and perhaps defines Moore's musical career and legacy. 'I went back to the music that I always loved', Moore explained, and that decision brought him the biggest commercial success of his career with the release of his eighth studio album, *Still Got The Blues* (1990).[5]

The pages that follow will trace this musical journey, from Moore's early experiences in Belfast, his stints in Thin Lizzy playing melodic rock and in Colosseum II playing jazz-rock fusion, and his solo career, which saw him become a heavy rock 'guitar hero' and then, finally, a modern-day blues legend. On this journey, recurring themes will emerge about Moore's character and motivations.

For instance, Moore had a single-minded determination to follow his own path regardless of the consequences. This was perhaps the main factor that shaped his music career.

A further recurring theme was his desire for perfection, which resulted not only in him being his own worst critic, but also led to numerous disagreements with fellow musicians. Connected to that was a kind of restless search for musical self-satisfaction, most evident in his embrace of a variety of musical genres.

Moreover, Moore worked hard to gain the respect of his musical peers, and in the process transformed himself from a guitar player who could, in a pinch, provide occasional backing vocals, to a fully-fledged singer-songwriter, composer, and lyricist. Almost every decision

Moore made can be understood by referring back to these character traits, and the challenges he set himself.

There are also recurring themes in the critical reception of Moore's music, some of which are positive and supportive, and some less so. Foremost was almost universal acknowledgement that Moore was an exceptional guitar player whose skill and passion raised him to a level above his rivals.

A further recurring conversation was about Moore's supposed peripatetic nature, which, many critics charged, hindered his path to popular success. There was also a perception that he was a prickly character who found it hard to play second fiddle to other musicians that he didn't respect.

Moreover, many critics viewed Moore as somewhat humourless, until they actually met him when they discovered he was actually personable and funny. Critics also often speculated as to why Moore's music never made much of an impact in the American music market, despite concurrent accusations that he 'chased trends' in search of success.

Moore, after all, was a perfect example of the hardworking everyman who should have achieved the 'American Dream' in the land of opportunity. And when that finally happened in 1990, when Moore's *Still Got The Blues* album sold millions of copies, some critics dismissed Moore's blues as 'inauthentic' and mere imitation.

I've titled this book *Back On The Streets: The Gary Moore Story*, not just in reference to his debut solo album, but because Moore was a street fighter, not in the physical sense, but in his attitude towards adversity. His life began in the tough streets of Belfast, and that helped forge a man determined to follow his own path to success and musical self-satisfaction.

Often derided because of his looks — he was an overweight in childhood, and in adulthood his face was badly scarred — Moore worked tirelessly to build a career as a professional musician, then to ascend the ladder of popular musical success. He was often decisive, perhaps even ruthless in his decision-making, and he frequently raised the heckles of even his close friends.

While he was a polarising figure, Moore thought the truth could be found in his music, and especially in the passion of his guitar playing. Since he first picked up a guitar at age ten, all he wanted to do was *play*. He had something to say, and the guitar allowed him to do that. With the instrument in his hands, he was no longer just another anonymous kid from Belfast: the guitar allowed him to express his personality, provided him with a livelihood that was the envy of many, and entertained millions over the course of a five-decade long career.

***

Many thanks to Dr Nic for some helpful feedback on early draft chapters.

Dedicated, as usual, to Morgan and Myles.

Belfast And Dublin

'There are no drum heroes. There are certainly no piano heroes. Nor are there saxophone heroes, harmonica heroes, or even bass guitar heroes. There are, however, guitar heroes.'

David Hepworth[6]

Robert William Gary Moore was born in Belfast, Northern Ireland in 1952. His family lived on the outskirts of Belfast, on a street off the Upper Newtownards Road, opposite the main entrance to Stormont Estate, where the Northern Ireland parliament sat, and where some of the state's civil service was based. It was an area populated largely by middle class protestant families whose politics were unionist and conservative.

Moore's father, Robert, was a concert promoter who ran the Queen's Hall ballroom in Holywood, Co Down, a small town on the southern shore of Belfast Lough. Young Gary would sometimes tag along to these concerts, and on one occasion when he was around six years old, and with his dad's encouragement, he got up on stage and sang a song called 'Sugar Time'. Moore recalled that it was on those occasions that he first became fascinated with live music, mainly because he had never before seen it performed on stage. 'That was it. I had the bug', he reflected.[7] At age ten, Moore's dad bought him a Framus guitar as a gift. Moore recalled that before he picked up the Framus he had wanted to be a journalist but with the guitar in his hands, 'everything else went out of the window.'[8] It had a very high 'action', which made it difficult to press and hold down the strings on to the neck in order to play notes and chords.

Despite this, Moore had an aptitude for the instrument and, in fact, the guitar's difficulty to play helped him develop the hand and finger strength needed to master the instrument and to progress to techniques such as string bending. Despite being left-handed, Moore played guitar right-handed simply because that was the norm at the time, and he didn't know any better. Among the first songs he learned were chart hits such as 'Wonderful Land' by The Shadows and 'Picture of You' by Joe Brown.

In due course, when Moore moved from the beginner stage to playing in a band, he moved on from his Framus to a Fender Telecaster. 'I got the idea from watching the Yardbirds', Moore told *Guitar World's* Steven Rosen. 'There were three Telecasters coming into Belfast at that time and two were spoken for and I got the last one. It was white with a maple neck. I was really influenced by [Jeff] Beck.' Moore also owned a Gibson SG, but that was quickly stolen, and he only rarely picked up an SG again in his professional career.[9]

As a teenager, Moore's interest in music took him to various music venues around Belfast, either to larger venues such as the Ulster Hall to see some of the beat bands from England, or to smaller music hubs such as the celebrated Maritime Club in Belfast city centre. Also known as Club Rado, it was the heart and soul of the Belfast blues scene in that era. Van Morrison's Them got their break at the club when they were spotted by a Decca music scout. Rory Gallagher's Taste also played there, sometimes with Moore as his support act. Moore had fond memories of those days and of Gallagher in particular: 'I remember an occasion when we didn't have any spare strings between us so we decided we'd leave one of the guitars up on stage for both of us. It was like that. And Rory was always really friendly and very courteous.'[10]

Many years later Moore wrote of these interactions with Gallagher in the song 'Business As Usual', from his 1997 album *Dark Days In Paradise*. The lyrics recall Moore's earliest memories of Belfast in stream-of-consciousness fashion. Moore was impressionable, and something of a musical sponge. He learned from Gallagher, particularly how the Cork bluesman carried himself in such a down-to-earth fashion, with no airs and graces, but also from Gallagher's refusal to make any musical compromises. This gave Moore a template for how to behave in the rock business.

While going to live gigs was an escape from some of the usual adolescent problems Moore would later write about in his 1983 song 'Teenage Idol', he could not totally escape Belfast's often mean streets: for example, Moore spoke about the gangs who would wait outside Club Rado late at night and rob him of his bus fare. He then had to walk home, about four miles over the Queen's Bridge and through a neighbourhood where the same people who robbed him earlier would again be waiting to give him a hard time.[11]

Moore wrote about some of these experiences in 'Livin' On Dreams', a track from his 1989 album, *After the War*, about listening to a band called the Alleycats (actually the Alleykatz) on a Saturday night at the Maritime Club, standing on street corners, smoking cigarettes, showing attitude, and all the time dreaming of a better life.

Moore said of his Belfast upbringing, 'It was more peaceful when I grew up there… It was a pretty rough place though, but I'd imagine it was just like growing up in Glasgow or somewhere [similar]. I mean, it wasn't Beverley Hills, that's for sure!'[12]

Among the visiting bands Moore saw in his youth were The Who, Peter Green, Jimi Hendrix, and Cream, all of whom played live in Belfast, and all of whom had an impact on his musical development. Moore recalled: 'there was a great scene in Belfast then. I remember seeing The Who at the Top Hat [actually in Lisburn, just south of Belfast]. I had a band called Platform Three by that time and we had to do a gig that very night. I remember finishing the gig and running all the way to where The Who were playing, hearing the sound of 'The Kids Are All Right' from way up the street, throwing my three shillings… at the guy on the door and pushing my way up to the front. It was a wonderful moment, and a great time to be growing up.'[13]

Like most teenagers in that era, Moore's initial musical influences were The Shadows and The Beatles, but as the British blues scene became popular, Moore became hooked on the likes of Clapton, Green, Mick Taylor, and Hendrix, as well as Jeff Beck of The Yardbirds, all of whom influenced his guitar development. 'You can hear all of those people in my playing', he explained.[14]

Along with Bill Downey, one of Moore's friends from the local Ashfield Boys School, at age 11 Moore formed his first band, which they called The Beat Boys.[15] As their name suggests, The Beat Boys modelled themselves on the 'Fab Four', complete with pudding bowl haircuts and matching red satin shirts. They played Beatles' covers in local talent contests, achieving some success. For example, in Summer 1965 The Beat Boys won their heat in a talent competition at Pickie Pool in Bangor, Co. Down. Moore told the *Irish Times*, 'I also remember doing another one around that time, run by Eddie Kennedy at the Club Rado in Belfast. We actually won — the prize was £15 — and he handed us this empty envelope on the stage and said: "Don't worry, lads, we'll sort out the cheque later." I'm still waiting!'[16]

Moore's father also let the band perform at his Queen's Hall venue. The Beat Boys was the first of a series of youthful bands in which Moore played, and about which not much is known. These included Dave and the Diamonds, The Barons, and a blues band called Platform Three. Moore began to develop a reputation as a hot young guitarist and at age 16 he was asked to deputise for the injured lead guitarist in a band called The Method, whom he had seen perform at the Maritime Club. The Method had a regular Wednesday night gig at the Club-A-Go-Go in Dublin, and Moore jumped at the chance.

It was while visiting Dublin with The Method that Moore met Brush Shiels, founder and bass player for a band called Skid Row. Shiels knew of Moore's reputation and invited him to join his band.[17]

Initially, Moore was reluctant because Skid Row covered pop songs and Shiels told Moore he wanted the band to develop an American West Coast sound similar to The Byrds, whereas Moore was more into blues music. However, Shiels' offer to provide accommodation for Moore in Dublin, plus a £15 a week retainer, was too tempting, and Moore left home to start a new life in Dublin. It's perhaps surprising that such a young man from a relatively sheltered background would choose to leave the family home so early in his teenage years but there is some suggestion that Moore's parents Robert and Winnie were in conflict at this time: 'there were loads of troubles in our house', Moore would later reveal.

Some of this cropped up in autobiographical songs such as 'Business As Usual', wherein Moore recalled: 'Trembling at night from the violence I heard from my bedroom'. A year after he moved to Dublin, his parents split up.[18] Moreover, Moore's relocation to Dublin demonstrates that from an early age he was driven to succeed, was willing to take risks, and had a fair amount of intrepidity in moving to a new, strange city, to play with older musicians he barely knew, and with no guarantee of future happiness or success.

Moore recalled his first night in Dublin in an interview with Neville Marten of *Guitar World*. He told Marten that he was basically a naïve 16-year-old who tried to impress Shiels by pretending to be into drugs when, in fact, he had never tried them before.

In fact, Belfast was hardly a hip scene in the 1960s and illegal drugs were hard to come by. Moore recalled that Shiels was shocked by Moore's revelation, telling the young Belfast guitarist that the lads in Skid Row were into beer and football, but not drugs. Moore told

Marten that the big difference between Belfast and Dublin was the influence of the Catholic Church in the south which caused everyone to feel guilty if their actions or views conflicted with the Church's teachings on morality and order.[19]

No doubt Moore's observation was influenced by his protestant upbringing in the North, but religion played no obvious role in shaping his music, nor did he discuss it in his lyrics or in interviews.[20]

The next milestone to occur in Moore's life was when Shiels introduced him to Skid Row's charismatic lead singer, a tall, dark-skinned young man named Phil Lynott. The two hit it off immediately. One of Moore's oft-told stories about Lynott goes some way towards illustrating their relationship, which can best be characterised as one of friendly rivalry: 'One time he got me to order something from a Chinese restaurant which he knew I wouldn't like, and he ate my food. From then on that's how our relationship was — Phil was pulling things on me, and I was falling for them.'[21]

However, Lynott didn't last much longer in Skid Row, mainly as Shiels wanted to make the band a three-piece in the style of Cream or Rory Gallagher's Taste. Lynott would, of course, go on to form his own bands, including Thin Lizzy, where he would reunite with Moore to form a fruitful, but tempestuous on-off music relationship that would last until Lynott's untimely death in 1986.

But for the moment, Moore saw his future with Skid Row. Along with Shiels, he took over from Lynott on lead vocals, and he made his first trips to London with the band. Skid Row developed a good reputation as a live act and got their first recording contract in 1969. They would proceed to release three albums, two of which featured Moore, and they toured Britain, Europe, and the United States, opening for the likes of Fleetwood Mac, Canned Heat, and Frank Zappa. They were one of the first Irish rock bands to garner a degree of international recognition.

Moore's first record releases with Skid Row were also the only ones involving Phil Lynott. The band's first single in 1969 was 'New Places, Old Faces', written by Brush Shiels and sung by Lynott, coupled with 'Misdemeanour Dream Felicity', written by Moore. These tracks were a world away from the blues and rhythm and blues that Moore had been listening to and playing thus far.

'New Places, Old Faces' has a pastoral feel, somewhere between traditional Irish music and the California hippy music that had, by this point, already come and gone as a popular musical style. For example, it features a penny whistle, which gives the song an arcadian feel, and Moore eschewed his electric lead guitar for gentle acoustic patterns. 'Misdemeanour Dream Felicity' is a kind of abstract folk jazz composition, with Shiels providing lead vocals, including some scat singing. Moore plays acoustic jazz chords and fast fills that are a little rough around the edges. This seems more like a recorded jam session than a polished studio recording. In tone and style, it is a little reminiscent of Van Morrison's early solo work.

The band released a second single in 1969 entitled 'Saturday Morning Man', with 'Mervyn Aldridge' on the B-side. The former features Moore on lead vocals. It is another change in pace for the band, very much in the pop style of The Kinks or Small Faces and lacking any Irish folk or jazz influences. Moore plays an electric lead guitar rock solo when a more psychedelic-style solo would seem more appropriate, whereas on 'Mervyn Aldridge' Shiels takes on lead vocal duties while Moore plays jazz guitar stylings on an acoustic guitar, together with some electric lead fills.

A third single, 'Sandie's Gone (Part 1)', coupled with 'Sandie's Gone (Part 2)', was released in April 1970. Written by Shiels, and with Shiels and Moore sharing lead vocals, 'Sandie's Gone' is a further divergence in style, with Skid Row now sounding somewhere between the country-rock stylings of The Band or The Allman Brothers Band, and the 'cosmic country' vibe of the Flying Burrito Brothers. Moore plays a tasteful electric lead solo, seemingly plucking with his fingers rather than picking, which is a technique often used by country and western style guitarists.

The overall impression of these singles is of a band searching for an identity, with Moore playing accomplished and tasteful guitar but more in the style of a session player rather than someone who is capable or willing at this point to stamp his own sound and identity onto the recordings. Indeed, it's very possible that Moore did not yet know what his own sound was.

In early 1970, Skid Row got a big break when they supported Fleetwood Mac at the National Stadium in Dublin and Moore got to meet one of his music heroes, the multi-talented Peter Green. Moore recalled these events: 'Peter had said to this DJ guy who was hosting the show that he'd like to meet me... so I just went up and said hello and he said, "Oh I really like your playing, do you want to come back to the hotel afterwards and we'll have a chat?" I went up to the room and there was Mick Fleetwood and Peter sharing a room… We both sat there and talked all night and played together.'[22] Moore then travelled with Green to the next gig and Green persuaded his manager, Clifford Davis, to bring Skid Row over to England where he signed them to CBS Records.[23]

The band's debut album for CBS, *Skid Row* (May 1970), was comprised of original material written by all three members of the band, and it included two of the band's first three singles ('New Faces Old Places' and 'Sandie's Gone'), plus Moore's B-side, now renamed 'Felicity'. Its cover was a group photograph of the band standing in front of a sign saying, 'Dublin Gas Comy. Cooker and Meter Factory'. The sleeve credits read: 'Gary Moore, 17 years old, lead guitar and vocals - Noel Bridgeman a little older than 17, drums and vocal - and myself, Brendan Shields, commonly known as "The brush", older than Noel, bass, guitar, and vocals - together we make up SKID ROW.'

As promising as this seemed, Clifford Davis wanted the album withdrawn as he believed it needed further polishing. CBS agreed and the album was reissued in October that year, retitled simply *Skid*, and with a different cover and track listing. From the withdrawn release, only the tracks 'The Man Who Never Was', Unco-Up Showband Blues', 'Heading Home Again', 'Virgo's Daughter' and 'Felicity' appeared on the reissued album. Two of those tracks, 'The Man Who Never Was' and Unco-Up Showband Blues' were co-written by Moore, Shiels and Bridgeman, while 'Felicity' was written solely by Moore. A new track, 'For Those Who Do', was co-written by Moore, Shiels, and Bridgeman.

Skid (October 1970)

The opening track, 'Mad Dog Woman', was written by Shiels, who appears on this occasion to have been channelling prog rock band King Crimson. It features some electric lead guitar acrobatics from Moore, no doubt encouraged by Shiels, who hoped Skid Row might emulate the dynamic drums, guitar, bass and vocals of power trios like Cream, Taste and maybe even The Jimi Hendrix Experience.

'Virgo's Daughter' follows, a brash prog rock song with psychedelic influences and which makes reference to the hit song 'The Age of Aquarius', from the movie *Hair*. It features a number of time signatures — one of the characteristics of prog rock — and incorporates native American rhythm, chanting, and drumming at the beginning and end. In that respect, it is a little reminiscent of the Thin Lizzy track 'Sitamoia', which it predates by a few years. Moore's playing is frenetic but remains controlled throughout.

The next track is 'Heading Home Again', which was written by Shiels. It showcases some intricate and melodic country-rock playing by Moore in the style of Scotty Moore. A further Shiels track follows. Entitled 'An Awful Lot Of Woman', it is another fast paced Frank Zappa-style romp, with Shiels doing his best vocal impression of Rory Gallagher and Moore playing a fast, recurring pattern throughout. At one point, the song descends into a slower 12-bar rhythm, and Moore unleashes a rock guitar solo easily as fast and exciting as anything played by blues-rock guitarist Alvin Lee, who many regarded then as the fastest player on the scene.

Side one ends with 'Unco-Up Showband Blues', which is probably the closest Moore has come to writing in the style of Robert Plant and Jimmy Page. Moore, though, wasn't a fan of Page's playing, claiming that Page was by far the weakest player of the crop of British guitarists that emerged from this era. In fact, when someone later told Moore his guitar sounded a bit like Page's signature sound, Moore immediately changed the effects he was using. Nevertheless, this is a hard-rock blues track reminiscent of the first Zeppelin album. It features a somewhat redundant and hackneyed musical conversation/duel between bass and lead guitar.

Side two of *Skid* begins with 'For Those Who Do' a track co-written by Shiels, Moore, and Bridgeman. A few years later Moore joined a jazz-rock fusion band entitled Colosseum II and one can see the birth of that style of playing in this indulgent and over-the-top progressive rock song.

The same might be said of the following track, 'After I'm Gone'. Time signature changes and frenetic duetting between Moore and Shiels mark this as a further statement of musical virtuosity, if not potential widespread popularity.

Like 'For Those Who Do', the album's penultimate track, 'The Man Who Never Was', is another co-written song between Shiels, Moore, and Bridgeman, and like that song, this is another track that foreshadows Moore's work in Colosseum II. It is perhaps a little easier on the ear than 'For Those Who Do' in that it maintains a consistent time signature, although it is just as intense, with Moore playing fast and precise riffs throughout.

The album's final track is Moore's 'Felicity'. On this version, Moore sings and plays electric lead guitar. It is a reworked and extended version of the original single with some effects added during an instrumental interlude, as well as a bass solo by Shiels. On all these tracks, Bridgeman's impeccable drumming provides the glue that keeps the band tight, but he also adds tasteful fills and provides emphasis at just the right time for dramatic effect, as can be heard during 'Felicity's instrumental interlude. Moore plays very fast and colourful fills, which would become one of his trademarks.

Skid entered the UK album charts, and peaked, at 30, eight places above Paul McCartney's debut album, *McCartney*.[24] Nevertheless, *Record Mirror* called it 'rather a mediocre album' while citing 'Felicity' as its highlight.[25] While that comment may have been a boost to Moore's confidence, and the top 30 status the album achieved was certainly promising, *Skid* far from established the band as a financially viable or professionally acclaimed new band, and as Moore's career would later evidence, these were the two measures of progress that Moore most desired.

34 Hours (1971)

The band released its second album, *34 Hours*, in early 1971. The album was so-called because it took only 34 hours to record. Moore explained to *Record Mirror* the differences between the debut album and its follow-up: 'The speed thing, unison playing and riffs got us across at first but that in itself is not enough anymore. We are going for a more funky sound now, something like the Stones.'[26] The album was preceded by the single release, 'Night Of The Warm Witch' coupled with a non-album track entitled 'Mr. De-Luxe'.

Four of the album's six songs were co-written by Shiels, Moore, and Bridgeman, with the remainder written solely by Shiels. The opening track, 'Night of the Warm Witch', begins with some bass guitar harmonics from Shiels and lead guitar effects by Moore, including the technique of adjusting the guitar's volume control each time he played a chord to get a fade in/fade out effect. Using the volume control in this way allowed Moore to introduce the note or chord slowly, without the initial abrupt striking sound. Moore also used distortion and tremolo effects to create a dream-like, vaguely disconcerting atmosphere. The song progresses with funky bass and lead guitar riffs, and some aggressive drumming from Bridgeman. An instrumental interlude sees Moore use the same tone fade in/out effect, then a tempo change is Moore's cue to play some fast patterns. The song ends as it began, with atmospheric bass and lead guitar effects. Some misogynist lyrics that were par for the course for some rock and pop lyricists in 1971 haven't aged well.

'First Thing In The Morning' is a brief, fast-paced rocker, with Moore playing dynamic lead fills. The lyrics describe a man disingenuously trying to persuade his partner that he sees her as something more than a sexual object, and at less than two minutes in length its impact is inconsequential.

'Mar', the final track on side one, is a change of pace and style. It begins in country-rock style, then transforms into a mid-paced rocker with an extended lead guitar solo from Moore. In addition, Moore teases some steel guitar effects from his lead instrument to add to the track's countrified feel.

Side two opens with 'Go, I'm Never Gonna Let You, Pt. 1', a dynamic prog rocker with a tricky, recurring riff played by Moore and Shiels, and some Hendrix-style fills by Moore. Moore uses a wah-wah pedal during the solo, in the style of Jimi Hendrix. 'Pt. 2' of the song, is a 12-bar shuffle with Moore providing a lively extended rock-blues solo.

'Lonesome Still' is another track in the country-rock genre, with Moore once more creating pseudo steel guitar stylings. The track features an accordion, probably to add some colour. While the instrument went uncredited on the album notes, it could have been played by Moore who, a few years later, would play an accordion on his hit song 'Parisienne Walkways'. On 'Lonesome Still' Moore provides some tuneful harmony vocals to Shiels lead.

The album's closing track is 'Love Story', which, despite being only five minutes in length, is nevertheless listed on the album credits in typically pretentious prog rock fashion as a four-part track. It is essentially an extended drums, bass, and lead guitar work-out with Shiels providing dynamic vocals. The first three-and-a-half minutes is prog rock reminiscent of King Crimson, then the song transforms dramatically into Hendrix-style blues rock.

34 Hours is a more focussed and better-produced album than Skid Row's debut effort, while retaining some prog-rock attributes such as style changes, complicated riffs, and time changes. It firmly established

Skid Row as an interesting, innovative and ambitious prog rock band, comprised of virtuoso musicians, but with little chance of achieving the hit single release that could lead to wider popular exposure.

CBS released the album in a gatefold cover, which was more expensive to manufacture, and which indicates that the record company had enough confidence to invest in the release. However, the single that preceded the album, 'Night Of The Warm Witch' failed to chart, as did the subsequent album. This was despite a solid *Billboard* review, which praised the album's 'hard stuff and the originality' and which singled out Moore's guitar playing and vocals as 'distinctive'. 'These heavy lads will travel far!', *Billboard* predicted.[27]

After the band signed with CBS they moved to England on a semi-permanent basis and began touring. By the time the second album was recorded, the band was playing around six gigs a week, mainly in clubs, at universities, or at an occasional mini- festival.

For example, in December 1970 Skid Row performed at the Sisters Club in London and the Gin Mill in Godalming. In April, 1971, they played the Quaintways club in Chester and later in July, Tofts club in Folkestone. On October 22, the band performed at Exeter University sandwiched between headliners Atomic Rooster and Genesis, who were bottom of the bill behind Skid Row. In September, the band appeared on the second day of a two-day festival (September 4-5) in Bearsden on the outskirts of Glasgow. On the bill that day were The Move, The Electric Light Orchestra, Uriah Heep, Skid Row, and Slade. On November 26, they played the Van Dike club in Plymouth, which could accommodate around 500 people, and on December 4, they performed at the Town Hall in High Wycombe.

Moore stated a preference for gigs outside London, as he thought the audiences were more responsive. He also gave an early indicator of his need for professionalism, telling *Record Mirror* that university gigs were the worst as, 'they're so badly organised because the people that run them are so irresponsible.'[28] Nevertheless, these indicative examples illustrate that in terms of venue bookings and drawing power, Skid Row made no real progress in the time period from when they first based themselves in England until Moore decided to quit the band in December, 1971.

Skid Row made a number of television and radio appearances, some of which fared better than others. After a particularly poor vocal performance from Lynott on RTE television, caused by inflamed tonsils, Shiels decided to fire Lynott and make the band a three-piece. An appearance on John Peel's BBC radio show in July 1970 was more successful — although beginning the show with a nine-minute drum solo hardly added to their radio appeal — as did their performance on German television music show *Beat Club* on March 18, 1971.

The set list that day included 'Unco-Up Showband Blues' and 'An Awful Lot of Woman'. It's unclear whether that performance enhanced or hurt their reputation: although it was energetic and the trio cut quite a scene, with for example a bearded, crucifix-adorned Moore dressed in a white shirt, waistcoat and red beanie hat, playing his Les Paul like a demon, unfortunately Shiel's bass was out of tune, which is particularly noticeable on 'Unco-Up Showband Blues', and the performance is therefore a little difficult to listen to.

There were also international tours, for example, to Europe in October 1970, supporting Canned Heat, who were in great demand after their Woodstock performance the previous year, and American tours in November 1970, April and November 1971 opening for the likes of the Grateful Dead, Jethro Tull, the Allman Brothers Band, and Mountain.[29]

In an interview with *Sounds* in December 1970, the band tried to put a brave face on their first America gigs as an unknown support band, saying they had learned a lot from the experience. However, disillusionment wasn't far from the surface: Shiels called the Whisky A Go-Go in Los Angeles 'a groups graveyard… If you are too loud for them to talk over, or if they can't dance to you, they just don't want to know.'

Bridgeman said: 'I never realised before just how good British audiences are. The only place over there where they were as good was Boston.'[30] Nevertheless, a high point of the last tour was when members of Led Zeppelin came to see the band play at the Whisky A Go-Go. Moore recalls: 'We were all staying at the Holiday Inn in Los Angeles. They were playing at the Forum and they used to come and see us every night. They got pissed one night and John Bonham and Robert Plant got up. John sang and Robert played the drums.'[31]

Moore soon quit Skid Row as he wanted to play more blues music, which put him in conflict with Shiels who believed that would limit the band's potential. Shiels had too many ideas to be strait-jacketed into just a single musical genre, a point noted in a *Sounds* review of Skid Row's appearance at the Country Club, Hampstead in December 1970.

Reviewer Ray Telford said of the band: 'On paper Skid Row sound as though they could be one of a thousand groups all of similar ideas and musical format, but the difference lies in their constant inventiveness.' Telford singled out Moore for particular praise, as 'a very talented guitarist who commands a lot of attention through his individualistic playing which refreshingly owes nothing to B. B. King or Jimmy Page.'[32] In a similar vein, Eric Bell, who would briefly replace Moore in Skid Row, said Skid Row 'was an absolutely incredible three-piece band… it was… technical [with] very, very intricate riffs and time changes'.[33]

Moore, however, had decided it was time for a change. While he remained friendly with Shiels in particular, in later years he spoke less than fondly of Skid Row, saying, for example, 'I don't have great memories of [the band]… the rhythm section was so busy. It was just like everyone was showing off… Brush Shiels, I think he saw me as this kind of little prodigy — because I was 16 when I joined the band — someone to show off to people. And he was encouraging me to play faster and faster, just so much emphasis on speed, showing off chops and all the shit that meant nothing, really. But I was so young at the time, I didn't really know what was going on so I went along with it.'[34]

As to why he quit the power trio, Moore revealed: 'Recording-wise, we were such amateurs. We got to the stage of doing twenty-minute versions of 'Johnny B. Goode', getting drunk and playing as fast as we could, so I left because I wanted to do something more musical, a dual guitar band in the Allman Brothers direction.'[35]

Moore had, of course, witnessed the Allman Brothers Band at close quarters when Skid Row supported the band in the United States. Furthermore, the Allman Brothers played covers of many of the blues tracks that Moore loved.

So, Moore quit and soon put his own band together, going out on tour in England and Scotland in support of the English prog-rock band Curved Air. Between March 29 and May 6 1972, the newly formed Gary Moore Band played twenty-two support gigs. A record contract with CBS would soon follow, and Moore decamped to the studio to make what in essence was his first solo album, *Grinding Stone*.

Grinding Stone (1973)

Produced and engineered by Martin Birch, who had previously worked with Moore in his role as studio engineer for the second Skid Row album, *Grinding Stone* marks another change in direction for Moore.

The album cover is a striking indicator of this, marking a significant change from the Skid Row albums, which originally featured group photos of the band on and off-stage. However, the cover of *Grinding Stone* is a suggestive, colourful illustration of two scantily clad women, accompanied by a number of phallic symbols. While such lowest-common-denominator album art might indicate a move towards a puerile form of glam rock, a first spin on the turn table offered listeners a surprisingly mature album.

The opening track, 'Grinding Stone', is an instrumental, nearly ten minutes in length. It begins with a slow-paced guitar and bass melody that builds to a mini crescendo, which serves essentially as an introduction to the main melody, which then reveals itself as a mid-paced, guitar-driven piece of progressive funk-rock. Moore uses a wah-wah pedal to play fast lead breaks, while drums, bass and keyboards provide a funky back beat. (Jan Schelhaas from the prog rock band Caravan plays keyboards.) This opening track is like a more melodic and simplified version of a Skid Row track, which perhaps illustrates Moore's desire to reach a wider audience than had his previous band.

The next track, 'Time To Heal', is in the style of the Allman Brothers Band, with Moore providing gruff lead vocals that are somewhat similar in delivery and tone to those of Brush Shiels. It is a mid-paced, blues-rocker with lots of energy and rhythm. Moore's fills are a lot more melodic than on his Skid Row albums, as if he no longer felt the need to prove his guitar ability and instead was trying to play more euphonious patterns that would be more accessible to a broader audience.

Side one ends with 'Sail Across The Mountain', a beautiful slow-paced country ballad. Previously, the Rolling Stones had success with country crossovers, for example the track 'Let It Bleed', from the *Let It Bleed* album (1969), 'Dead Flowers' and 'Wild Horses', from *Sticky Fingers* (1971) and 'Sweet Virginia' from *Exile on Main St.* (1972). Keith Richards had become fascinated with the country-rock style of Gram Parsons and in the same way, Moore seems to have become enamoured with the genre's evocation of rural Americana, particularly when done by the likes of the Allman Brothers Band, whose style this song resembles.

The opening track on side two is 'The Energy Dance', a two-and-a-half minute instrumental written by Moore featuring only piano and synthesiser. This leads into the epic, 17-minute track, 'Spirit', which approaches the prog rock complexity of Emerson, Lake & Palmer, but with guitar stylings by Moore that are more reminiscent of the Allman Brothers Band, particularly their 1973 song 'Jessica'. After some vocals by Moore, a samba beat leads to some Santana/Peter Green-style guitar patterns. A quieter section sees Moore once more use his guitar volume control to create eerie sounds. Arpeggiated synthesiser chords then kick in, gradually forming a recurring pattern, before Moore lays down a David Gilmour-style extended guitar solo.

The album's final track is 'Boogie My Way Back Home', a 'down home' style blues track. Moore plays acoustic guitar chords and a slide to get that country-blues effect, before the tempo quickens into a mid-paced blues shuffle. Moore provides passionate vocals, in authentic blues style.

Billboard magazine gave the album a positive review, stating that it had a 'Good mix of rock, blues and synthesizer orientated material', and that its strongest points were 'lengthy instrumentals which should appeal to the audience already enjoying electronic rock.'[36]

In contrast, a retrospective review by Martin Popoff adjudged the album a 'ragged, bluesy affair', which made little impression on the music world or the music charts.[37] Brush Shiels thought *Grinding Stone* was derivative of Skid Row and offered nothing innovative: it was, he claimed, 'a forced album… a poor man's album of us.'[38]

Yet *Grinding Stone* is a surprisingly mature album from a 21-year-old Moore who had embraced the responsibility of band leader. It was certainly not the pure blues album that fans might have expected after his departure from Skid Row; instead it prefigures Moore's later involvement with Jon Hiseman's prog-jazz-rock band, Colosseum II. Nevertheless, in the promotional tour to support the album from July to October, in a line-up featuring Moore on lead guitar, Pearse Kelly on drums, and John Curtis on bass, Moore added a few blues songs to his set list, such as Peter Green's 'The Same Way', a blues standard called 'Third Degree', and 'Eyesight To The Blind', which had been recorded by Sonny Boy Williamson, Eric Clapton, and the Allman Brothers Band. It's intriguing to speculate how Moore's career might have developed if he had fully committed to the blues at that point.

However, the album did not chart, and Moore was short on cash. Perhaps going solo was a mistake and he clearly felt out on a limb. In early 1974, Moore told *Disc* magazine, 'I began to feel more and more pressure on me and I began to feel that things weren't being handled properly. Eventually it got to the stage where we couldn't go on. Things just weren't working out.'[39]

Some years later he admitted: 'I didn't know what I was doing. We did one album, *Grinding Stone*. At the age of 19 I nearly had a nervous breakdown, so when I had the opportunity to join a band and have the pressure of being a leader taken off me, I jumped at it.'[40] That band was Thin Lizzy.

Gary Moore
And Thin Lizzy

From an early stage, Moore and Thin Lizzy were interconnected. The music scenes in Belfast and Dublin were energetic and close knit, and Moore met Brian Downey in Belfast while Downey was the teenage drummer in a Dublin-based blues band called Sugar Shack.

Moore and Lynott met when Lynott was lead singer in Skid Row, and the two remained friends after Brush Shiels ousted Lynott from the band. Moore met Belfast-born Eric Bell after Bell, Lynott and Downey (and another Belfast-born musician named Eric Wrixon), formed Thin Lizzy. Moore was also present when Lizzy recorded their first demos at Trend Studios in Dublin in 1969, although he didn't perform on any of these recordings.[41] The lives of Moore, Downey, Lynott and Bell would intertwine over the next four decades.

In these early days the relationship, on occasion, provided useful, practical benefits. For example, during the early Irish dates of Lizzy's tour to promote their *Vagabonds of the Western World* album (1973), Pearce Kelly from the Gary Moore Band helped Downey co-perform at a gig as the Thin Lizzy drummer was suffering from badly blistered hands.[42]

In addition, Moore sometimes guested with Lizzy: for example, when the band played London's Marquee club on June 28, 1973, Moore appeared onstage during the encore to perform a cover of the Fleetwood Mac song 'Stop Messin' Around'.[43] He gave a further guest performance when Lizzy performed at The Greyhound, Fulham, London, on July 22.

The failure of *Grinding Stone* was a chastening experience for Moore, whose plans to make a living as a professional musician were stretched to breaking point. However, Moore's links to the Dublin music scene, and to Thin Lizzy in particular, would soon provide him with a further opportunity to express his musical talent.

'We're going to get Gary fucking Moore to finish it' – **Chris Morrison, Thin Lizzy manager**

After the departure of guitarist Eric Bell, who quit Thin Lizzy in the middle of a gig at Queen's University, Belfast on New Year's Eve 1973, Lynott recruited Moore to help finish the band's ongoing Irish tour through early 1974. Everyone involved with Thin Lizzy knew that Moore was up to the task. He was already familiar with some of the band's recordings and was such a talented guitarist that he could make up for any potential shortcomings in that area with his virtuoso guitar playing. As it turned out, he had around six hours rehearsal time before his first performance with Thin Lizzy at Red Island, Skerries on January 4, 1974.[44]

Ten further Irish dates followed, including gigs in Northern Ireland at small venues in Newtownards, Omagh, Coleraine, and Dromore, and a showpiece gig at the Ulster Hall in Belfast. Ironically, Lizzy played the Ulster Hall on Saturday, January 12, exactly one week after Moore and Lynott's old band Skid Row headlined the venue.

If the Ulster Hall was Lizzy's showcase gig in Northern Ireland, the showcase gig in the South was on January 16 at the National Stadium. Such was the short notice Bell gave of his resignation from Lizzy, his image remained on an advertising handbill for this gig. Perhaps it was also too expensive to print new handbills featuring Moore's image instead of Bell's. A local music reviewer was particularly enamoured with Moore's guitar playing in Dublin, making Moore the main subject of his gig review, while ignoring Lynott entirely. Moore 'starred for a lot of the time', the reviewer wrote in the *Irish Times*, 'and indeed his technique is remarkable — particularly noticeable in a sort of pastiche of classical-sounding odds and ends tied together with fluttering runs and odd thoughts apparently of his own devising; showy but frankly so, entertaining and fascinating.'[45]

A tour of Britain followed in February, with Lizzy playing sixteen club and college venues in England, Scotland and Wales. Moore did not immediately join the tour but instead gave his first live performance on this British tour in Birmingham at Barbarella's on February 10. The most prominent gigs were at venues such as the Marquee and Roundhouse in London, and in Liverpool at the Cavern. This was a tour mainly of major cities such as Birmingham, Manchester, Cardiff, and Glasgow, but which took Lizzy as far north as Aberdeen and also to off-beat towns such as Merthyr Tydfil in Wales and Spennymoor in Durham, which not coincidentally were two working class, coalmining towns and likely therefore to attract receptive audiences for Lizzy's style of no-nonsense rock music.

Lizzy continued touring through March with four gigs in Dublin and five in southern England. After a ten-day break at the beginning of April, Lizzy continued touring with five gigs in England and a one-off gig in Belfast at The Carousel Ballroom. A bootleg of the Locarno gig in Bristol entitled 'Gary's Jig' reveals the Thin Lizzy setlist for this time period, which included a Gary Moore guitar solo which begins with some intricate jazz-style picking then develops into a heavier section that is basically an Irish jig played at speed and with power. Moore would reuse this part of the solo a few years later in the song 'Róisín Dubh (Black Rose): A Rock Legend', which is based on a number of traditional folk songs but with co-writer credits attributed to Moore and Lynott.

Also on the setlist was 'Things Ain't Working Out Down At The Farm', the band's current single 'Little Darlin'', 'Crawling' (with Moore providing lead vocals),[46] 'Little Girl In Bloom', 'Showdown', 'Suicide', 'Slow Blues', 'Black Boys On The Corner', Whiskey In The Jar', 'The Rocker', 'Hard Drivin' Man', 'I Love Everything About You', 'Rock 'N' Roll With You', and 'Sitamoia', which provided space for a Brian Downey drum solo and some Celtic guitar phrases by Moore.

On the band's rendition of the Stevie Wonder song 'I Love Everything About You' Moore provided backing vocals and then took over mid-song from Lynott to sing lead. Moore also sang lead vocals on 'Crawling'. The handbill for this gig includes an illustrated image of Lizzy featuring Eric Bell, with Moore once more missing from most publicity material for the tour. Moore's last live gig with Lizzy in this particular iteration was at the Corn Exchange in Cambridge; when Lizzy began a German tour on May 11, it featured a new line up of Lynott, Downey, Andy Gee, and John Du Cann.

Before that, however, Moore did his most substantial work with Lizzy to date. In April 1974, Lizzy recorded songs in London for the John Peel radio show, *Sounds of the Seventies*. Some of these songs would later appear on Lizzy's *Nightlife* album, including 'It's Only Money' and 'Still In Love With You'. For Peel, Lizzy also recorded 'Little Darlin'', as well as an alternative version of the previously recorded 'Black Boys On The Corner', and the Lizzy rarity, 'Sitamoia'.

In this session Moore did not simply copy Bell who, on the most recent Lizzy album *Vagabonds Of The Western World*, had been moving towards a cleaner guitar sound. In 'It's Only Money', for example, Moore plays distorted rhythm and lead guitar. On 'Little Darlin'', however, Moore begins with a riff reminiscent of Bell's performance on 'The Rocker'. This opening riff did not appear on the studio version of the song that was released as a single in the UK on the Decca label and wouldn't appear on a 12-inch vinyl LP until the release of the 1976 compilation album *Remembering – Part 1*. Moore plays a solo with a slide effect, ending with a lengthy sustained note. On 'Still In Love With You', Moore shares vocals with Lynott in a relaxed and informal version of the song. This bluesy ballad was a perfect fit for Moore's voice, and at one point Moore pulls off a creditable falsetto. Moore plays both rhythm and lead guitar parts, with stereo effect separating each to left and right speakers. Peel called this performance of the song 'Gary Moore at his most mellow and laid back'.

On the drum-driven song 'Sitamoia', which was written by Brian Downey in 6/8 tempo, Moore plays Celtic-influenced electric guitar reminiscent of some of the guitar lines that would later appear on the song 'Róisín Dubh (Black Rose): A Rock Legend'. On the original recording of 'Black Boys On The Corner', which appeared on Lizzy's *Shades Of A Blue Orphanage* album in 1972, Eric Bell appears to be channelling Led Zeppelin's Jimmy Page; however, on this rendition, Moore's soloing seems influenced more by Rory Gallagher than Bell or Page. On the whole, this is a punchier, more aggressive rendition of the song, with both Moore's guitar and Lynott's vocals proving more aggressive than the earlier recorded version.

'Little Darlin'' perhaps surprisingly made no impact on the UK singles chart. Credited solely to Lynott as songwriter, 'Little Darlin'' was a catchy rocker, and the single release had a melodic brass arrangement.

According to producer Nick Tauber, Moore played through two Fender Twin Reverbs and two Echoplexes, which gave the song an interesting vibe.[47] The track bears some resemblance to The Rolling Stones' song 'Doo Doo Doo Doo Doo (Heartbreaker)', which the Stones released as a single the previous year, so perhaps Lizzy took some inspiration from that release.

Neither 'Sitamoia' nor 'Little Darlin'' made it on to Lizzy's next studio album but both later appeared on the 1976 Decca compilation album *Remembering – Part 1.*, which was released by London Records in the United States in 1977 but retitled as *Rocker (1971-1974)*. The album includes a studio version of the aforementioned rarity 'Sitamoia' as well as the single version of 'Little Darlin'', both of which feature Moore. A *Billboard* magazine review singled out Moore's 'high energied [sic] guitar support' and listed 'Little Darlin'' as one of the album's best cuts.[48]

Moore was with Lizzy just long enough to be involved in the *Nightlife* recording sessions, which caused some issues for Lizzy after Moore parted company with the band. For instance, 'Still In Love With You' is an amalgam of a song of that name penned by Lynott, and a tune written by Moore called 'I'll Help You See It Through'. Because Lizzy had just ended their contract with Decca, the last obligation of which was a final single release ('Little Darlin''), and as the band did not want anything to undermine negotiations with their new record label, Phonogram, Lynott took sole song-writing credit when 'Still In Love With You' appeared on *Nightlife*.

New Lizzy guitarist Brian Robertson, who now formed one half of Lizzy's new twin guitar attack alongside Californian new boy Scott Gorham, declined to re-record Moore's guitar parts as he did not think he could improve upon Moore's performance. No one mentioned this to the record company, so Gary Moore went uncredited on the album despite performing on the song, as well as being its co-writer.[49] Ironically, the demos recorded with Moore had helped secure the new contract with Phonogram.[50] Another song on *Nightlife*, called 'It's Only Money' was demoed previously with Moore, but unlike with 'Still In Love With You', all Moore's parts were re-recorded for the album.[51]

A few short months after Moore left Skid Row, Moore once more made the decision to leave an up-and-coming band. It is difficult to be certain if Moore had any intention to stick with Thin Lizzy or if he always planned to leave after fulfilling some live dates as a favour to Lynott. Certainly, when Moore spoke to *Disc* magazine in early 1974 he gave no impression of this being a temporary arrangement, and he told *Disc* that Lizzy gave him more scope for musical fulfilment than his previous efforts. 'I'm finding Thin Lizzy a lot more versatile than my old band', he explained. 'I'm one of those people who doesn't like to get too stuck into one thing, but likes to try various styles. In Lizzy they're into all sorts of things like Irish music and of course a lot of heavier stuff.'[52]

Eric Bell would later claim that Moore had been teetotal for two years before joining Lizzy but such was the band's party culture that it began to affect him adversely. He 'started developing a drink problem', said Bell.[53] Manager Ted Carroll claimed, however, that the drinking culture around Thin Lizzy was merely social and not a serious issue. Instead, Carroll thought Moore left Thin Lizzy because 'he wanted to do his own thing… jazz-rock, technical stuff.'[54] Lynott told *Sounds*, 'When Eric split our first reaction was to ask Gary, it was natural, he was a good mate of ours. We had such a laugh on the Irish tour that he decided to stay for a while although we all knew it wasn't going to be a permanent thing 'cause musically we were both at opposite ends.'[55]

It remains unclear then whether the impetus for Moore's departure lay in Lizzy's drinking culture, or in Moore's dissatisfaction with the progress of his own ambitions. In a 1979 press interview Moore explained: 'When I first joined Lizzy I thought: "This is fantastic," I was totally into it, and at the end I had almost destroyed myself. That was a very bad period of my life.'[56]

In addition, Moore anticipated that the Lizzy single 'Little Darlin'' would be successful. He told *Disc* he was 'very hopeful' about its release, noting that when Lizzy performed it to an audience it 'went down very well.' Therefore, the single's failure to chart could have given him cause to consider if Lizzy had the right ingredients for commercial success.

A number of scenarios therefore are plausible: Moore may have had the self-awareness and discipline to quit Lizzy before the drinking affected his health. He wanted to be a professional musician, not merely a 'rock star', with all its pitfalls. In retrospect, given the addictions that would befall Lynott and Scott Gorham in later years, Moore's concerns proved well-founded. Yet Moore also wanted to attain a level of commercial success, and when first *Grinding Stone* and then Lizzy's 'Little Darlin'' failed to sell, Moore may have concluded that his financial needs wouldn't be secured with Lizzy.

However, if he left solely for commercial reasons, his decision in November 1974 to join much-respected drummer Jon Hiseman in a new prog-fusion band called Colosseum II seems odd. In fact, despite his initial embrace of Lizzy's eclectic sound, Moore felt limited in the band. He later admitted that he joined Colosseum II to work within a more professional set-up, as well as broaden and develop his musical knowledge: 'I wanted to play with some of the more respectable musicians in Britain. I needed to discipline myself, to find out if I could do it. That whole period really toughened up my music.'[57]

Lynott's assertion that he never intended Moore to be a full-time replacement for Bell may have been a face-saving exercise: losing one guitarist could be explained away as 'exhaustion' on Bell's part but losing his replacement just a few months later could suggest problems within Lizzy that had potential to generate bad press. Asserting that Moore was only a stop-gap replacement sidestepped any bad publicity that could arise from his abrupt departure. In any event, Lynott expressed public gratitude to Moore, telling UK music trade magazine *Music Week* that Moore 'pulled us through the worst'.[58]

Moore was to return to the fold just a few years later, albeit once again on a temporary basis. In April 1976, Lizzy planned to travel to the United States for a series of gigs through to June where Lizzy should have played thirty-seven gigs in thirty-eight days supporting Aerosmith, The Tubes, Be-Bop Deluxe, Journey, Aerosmith, REO Speedwagon, Styx and Rush at different gigs, followed by dates with Rainbow.

To this point, Lizzy were not that well-known in the States, but their single 'The Boys Are Back In Town' from the *Jailbeak* album (1976) reached the top ten in the UK and top twenty in the States. Lizzy was unable to capitalise on the success of the single because their 1976 American tour was cut short due to Lynott contracting hepatitis.

Scott Gorham, speaking with *NME* in the June 26, 1976 issue said: 'We never played a single note on that tour because Phil was suffering from hepatitis weeks before we even got to Ohio where the tour was to begin. The day we got to Ohio Phil more or less nearly collapsed with exhaustion and was taken to the hospital where he was told that he had contracted hepatitis and was to immediately fly back to London. Back in London he was put in the intensive care unit for a couple of weeks. It's a shame, 'cause it would have been a great tour for Lizzy.'

The planned November tour was intended to make up for these earlier cancelled dates. However, on the eve of the band's planned departure, Lizzy guitarist Brian Robertson injured his hand in a bar fight in London and the tour had to be cancelled. Although it wasn't clear at the time, this was the beginning of the end for Robertson's position in Lizzy; although he would re-join the band after the tour, play a part in the recording of their next album, *Bad Reputation* (1977), and tour with Lizzy again through to December 1977, like Eric Bell a few years earlier, Robertson was becoming unreliable just as Lizzy was achieving a measure of popular success.

The cancelled late-1976 US tour was a lost opportunity for Lizzy to raise their profile and perhaps progress from a support act to headliners in the States.

However, another opportunity arose almost immediately, when Roger Taylor and Brian May of Queen approached Lynott to request that Lizzy be the support act for Queen on their forthcoming US tour from January through March 1977. Drummer Taylor told *Melody Maker*, 'There were about a dozen bands that wanted to do this tour with us. We thought that Lizzy suited our audience better than any of the others, and they're probably better that any of those bands anyway. I mean, there's no point in making it easy for yourself. We wanted a good all-round show. It's a good tour for both bands anyway. Lizzy playing to tremendous audiences, 10-20,000 a night.'[59] The 'Queen-Lizzy' tour, coming as it did in 1977 during Queen Elizabeth II's Silver Jubilee year, was a stroke of marketing genius; it also became legendary for the quality of performances from two bands arguably at their peak.

Lizzy needed a second lead guitarist to replace Robertson, and that's when Gary Moore re-entered the Lizzy story. Moore formed Colosseum II with John Hiseman late in 1974, although it took time to finalise their line-up. When that finally occurred, the band released two albums in quick succession, *Strange New Flesh* in April 1976, and *Electric Savage* in January 1977. (A third and final album appeared in November that year.)

Moore was musically content with the band, which played challenging jazz-rock fusion that he enjoyed. Nevertheless, the band had yet to achieve any commercial success, and Moore was determined to persevere until they did. Therefore, while Moore was happy to aid his old friends in Lizzy while Robertson recuperated, he did not intend to stay with Lizzy beyond the American tour with Queen. This was reflected in a press release by Lizzy's American record label, Mercury, which explained that while Moore would 'record and perform with the group on all future gigs', he was still only a 'temporary replacement' for Robertson.[60]

Moore's first gig in his second spell with Lizzy was in London on January 3, 1977, and it acted as a warm-up for the American tour. Billed as 'The Dire Ear Band', Moore performed onstage with Gorham, Robertson, and Lynott, and a few other musicians at a farewell gig at the Hope and Anchor pub, which was closing down.[61]

Moore then had around eleven days of rehearsals with Lizzy in New York to learn new songs and, in particular, to find his feet in a dual-guitar band. Previously, when Moore took over from Bell, Lizzy remained a three-piece band of bass, drums, and guitar, but Lizzy had transformed since then into a four-piece with Robertson and Scott Gorham sharing rhythm and lead guitar parts. How would Moore and Gorham blend?

Gorham told *Melody Maker* that the two 'clicked' almost immediately. According to Gorham, Robertson had become less interested in playing harmony guitar and instead preferred lead work, while Gorham was relegated to rhythm. In contrast, Moore liked Lizzy's harmony guitar arrangements and was happy to play them with Gorham. In addition, and contrary to one of the criticisms that has often been levelled at Moore that he is something of an attention hog on stage, during the tour Moore encouraged Gorham to share lead guitar parts.[62]

Moore said of his relationship with Gorham, 'I didn't try to overshadow him at all — in fact, I tried to restrain myself most of the time, because I realised I was just one quarter of the band, not a solo artist'.[63]

This was an intensive and challenging tour for all involved. For example, in January Lizzy played nine gigs in twelve days in the United States and Canada. A further seventeen gigs followed in February; and in March Lizzy performed thirteen times in eighteen days. Lizzy was under pressure as a support act whose job was to bring in some of their own fans but also to warm up the crowd for the main act, Queen.

As support, they played a one-hour set whereas Queen played for ninety minutes. They weren't allowed to use pyrotechnics; Queen management wouldn't let Lizzy hang their logo above Taylor's drum kit; sometimes Lizzy never got to do a full soundcheck because the Queen soundcheck lasted longer than scheduled; and Lizzy was denied access to some areas of the stage that were reserved for Queen use only. At one gig, when Moore ventured astray on to a catwalk that was designated for Queen's use only, Queen's management reminded him afterwards of his contract stipulations.[64]

Although at first glance these constraints seem petty, they were, in fact, practical and routine: for example, these precautions ensured none of the equipment Queen had tested at the soundcheck was disturbed. Besides, it wasn't the job of a support band to upstage the main act, although that sometimes occurred anyway.

Lizzy had been in this position numerous times before: for example, supporting Slade's UK tour in late 1972 was a particularly difficult task given the hostility shown towards Lizzy by Slade's fanatical supporters.[65] However, the Queen tour was on a different level in terms of the size of the venues and crowds. Gorham mused: 'we're playing in a lot of places we've never played before and we're playing in places where they haven't even played our record, so that's the real challenge.'[66]

The opening gig of the tour was at Detroit's Cobo Hall on January 18, and the tour ended in Edmonton, Canada on March 18. Lizzy played a truncated support-band set consisting of the following songs: 'Jailbreak', 'Massacre', 'Emerald', 'Still In Love With You', 'Johnny The Fox Meets Jimmy The Weed', 'The Boys Are Back In Town', 'Cowboy Song', 'Warriors', 'Sha La La', 'Baby Drives Me Crazy', and 'Me And The Boys'.

This was, by and large, the same setlist as Lizzy's gigs in England in November 1976, minus 'Rosalie', 'It's Only Money', and 'The Rocker', but with 'Emerald' included on the American setlist. In addition, there was at least one performance of 'Sitamoia' on the tour, in Saginaw on January 20.

Although Moore had one warm-up gig with Lizzy, underwent eleven days of rehearsals, and was familiar with some of the Lizzy catalogue, the opening show in Detroit on January 18 was still a challenge for him. When *Creem* journalist Patricia Goldstein met the band post-gig in the bar of their hotel, Moore was nursing a drink and appeared a little unsettled. Goldstein wrote: 'Talk about nerves. Moore is still shaking hours after the gig.' Moore told Goldstein, 'It's weird, I still remember a lot of the old Lizzy tunes, but they're none of the ones we do on stage. That's all new material.'[67]

Steve McDonell witnessed the second show of Lizzy's tour, which was at the Saginaw Civic Center. He called their performance 'badass' and Lizzy a 'band to be reckoned with.' McDonell compared Moore's looks unfavourably with Robertson, but was more complimentary about his guitar playing, claiming Moore played 'one pig of a guitar', slang indicating Moore played some difficult guitar parts.

The climax of this show, in McDonell's view, was the song 'Warriors', in which Gorham and Moore 'go at it with a passion that left their Detroit show in the dust. Their solos do in your senses. Kinda like putting salt in a wound.' McDonell finished his review expressing hope that Lizzy would make a welcome return.[68]

Journalist Harry Doherty, having witnessed Moore's playing at Madison Square Garden, Nassau Coliseum, Syracuse Civic Center, and the Boston Garden, claimed that Moore's input, 'reflected his own effervesce[ce]... adding a powerful injection of axe style.' Doherty thought Moore's soloing at the Nassau gig in particular was stunning.[69]

A slightly downbeat note came from journalist Sally Rayle, who reviewed the March 2 Inglewood Forum gig for the *Los Angeles Free Press*. Rayle considered Lizzy 'a personal favourite' but sensed some on-stage tension: 'their hard rock macho image appeared a bit tired', she claimed.' It was as if each of the four members were fighting for the centre stage spotlight (usually leader Lynott's space).'[70]

Again, one is reminded of that accusation about Moore's domineering stage presence. Finally, journalist Fred Seegmuller reviewed Lizzy's gig on March 12 at the Paramount Theater in Portland, Oregon, praising Moore and Gorham's energy around the stage as they 'took turns unleashing torrid leads'.

Reviews of Lizzy's performances, and bootlegs of this tour, are few and far between. Where they exist at all, reviewers tend to focus on Queen, and if Lizzy is mentioned the focus is usually on the totality of their performance rather than with a particular focus on Moore, so it is difficult to gauge Moore's impact and reception aside from the few aforementioned sources. Nevertheless, based on those journalists' comments, what can be said is that there was no negativity about Moore, only positive comments about his energy and playing. Indeed, Brian Downey is on record as singling out Moore's 'great performances' on the tour.[71]

Overall, the tour was a boon for Lizzy. They had to cancel or cut short two previous American tours and to cancel a third could have been disastrous for their standing in the country. 'We couldn't let America pass by again', Lynott admitted.[72] Lizzy were fortunate that Queen then asked them to tour as their support, and fortunate also that Moore was available at short notice, having just completed his recording duties for Colosseum II's second album. The band likely had more exposure on this tour than they would have had on the one cancelled in late 1976 due to Robertson's injury, not just because of their support slot for the high-profile headliners Queen, but also because Lizzy got to headline twice when Queen had to cancel gigs due to problems with Mercury's voice.[73]

Lynott told the *Los Angeles Times*, 'This was a quick way of doin' a tour for 3/4 of a million people. If we can get through to the promoters and remind the kids that we're still alive and well and get some reliability into our reputation, then we can come back in the end of summer and do it the way we like to do it.'[74]

Scott Gorham saw it that way too: 'That was the tour that really helped out Thin Lizzy a lot in terms of getting us out in front of a lot of people, in introducing us to a lot of potential new fans.'[75] The same applies to Moore, whose tour with Lizzy only added to his reputation and elevated his profile as a guitarist capable of rising to a challenge. Gorham said that playing with Moore refreshed his own playing, while music journalist John Tiven called Moore 'a very fine player' who 'complemented Gorham perfectly.'[76]

Lynott, too, was impressed: he asked Moore afterwards if he would like to join Lizzy on a full-time basis, but Moore declined as he was still committed to Colosseum II.[77] In fact, though, due to Robertson's unreliability and volatility, it wouldn't be long before Moore and Lizzy crossed paths again.

Robertson re-joined Lizzy in late-Spring 1977 but he had already lost Lynott's confidence. Lynott, in fact, continued to court Moore, complementing him widely and profusely in the press. He told one journalist:

> I think Gary Moore is the best living rock 'n' roll guitarist in the world today, but he is in what I consider to be a jazz-rock field. In that field, there's a lot of great guitarists. Like the competition is heavy! That's basically the paradox that Gary is in, but all the great guitarists go after that. You either do what Clapton has done and go simpler and become a songwriter, or you do what Beck is doing and chase it into the realms of where it becomes musicianship. That's what Gary is doing. He is just ahead of his audience. When Gary Moore was playing rock, the audiences should have been there to hear him. But it might dawn on Gary, "I've got this down; I want to play rock again." He has these two sides to him all the time: the musician

side and this basic energy side where he just wants to go out and boogie, and he gets that chance occasionally to blow out as a rock guitarist with Lizzy. But with Colosseum, he satisfies a much more demanding need, playing with excellent musicians such as Jon Hiseman.[78]

When Lizzy travelled to Toronto to record their next album, *Bad Reputation*, (1977), Robertson wasn't invited to take part until late in the recording sessions. Lynott believed that Gorham could handle all the guitar parts, but Gorham wanted Robertson to be involved. On the finished album Robertson was only credited on three tracks.

Clearly, he was slowly being edged out of Lizzy, mainly at Lynott's insistence, a point confirmed somewhat by the album's cover art, which depicts Lizzy as a trio featuring only Downey, Gorham and Lynott: Robertson's image was relegated to the back cover and record sleeve. It is possible that the song 'Southbound' from this album derived from an earlier Moore tune. Biographer Martin Popoff wrote, 'Gary swears up and down the writing of the song originated with him and that he even extracted some money out of Phil for it years later.'[79] Moore, however, remains uncredited for the song.

Lynott continued to praise Moore in the Press. For instance, in August 1977 he told *Sounds*, 'Gary is strongly into a musicianship of a very high standard, really intense y'know, people of that really high standard. But on another level I feel he's a great guitarist who just likes to play music generally'. Lynott also spoke about his relationship with Moore: 'me and Gary can work very intensely together over a period of three months and then we have to go away from one another for a while. So you'll probably see us working together on me solo album or if he gets an album together I hope he asks me to do something. It's that type of relationship, hot and cold. Now I don't mean that personality-wise, I mean it just musicianship-wise.'[80]

It was, therefore, no surprise when Moore — still with Colosseum II — worked with Lynott in January and February 1978 on a handful of demos, some of which would appear later that year on Moore's solo album *Back On The Streets*. These were the Lizzy song 'Don't Believe A Word', recorded here in slow blues style, a track written by Lynott called 'Fanatical Fascists', and a track co-written by Moore and Lynott entitled 'Parisienne Walkways'. A further co-written song called 'Spanish Guitar' was recorded, with vocals by Lynott; late in

1979, after the pair parted ways, Moore added his own vocals for the song's release as a single.

Given these fruitful collaborations, it was only natural that when in July 1978, a heated argument between Lynott and Robertson led to their estrangement, Moore was once again Lynott's first choice to replace Robertson for Lizzy's forthcoming American tour beginning in August and ending in October.

Press reaction to the news was generally favourable: *Record Mirror* wrote, 'Despite Brian's departure I can't see Phil Lynott and the boys giving in very easily, and with an accomplished guitarist in Gary Moore, Thin Lizzy's future still looks healthy.'[81]

A warm-up gig was arranged on July 29 at the Electric Ballroom, Camden, to reintroduce Moore to the band. They performed using the 'Greedy Bastards' band name, which featured Lizzy plus musical guests including Steve Jones and Paul Cook of The Sex Pistols. At this gig, Moore provided lead vocals on the Clifford Davis/Peter Green track 'Stop Messin' Around'.[82]

Lizzy's 1978 American tour began on August 8 at the Coliseum in Jackson, Mississippi, before moving to the southwest for a series of gigs in Texas and Arizona. The tour then travelled to the west coast for some California gigs, before proceeding through the Midwest and onwards to the east coast for big-city gigs in Boston, and then back through the north-west before returning to New York City for three gigs at the Palladium. After a short break, the tour began its final stage in Denver, before moving on through Salt Lake City and then to Seattle.

The sole Canadian gig took place in Vancouver on October 12, after which Lizzy returned to Texas and then Pasadena, California for the tour's final date on October 15. If that peripatetic schedule wasn't exhausting enough, the band immediately left for a short, five-date tour of Australia. Brian Downey took one look at the punishing itinerary and decided to stay home: American drummer Mark Nauseef toured as his replacement.[83]

This would not be the full headline American tour that Lizzy had hoped for but they did fill support slots for some of the elite of American rock and pop, including Kansas, Journey, REO Speedwagon, Blue Öyster Cult, The Cars, The Doobie Brothers, and Styx. Furthermore, they did headline a handful of gigs, for example in Philadelphia on September 8, Royal Oak, Michigan on September 13, Cleveland, Ohio on the 16th, Chicago on the 22nd, Kansas City, Missouri on the 23rd, and Omaha, Nebraska on September 24th. On all these occasions, Scots-Australian powerhouse rockers AC/DC filled support slots.

As well as being exhausting, this was an eventful tour for Moore. In Memphis, the limousine he and Lynott travelled in was involved in a car chase with an armed man. A little earlier the limo driver was involved in an altercation with this man, and when the limo driver came to collect Moore and Lynott the armed man returned and gave chase. Eventually, they were able to find their way back to the safety of their hotel.[84]

Moore also had some on-stage issues. Mike Flanigan was in the audience when Lizzy played the Uptown Theater, Kansas City, Missouri. Flanigan was astounded by Moore's guitar playing but also recalls Moore's volatile nature: '[Moore] was jaw droppingly good… [his] performance left a lasting impression. He was absolutely on fire. I was a seventeen year old at the time and I'd already seen the likes of Iommi, Blackmore, Brian May, Buck Dharma, Ted Nugent, Alex Lifeson and had recently seen Van Halen no less than four times in one year on their first tour across America but what I saw out of Gary Moore had me convinced that he was as good if not better than all of them.'

However, both Moore and Lynott experienced sound problems, and Moore's response was volcanic. Flanigan recalled, 'I've never seen anyone get so angry on stage as he did that eve… Not once but twice Gary's guitar cut out on him while he was soloing. The first time it happened he was visibly angry but a roadie got things squared away. The second time it happened was during his extended solo during 'Me And The Boys'... and he came unglued. He literally took off his Les Paul… and threw it at a roadie. Not figuratively, he literally threw it at him. Hard! And then he walked off the stage and let the band finish the song. The roadies got things squared away, again, and he came back out but they wrapped up the show quickly from there.'[85]

Off stage too, Moore sometimes appeared unhappy. Ross the Boss, guitarist for The Dictators, who were one of Lizzy's support acts, was a Fleetwood Mac and Peter Green fan, and he was excited to discover that Moore had brought with him Green's 1959 Gibson Les Paul Sunburst. Nevertheless, despite their shared love of Green's music, Ross the Boss found Gary to be a 'moody fellow' on this tour and he kept his distance.[86]

Bootlegs of this tour suggest the setlist followed closely the track listing of Lizzy's *Live And Dangerous* live double album, which captured the band in concert from November 1976 to October 1977. The 2022 release of Lizzy's performance at the Sydney Opera House in October 1978 also confirms this point. Few reviews of the American leg of the tour have surfaced thus far. As well as Flanigan's recollections of the Kansas City gig, a local Memphis newspaper gave Lizzy a few lines, stating that in spite of the line-up having only been together for a short time, songs such as 'Jailbreak' and 'The Boys Are Back In Town' still 'came off well'.[87]

As soon as the American leg of the tour concluded, Lizzy travelled to Australia for five headliner gigs. Of these, the Sydney performance on October 29 is prominent in Lizzy lore as it was filmed for documentary and television broadcast. As such, it is probably the best recorded visual documentary of Moore playing live with the band. The setlist is once again based on that of *Live And Dangerous*. Of note is that although Moore played most of gig with a Les Paul, when the band returned to the stage towards the end of their set Moore took to the stage with a Gibson Melody Maker. He then proceeded during the song 'Me And The Boys' to do some shredding, including a short guitar rendition of 'Waltzing Matilda'. Also of note is that the setlist included a live debut of a new song entitled 'Waiting For An Alibi', which featured some magnificent harmony guitar playing between Moore and Gorham, before they began trading killer licks.

When Lizzy returned home after the US and Australian tour in 1978, Moore gave a series of live performances in London and Ireland with The Greedies, and was involved in a special Lizzy Christmas show at the Hammersmith Odeon on December 17, supported by Londonderry punk band The Undertones. During this performance, Moore chased a roadie off the stage after the unfortunate man had handed Moore a guitar with the strap fitted insecurely, causing it to fall on to the stage.[88]

Barry Cain, reviewing the show for *Record Mirror,* had this to say about the guitarist: 'The mercurial Mr Moore grabs nearly as much attention as Lynott simply by his interminable acrobatic histrionics. He devours the stage with exhausting runs, leaps. sweat showers and spent more time under the spotlight than anybody else. And it was Moore who pumped the atom heart mother into the proceedings with his "Still In Love With You" solo which was as formidable as

Robertson's vinylised [sic] contribution.'[89]

Lizzy performed a few as-of-yet unreleased songs, including 'Róisín Dubh (Black Rose): A Rock Legend', 'Waiting For An Alibi' and 'Get Out Of Here', as well as 'Back On The Streets', which was sung by Moore and would later be included on his solo album, and released as a solo single.

In December 1978, and at the beginning of 1979, Lizzy travelled to Paris to record their next album, *The Black Rose: A Rock Legend*. It is the only Lizzy album on which Moore made a substantial contribution. Some demos with Moore had been recorded a year previously, including 'Waiting For An Alibi', 'With Love', 'Róisín Dubh (Black Rose): A Rock Legend', 'Got To Give It Up', and 'Toughest Street In Town'.[90]

On the album, Moore plays on all these tracks but is given co-writer credit only on 'Toughest Street In Town', 'Róisín Dubh (Black Rose): A Rock Legend', and another track called 'Sarah', which was recorded at Morgan Studios in London. Moore also worked on a track entitled 'A Night In The Life Of A Blues Singer', which didn't make the cut for the *Black Rose* album and would only appear as a Lizzy B-side in 1983, long after Moore left the band. It features a memorable blues solo by Moore, but the overall mood of the song wasn't in keeping with the rest of the *Black Rose* album and that is likely why it was omitted.[91]

Moore explained why he shared writing credits with Gorham and Lynott on 'Toughest Street In Town': 'That was a riff I had before I joined the band and we built it up from there. The middle eight was a riff that Scott had hanging around. The title was mine and again, I lead off some of the lyrics. I would write some of the lyrics for the first verse and a chorus, and Phil basically filled in all the holes for me. So that's how that one came together. But the main idea was something I had.'[92]

Moore also explained how he co-wrote 'Sarah' with Lynott: 'I wrote most of that song, 85% of that song and he wrote most of the lyrics. But even some of the lyrical ideas, was my idea [sic] that it should be about his kid basically, which is a really weird thing to have happened.'

Moore explained how the initial demo was recorded on acoustic guitar, with a drum machine, and how for the final album version he spent a lot of time working alone with producer Tony Visconti trying to get the exact guitar sound he wanted. In the end, Moore played all guitar on the song (except bass) and his solo was multi-tracked seven times. He called 'Sarah' 'the best showcase of my playing on that record.'[93]

Critics seemed to agree: for example, *Melody Maker* called it 'a beautiful and exquisitely organised ballad'.[94] Lizzy released 'Sarah' as a single in September 1979, after Moore had left the band. It was a moderate hit, reaching the top 30 in the UK. Finally, Moore is credited as co-writer of 'Róisín Dubh (Black Rose): A Rock Legend', which incorporates some traditional folk songs into an epic tribute to Lizzy's Celtic roots. Moore had some of the guitar arrangement figured out years earlier, and he played those onstage during his first live tour with Lizzy as part of an extended guitar solo.

For the most part, the album received good press reviews, and Moore's contributions were recognised. For example, *Creem* said: 'Gary Moore's taken Brian Robertson's place but the crazed quotient don't [sic] drop an iota; just listen to that solo on "Toughest Street In Town." Also, Gary's presence means more variety in the writing, from the soothing salves of "Sarah" to the Irish-history-as-seen-through-the-eyes-of-a-fuzztone of the title track.'[95]

In praising *Black Rose* as Lizzy's 'strongest, most consistent album in a number of years', *Cash Box* called Moore's reunion with Lizzy, 'an event, in some circles, akin to Danny Kirwan rejoining Fleetwood Mac. His presence as both a contributing songwriter and on the band's distinctive dual lead guitar work add a chemical element that should further their development as one of the better rock 'n' roll bands.'[96]

Melody Maker's Harry Doherty called *Black Rose* 'Thin Lizzy›s best studio album yet' and singled out Moore for praise as 'an inspired addition. He's no more potent, stylistically than Brian Robertson', Doherty argued, 'but his partnership with Scott Gorham is a hell of a lot more creative. "Waiting For An Alibi", for example, is traditional Lizzy lifted to extraordinary heights by the clash of the two guitarists.'[97]

Sounds wrote that *Black Rose* 'promises much, gives you quite a bit but still falls slightly into the trap of the band's own mythology.' Despite adjudging the track 'Róisín Dubh (Black Rose): A Rock Legend' to be 'grotesque hyperbole', *Sounds* nevertheless praised Moore's overall contribution to the album, which, it claimed, 'broadens and sharpens the sound.'[98]

Despite *Black Rose: A Rock Legend* being a fan favourite, in

Moore's judgement it wasn't a classic Lizzy album. He mused, 'we did some nice tunes together but again, the songs weren't up to what was going on before it either. There were a couple things there but it wasn't like a classic Thin Lizzy album… it wasn't like *Jailbreak*.'

Surprisingly, perhaps, Moore also said that he considered the Gorham-Robertson partnership to be the 'classic Lizzy line-up' and the one he enjoyed listening to most.[99] Gorham was more complimentary about the album, and he praised Moore's contribution. 'I thought the *Black Rose* album was great', he reflected. 'I thought Gary did a really good job on that. There were some great songs that came out of that.'[100]

On February 9, 1979, after recording *Black Rose*, but before setting off to the States for their latest American tour, Gary Moore and Friends (Lynott, Gorham, Don Airey and Cozy Powell) appeared on the BBC's *Old Grey Whistle Test*, performing the songs 'Back On The Streets' and the slow/fast version of 'Don't Believe A Word'. Lynott shared vocals with Moore on the former, although as this was an event designed primarily to promote Moore's solo album, Moore took the majority of the vocals, as he did on his solo album; on 'Don't Believe A Word' the two shared vocal duties. The latter ends with a frenetic burst of guitar energy that is more pronounced than the slightly tamer recorded version from Moore's solo album.

Lizzy released 'Waiting For An Alibi' in February as the first single from the *Black Rose* album. The B-side was the catchy Lynott-penned 'With Love'. Lizzy recorded promotional videos for both songs, with Moore featuring on both. Just twenty-four hours before Lizzy set off for the United States, they recorded another performance for television, this time on the *Kenny Everett Video Show*. At that time, Everett was a very popular disc jockey and television personality, and his show, aimed at younger people, was innovative and hip. The band performed 'Waiting For An Alibi' and seemed to be in good spirits.

Similar to the stage garb he wore in the official promotional video, Moore was dressed here in white shoes, black leather trousers, a white coat, dark shirt with white tie, and dark glasses. This style was probably influenced by the fashion of emerging 'New Wave' artists of the time, such as The Cars, The Knack, and Elvis Costello. Only Lynott's vocals were performed live, so for visual effect both Moore and Gorham forewent their usual guitars and instead Moore mimed playing a sunburst Fender Stratocaster with white scratch plate (Gorham used a striking, elaborately-shaped Danelectro). While

Moore returned to his usual Gibson guitars for the American tour, he retained his new fashionable clothes.

The American tour in support of Scottish rock band Nazareth was an opportunity once more for Lizzy to enhance their standing in one of the world's largest music markets. The Nazareth tour began in late February, but Lizzy did not join it until the beginning of March. In that month, twenty-two gigs were scheduled in twenty-four days, with only two rest days. The tour took Lizzy through the south and south-west, and then to the mid-west.

The *Black Rose* album had potential to break Lizzy in the States, so a number of songs from the album were included in their truncated set list, which was tailored to the fifty-minute slot Lizzy was allocated as support act. This caused some problems for Moore, particularly with the song 'Do Anything You Want To'. In the promotional video, all members of the band played kettledrums to add an interesting visual aspect to the performance. For the same reason, they decided to repeat this stunt in live performances. Moore recalled: 'We did it on the video, and it was on the record [*Black Rose*] and it just went from there. So we ended up having a couple of them on stage just as a visual thing. It wasn't my favourite thing in the world. Because you had to transfer quickly onto guitar.'[101]

There was also an issue with the song 'Róisín Dubh (Black Rose): A Rock Legend'. Moore had been playing parts of it live for a number of years previously, but during the recording sessions for the album, Gorham had to learn it from scratch. By his own admission, Gorham, who had only been playing guitar for around three years at this point, found Moore's intricate melodies difficult to play, but with Moore's help he was able to complete the recording. A live rendition was, however, a different prospect: 'We actually had to drop the title track of… *Black Rose*, because Scott couldn't play it live', Moore recalled.[102]

No sooner had Lizzy returned from their American tour than they began a hectic thirty-date UK Tour, which began late in March, then continued throughout April and into early May, 1979. There were only five rest days scheduled in this period. Lizzy played mostly songs from their *Live And Dangerous* album, which that March had been certified Platinum in the UK, and was developing a reputation as one of the best live double albums around.[103]

However, bootlegs from the period reveal that a number of songs from *Black Rose* were rolled out, including for example, the following, which were on the setlist for the Bournemouth, Glasgow and Preston gigs: 'Do Anything You Want To', 'Waiting For An Alibi', 'Got To Give It Up', 'Get Out Of Here', and 'Róisín Dubh (Black Rose): A Rock Legend'.

Although it wasn't played at the beginning of the tour, by the time Lizzy reached London for their Hammersmith Odeon gigs, 'Parisienne Walkways' had been added to the setlist to capitalise on the song's recent chart success. Live bootlegs indicate Moore was on top form during this tour, rarely missing a note despite some very fast and intricate playing.

A European tour followed in May 1979. Twenty gigs were scheduled in Sweden, Norway, Denmark, Switzerland, Germany, Holland, Belgium, and France. However, Lizzy had to cancel the last seven concerts scheduled in Holland, Belgium, and France. The official reason was that Lynott was suffering from food poisoning, although in retrospect the suspicion is that Lynott was instead struggling with addiction. The sole change to the set list since the previous UK tour was that Lizzy dropped 'Warriors' to make way for 'Parisienne Walkways', which for a time would become a regular part of their live show.

At the Cologne gig, Lizzy was joined onstage by Rory Gallagher, Moore's guitar hero from his early days in Belfast. *Melody Maker* journalist and Lizzy fan, Harry Doherty, who was following the band's German dates, reported mixed results for Lizzy, with a lacklustre crowd response in Hamburg, and a slightly better response in Saarbrucken. In Offenbach, Doherty thought that Lizzy's performance improved, and the crowd response was 'raucous'.

Lynott told Doherty that 'Whiskey In The Jar' had returned to the set list because Moore had only recently learned to play it. Doherty noted, however, that Lizzy tended to play 'Whiskey In The Jar' only if they were happy with the audience response on a particular night, as a kind of reward for their enthusiasm.

Docherty explained that Lynott had also been pondering Lizzy's longevity, saying that the band could fall apart at any time, but he was hopeful for the future because, 'Gary, for the first time, has given full commitment.'[104] In retrospect, Lynott seemed to be deflecting attention from his drug issues, and shifting responsibility (and blame) for Lizzy's future onto Moore.

Even before their second American tour of the year, it was clear that Lizzy was in danger of burn out. Constant touring, as well as the pressures of recording an album and various solo projects, were exacerbated by Lynott and Gorham's growing drug addiction. After only a week of rehearsals in the States, the tour began. Lizzy played a shortened version of their European tour set list. Of the *Black Rose* tracks from that set, they dropped only 'Get Out Of Here', which perhaps indicates the band made promoting the new album in the States a priority. 'Parisienne Walkways' was also dropped, likely because it wasn't a hit in America.

In the first week of the tour, just five dates into Lizzy's thirty-five-date schedule, Moore and Lynott got into an argument and Moore walked away. This was at promoter Bill Graham's Day on the Green show in Oakland. Lizzy carried on as a three-piece before Lynott's friend Midge Ure arrived to replace Moore. Privately, Lynott was furious with Moore, but in a press interview he made light of the situation, claiming his old friend 'didn't want to leave L.A. He missed a gig or two, didn't tell us what was happening.' Later in the conversation, however, Lynott described Moore's problem as 'delusions of grandeur'.[105]

A few years afterwards, Scott Gorham gave a fuller account of events: 'We only had a couple of hours before we had to get on a plane to Arizona and nobody had seen Gary for about two days. (Manager) Chris O'Donnell finally hunted him down at Glenn Hughes' home where Gary was a little bit worse for wear on the old drink front. We were all in the room while Chris had him on the phone. Gary kept screaming, "I get no respect from this band, nobody respects me!"'

According to Gorham, O'Donnell then asked Moore a few times if he was going to be on the plane but Moore just kept talking about lack of respect. When O'Donnell asked Moore a final time, Moore made no reply, so O'Donnell told him he was fired, before slamming down the phone.[106]

Moore had grown disillusioned with drug taking within Lizzy, and also possibly that Lynott had become something of a diva on tour. During the previous Australian tour, Lynott had treated support bands poorly, leading to what Martin Popoff described as 'further deterioration in his relationship with the comparatively more professional Gary Moore.' Moore described the group dynamics of working on the *Black Rose* album as 'a couple of smack heads [Lynott and Gorham] and me'.[107]

During the American tour, Moore complained that Lynott had been acting unprofessionally, was constantly keeping everyone waiting, almost missing flights, and made mistakes on stage such as forgetting lyrics or, on one occasion, singing over the top of one of Moore's guitar solos.[108]

Furthermore, although his solo album *Back On The Streets* had been released in Britain in September 1978, it wouldn't get an American release until August 1979. The title track from the album would also be released as a single in the States later in the year. Due to this schedule, American music magazine *Cash Box* asserted that Moore dropped out of Lizzy that July 'to pursue his solo career', and while it is possible these events were linked — that Moore quit Lizzy to focus on promotion of his solo album in the States — evidence for such a degree of cynical self-interest is in short supply.[109]

Nevertheless, Moore had already had a UK top ten hit single with 'Parisienne Walkways', which was released in March 1979, so it may have been on his mind at that time that a solo career was a better option than sticking with Lizzy, a band which, at that point, seemed to him to be on the verge of self-destruction. Furthermore, Lizzy manager Chris O'Donnell claimed that around that time Jet Records owner Don Arden was 'seducing' Moore into signing with Jet as a solo artist.[110]

Yet, the most obvious reason for Moore leaving Lizzy is likely the correct one, that Moore quit due to Lynott's heavy drug use, which led to erratic behaviour onstage and off. While Moore enjoyed an alcoholic drink, he did not use hard drugs, nor did he enjoy being around people who did. Musician Glenn Hughes explained: 'There were very few people in the industry who weren't doing coke, and Gary was one of them — he hated that drug.'[111]

To make matters worse, Lynott had begun using heroin during the Paris recording sessions for *Black Rose*, and heroin was a much more debilitating drug than cocaine, so it seemed a parting of ways was inevitable.[112]

Nevertheless, it was a setback for both Moore and Lizzy: Sharon Osborne, then at Jet Records, the record label that released *Back On The Streets* in the States, claimed that it was 'one of the worst mistakes of Gary's career... he just fucked it up.'[113]

Moore had high hopes for Lizzy when he left Colosseum II. He became a full-time member of the band, with a quarter share in revenue — a situation quite different to his earlier stints in the group. That he felt it necessary to once more part ways must have been dispiriting for the ambitious guitarist.

In a sense he would once more be starting over, albeit with an enhanced reputation for his musical ability, if not for reliability. In retrospect, however, his exit was more of a setback for Lizzy than for Moore, as his solo career was about to begin in earnest, whereas Lizzy never again hit the studio heights of *Black Rose*, or the live high of the *Live And Dangerous* tours. A few years later, Lynott reflected: 'when Gary came in — Gary's such a good player that the rest of us improved too, so we hit a high there. Then it got lost for a while...'[114]

Postscript

Although some hostility remained between Lynott and Moore, eventually the two ended their estrangement and began collaborating once more. These collaborations seem to confirm both men's assertions that musically they have intense periods where they are 'hot' and can collaborate, but which are so intense they both then need a break from each other. When Lizzy disbanded in 1983, Moore made a guest appearance at the Hammersmith Odeon on the band's farewell tour. Lynott said, 'Gary Moore was the first one to turn up. Gary rehearsed and we made up all our old arguments after not speaking for two years.'[115] Moore performed 'Still In Love With You' and 'Black Rose', and he appeared on the live album that was a record of this tour, 1983's *Life/Live*.

If the hatchet hadn't been completely buried by that point, the two old friends seemed to have put all their differences behind them the following year when Moore invited Lynott to his concert at the Ulster Hall, Belfast on December 18, 1984 — Moore's first appearance in Belfast for a decade.

On stage, Lynott joined Moore for renditions of 'Parisienne Walkways' and 'Stop Messin' Around', while backstage the two jammed together and seemed to be having a lot of fun. Lynott said he considered it a great compliment to be invited to the show, and that every time the two worked together it had been 'magical... always something creative came out of it'. Lynott concluded by saying it was 'an honour' to work with Moore.[116]

In early 1985, the pair worked together on songs that would soon appear on Moore's solo album *Run For Cover* (1985). These were 'Out In The Fields', 'Military Man', and 'Nothing To Lose'. They also worked on a new version of the Lizzy classic 'Still In Love With You'. 'Out In The Fields', coupled with 'Military Man', was released as a single in May that year, becoming a top ten hit in the UK. 'Still In Love With You' appeared on the 12-inch vinyl version of this single.

The pair collaborated on a video to support 'Out In The Fields', with both dressed in historic red army tunics. They also made a number of promotional appearances on television, including BBC's *Whistle Test*, during which they explained that their mutual animosity lasted for around three years until they met by accident at Heathrow Airport, shook hands, and began then to rebuild their friendship.

While *Whistle Test* showed the video of 'Out In The Fields', for Channel 4's *ECT* (Extra Celestial Transmission), Moore and Lynott gave live performances of 'Out In The Fields', 'Military Man' and 'Still In Love With You', although only a snippet of the latter was broadcast. The duo also made two separate appearances on BBC 1's *Top Of The Pops* chart show, on each occasion miming to a recorded version of 'Out In The Fields'. Moore invited Lynott to his wedding in July, and in September Lynott joined Moore on stage at the Manchester Apollo and two consecutive nights at the Hammersmith Odeon, for renditions of 'Out In The Fields' and 'Parisienne Walkways'. However, Lynott's well-documented, tragic descent into addiction and ill-health cut short his life and deprived fans of further collaborations between the two old friends.

Following Lynott's death in January 1986, Moore performed in May with members of Thin Lizzy at the Self Aid concert in Dublin. The following year, he dedicated his new album *Wild Frontier* to Lynott. Moore joined once more with former Lizzy members, as well as some of Lynott's family, in August 2005 when a bronze statue of Lynott was unveiled in Dublin. Moore was the anchor musician for a tribute concert to Lynott by an ensemble called 'Gary Moore and Friends', featuring Downey, Robertson, Gorham and Bell. A recording of the concert was released in 2006 as *One Night in Dublin: A Tribute to Phil Lynott*. And as it turned out, Moore's outstanding vocal and guitar performances were, indeed, a fitting tribute to the late, great Lynott.

Flying Solo 1974-1980

Outside of Skid Row and Thin Lizzy, Moore made a number of efforts to strike out on his own in search of both musical satisfaction and financial success. That both his stint in Skid Row and his first solo album, *Grinding Stone*, failed to meet his expectations left Moore confused as to which direction to follow. Over the next decade Moore would first embrace the opportunity to play a secondary, non-leadership role in Jon Hiseman's band, Colosseum II, but when that ended, he resolved to take control over his own musical career. In opting to succeed or fail from that point onwards only on his own terms, Moore was following in the footsteps of Rory Gallagher, a man who Moore admired and who showed little compromise in his musical vision.

Colosseum II

Moore's time with Colosseum II was one of the most musically productive and professionally rewarding times in his life. Formed primarily by drummer Jon Hiseman, formerly of John Mayall's Blues Breakers, but with Moore's input, the band was led by Hiseman and was mainly his attempt to redress the commercial failure of the band's previous incarnation, when it was known simply as Colosseum.

The original iteration had moderate success as a touring band and released three albums of jazz rock during its three-year existence from 1969 to 1971. While Colosseum was critically acclaimed, and had the respect of its musical peers, it did not achieve the level of commercial success necessary to ensure its longevity.

A few years later, after Hiseman had a similar experience with his band Tempest, he hoped to reform Colosseum with more well-known musicians, as a 'supergroup'.

In the late 1960s, this format of putting together a band from already well-known and popular musicians proved commercially successful for the likes of Clapton's Blind Faith. The 'supergroup' idea ensured immediate press attention and created a sense of expectation and anticipation that often precipitated a degree of commercial success.

In late 1973, Moore went to see Tempest at London's Marquee Club, where he suggested to Hiseman that the two form a band together.[117] Publicly, Hiseman said that the new band wouldn't have commercial or popular appeal; privately, however, Hiseman hoped that collaborating with hotshot guitar prodigy, Moore, would prove commercially lucrative.

Hiseman said of Moore: 'First I had to find a partner and I found guitarist Gary Moore, who sings as well. All I can say about Gary is that he is the greatest challenge to play with since Graham Bond... he's giving me a hard time. Tremendous speed.'[118]

But first, the two needed to set some ground rules. Years later, Moore revealed that he used to drink a lot and would dabble in drugs so he was grateful when Hiseman took him to one side and gave him a 'severe warning' about his behaviour. Moore said, it 'really made me think and having a musician who I really respected talk to me like that really upset me, because I thought I was losing his respect. I'd always looked up to Jon, and so in order to try to gain his respect I straightened myself out, and I haven't dabbled in drugs since.'[119]

It took a little longer than planned to find other musicians of sufficient stature: at one point, the band consisted of Moore, Hiseman, and bassist Andy Pyle, and the trio were offered money to record a film score. However, when details emerged that it would be a pornographic film, Moore and Pyle declined on moral grounds.[120]

When Pyle left the band soon after, Hiseman was able in May 1975 to secure the services of keyboard maestro Don Airey and bass player Neil Murray, both formerly of Cozy Powell's band, Hammer. The final line-up was secured when Moore and Hiseman invited the relatively unknown Scottish singer Mike Starrs to join the group. 'We've all been searching for a band like this', Moore told journalist Pete Makowski of *Sounds* magazine. 'We're all on the same level musically, all we have to do is take it by the reins and go.'[121]

Many years later, however, Moore said modestly that he did 'a lot of bluffing' with regard to the jazz aspect of the jazz-rock fusion direction that Colosseum II took. 'I thought I knew what I was doing but I really didn't, and the more I did it the more I realised I didn't know what I was doing. I came out of that band knowing a lot more than I did when I went in.'[122]

Nevertheless, Moore did improve his technique during his time with the band. He had to, otherwise he would not have been capable of playing the music the band was creating. 'I got into the picking thing then much more, instead of playing with one hand [meaning his left hand on the neck of the guitar, as opposed to his right hand, which he used to pick the strings nearer the guitar bridge]. Up until then I had been playing very orthodox sort of rock guitar... I really had to strengthen my picking technique.'[123]

The virtuoso line up was reflected in the musical content of the three albums the band released. Typically, the songs were co-written by Moore and Hiseman, and featured extended instrumental soloing, 'jousting' or dialogue between various instruments, technically proficient, often high-speed playing, songs with unusual time signatures and sometimes multiple time signatures within one song, and on occasion songs arranged into multiple sections, sometimes with a particular instrument favoured for each part. These sections functioned to showcase each musician's proficiency.

Technical prowess aside, Moore also wanted to achieve commercial success, after he had similar experiences to Hiseman with his other groups, Skid Row, Thin Lizzy and The Gary Moore Band, all of whom produced critically successful music and had the respect of fellow musicians but had not achieved enough commercial success to ensure financially stability.

According to Charles Waring, Moore was struggling to make ends meet, and in those early days Hiseman was paying him a £10 retainer.[124] However, Moore also wanted to be taken seriously as a professional musician, and a collaboration with Hiseman seemed to offer that opportunity. He told Makowski, 'We met out of musical frustration. We were both sitting at home thinking of packing it in. I didn't want to do anything unless it was with the best people.'[125]

Phil Lynott also noted Moore's need for professional acceptance. Lynott said: 'He has these two sides to him all the time: the musician side and this basic energy side where he just wants to go out and boogie, and he gets that chance occasionally to blow out as a rock guitarist with Lizzy. But with Colosseum, he satisfies a much more demanding need, playing with excellent musicians such as Jon Hiseman.'[126]

Moore was determined both to follow his own musical path and to take his musicianship seriously. He explained, for instance, that Colosseum II was a more professional outfit than his previous collaborations, and had been rehearsing five days a week, from 10am to 5pm. 'We're trying to set a different direction', he explained, 'not like Yes, but we're not going to blow people's ears off. I know we're going to have a hard time when we start gigging. I know we're going to get a hammering from the press or maybe go over people's heads but we're not going to change for anybody.'[127]

With Moore in the line-up, Colosseum II had a more powerful guitar-driven sound than its original iteration. Furthermore, while Colosseum played jazz-rock, with blues influences, Colosseum II developed a jazz fusion style that, after the release of their first album, increasingly relied on instrumental pieces without the need for lead vocals.

The band signed to Bronze Records, headed by Gerry Bron, who, a few years back, had been Colosseum's original manager. Bron listened to the new line-up's demo tape before signing Hiseman and Moore to Bronze. Knowing how important name recognition was for promotion and sales, Bron stipulated that the band change its name from Ghost to Colosseum, in effect, resurrecting Hiseman's old band but with different musicians.

Hiseman approached the old line-up for permission to use the name and no one objected; but to distinguish old from new, Hiseman and Moore agreed on the name Colosseum II. They planned to record their first album in October 1975, for a January 1976 release, with extensive UK and European tour dates to follow.[128] Colosseum II's debut album was recorded at the recently-opened Roundhouse Recording Studios, which was also owned by the Bron organisation. Moore played guitars and provided vocals on the album, which would be entitled *Strange New Flesh*.

Of the six tracks on the album, one was a cover of a Joni Mitchell song, one was written solely by Moore ('On Second Thoughts'), three were collaborations between Moore and Hiseman, and the other was a Moore-Airey song. Moore explained how the writing process typically unfolded with Hiseman: 'Jon gives me the lyrics and I take them home, take them apart and work melodies out.'[129] At least three other songs were demoed during that time period: 'Castles (version 1)' and the instrumental 'Gary's Lament', both written by Moore and Hiseman, as well as the Graham Bond composition 'Walking In The Park'.

The opening instrumental track, 'Dark Side Of The Moog', credited to Airey and Moore, is a statement piece, introducing Colosseum II to the world. It begins with a fast-paced work-out by the band, with intricate drumming, keyboards, bass and guitar. It is very precise and technical, as if to say, 'this is how good we are'. As well as fiery riffing, Moore wrings some tortured notes from his instrument for guitar fills. An abrupt change in time signature signifies a shift in tone, with Airey's keyboard now driving the song along, and Moore playing arpeggiated chords. The track is a surprising and daring introduction to a group of virtuoso musicians letting loose for the first time on record. 'Down To You' is a mellow extended rearrangement of the Joni Mitchell song, played at a slightly slower tempo than Mitchell's version, and with Mike Starrs providing vocals. Starrs is unable to replicate Mitchell's ethereal vocal delivery, but he provides a competent, emotional performance nevertheless.

Moore's playing here is reminiscent of Jeff Beck, offering tasty, delicate embellishments to the song, in which vocals, piano and keyboards take the lead. A lyric from this song provided the album with its title: 'When the closing lights strip off the shadows, on this strange new flesh you've found.' The third and final track on side one is 'Gemini and Leo', the album's finest example of jazz-funk fusion, with a great vocal delivery from Starrs. Moore plays a tasty funk-blues guitar break, as well as providing some background effects.

Side two opens with 'Secret Places', a medium-paced rocker, and probably the album's most commercial track. Moore provides some vocals on this track, as well as some fiery guitar fills and trills. The album's penultimate track, 'On Second Thoughts', was written by Moore, and is hard to categorise. It features complex interplay between all the musicians, which nevertheless creates a very mellow mood. For the first few minutes Moore's playing is restrained and services the song rather than the song simply being a platform for his virtuoso solo playing. A guitar fade-out leads to an abrupt change in tone that begins with some delicate and tasteful picking from Moore continuing until near the end of the track. As if to illustrate the song doesn't quite know its own identity, it ends with some oriental keyboard riffs from Airey, and some aggressive drumming from Hiseman.

'Winds' is the album's final and longest track. It is a statement of musical intent and defiance, and likely the track critics of this genre would find most irritating due to its beginning-to-end self-indulgence. The song's arrangement makes Pete Townshend's worst excesses on *Tommy* look tame in comparison. It is simply a showcase for complex interplay between the band, with Hiseman's energetic percussion underpinning instrumental indulgences from Airey and Moore. Moore uses a wah-wah pedal to good effect, adding colour to his musical palate.

Strange New Flesh was released in April 1976 to mixed reviews and poor sales as the band came to realise that virtuoso musicianship wouldn't necessarily lead to commercial success. As Moore had indicated, however, this was the reaction the band anticipated. While *Billboard* magazine called Colosseum II 'a very together band', and *Record Mirror* noted the quality of musicianship on offer, with Hiseman's drumming being 'energetic and keen', while the rest of the band 'play tightly', the whole was not greater than the sum of its parts. *Record Mirror* singled out poor lyrics as a particular weakness, as they tended to 'distract from the skill of the band'. Not coincidentally, *Record Mirror* adjudged the instrumental track 'Dark Side Of The Moog' as the album's best track, while Moore's 'On Second Thoughts' was deemed the only song 'where lyrics and music are tied in'.[130]

Journalist Chris Welch was a long-time Hiseman enthusiast and wrote positively about this iteration of Colosseum: 'Hiseman has assembled a team of young players whose first consideration is to write, improvise and perform to the best of their ability and create some excitement in the process.' Welch was particularly enthusiastic about Moore's playing on *Strange New Flesh*, saying: 'Gary Moore's guitars are heard either in sensitive mood or at their most wailing. Colosseum have enabled Gary to develop his style and technique. He is presented with challenges and responds magnificently.'[131]

Colosseum II toured extensively throughout Europe and the UK to promote *Strange New Flesh*.[132] However, as the album was a commercial failure, the new head of their record label, Lilian Bron, put pressure on Hiseman to cut costs and change direction by firing Starrs (which took place in July 1976). Neil Murray then quit, forcing Hiseman to reorganise the band as an instrumental four-piece, with John Mole now taking on bass duties in place of Murray. It made little difference as, soon after, Bronze dropped Colosseum II from their label altogether. Murray would go on to join David Coverdale's Whitesnake, which he compared favourably to Colosseum II, saying: 'At last I'm playing with my heart, not my head'.[133]

The new Colosseum II line-up regrouped after the break from Bronze. While their debut album wasn't a financial success, they continued to tour through 1976 and made a profile-raising appearance at the Reading Festival in August. A few months previously, the BBC organised a live recording of three Colosseum II songs, 'Dark Side Of The Moog', 'Siren Song', and 'The Awakening', all of which were co-written by Moore, for their BBC in Concert radio series.

There was, therefore, reason to be hopeful for future prospects, and this confidence helped the band negotiate for studio time at Morgan Studios in London to record their next album, and eventually to earn a new distribution contract with MCA.

Recording for the new album took place in December 1976. Before Colosseum II's debut album Moore said that it was going to have a very live feel, and that approach continued into the recording session for the new album, which would be entitled *Electric Savage*. On the album sleeve, for example, Hiseman wrote: 'Just before Christmas 1976 and a few hours after our return from a European tour, our exhausted crew set up the gear in Morgan No. 1. For seven days we continued playing music live. I Hope you enjoy it.'

In addition, the band may have taken note of the criticism that the song lyrics on their debut album were weak, as seven of the eight tracks on *Electric Savage* were instrumental: only one song, 'Rivers' written by Moore and Hiseman, had lyrics, with Moore taking on vocal duties. Of the eight songs on the album, five were co-written by Moore, and one other — 'Lament' — was a traditional folk song, arranged by Moore and Hiseman. Five other songs were demoed in mid-1976, all co-written by Moore, but none of them made it on to *Electric Savage*. These were 'Night Creeper', 'The Awakening', 'Siren Song', 'Castles (version 2)', and 'The Scorch'. A demo version of 'Intergalactic Strut', originally entitled 'Interplanetary Slut', was credited initially to Moore and Hiseman, but on the album credits it was attributed solely to Airey.

The playing on *Electric Savage* is tighter than on the band's debut album, and this is not surprising since the band had been performing these songs live for months previously. Moore is credited on the album cover for playing Fender and Gibson guitars, and for vocals. The opening track, 'Put It This Way', sees Moore play melodic funk-rock, which was a change in style for him. 'All Skin and Bone' is a relatively low-key track, whose skeletal frame is provided by Hiseman's impressive percussive skills, with Moore offering guitar ornamentation on top.

'Rivers' is another relatively subdued track, on which Moore provides a very respectable vocal performance. However, having been conditioned thus far on the album to instrumental tracks only, 'Rivers' seems oddly out-of-place here. Moore plays some interesting, melodic fills, although the guitar tone varies through the song as if the fills were added in stages and without a consistent guitar or amp setting. The final track on side one, entitled 'The Scorch', features Moore and Airey playing harmony melodies and engaging in some duelling, as one tries to outdo the other. Airey wins the battle on this occasion, but not the war.

'Lament', the opening track on side two, offers a change of mood. Credited as a traditional song, arranged by Moore and Hiseman, Moore's guitar carries the song along, first relatively gently in tone — with Airey playing atmospheric tubular bells — before offering more of an edge when Moore uses guitar effects to imitate the sound of Scottish bagpipes or Irish uilleann pipes.

'Lament' is followed by 'Desperado', a fast-paced jazz-rock fusion work out, which sounds like a stage jam that has lost its way somewhat. Moore and Airey once more joust together in fine fashion, but this track is probably the weakest of the album's high-tempo songs as it all adds up to less than the sum of its parts.

'Am I' is a medium-paced blues workout, featuring some interesting phrases from Moore that then ascend into something more like the 'cosmic rock' heard elsewhere on the album. The final track is 'Intergalactic Strut', a guitar and drum-driven *tour de force*, and probably the album's stand-out track. Moore first provides searing riffs, underpinned by Hiseman's drum beats and Airey's precise keyboards. A temporary change to a slower tempo provides breathing room and allows Moore to shine with more space-age guitar before the song picks up pace once more, with Airey and Moore duelling as if their lives depended on it. 'Intergalactic Strut' is a fantastic track upon which to end the album, and it indicates in which direction the band's music might go next if they remained consistent and persevered with fast-paced, intricate instrumentals and virtuoso playing.

Electric Savage was released in the UK in January 1977, and a few months later in the USA. It arrived to a mixed critical response. *Cash Box* said, 'the jazz/rock fusion sound is alive and well on this album which introduces a continental band [sic] to a worldwide audience after European success. Though their numbers are small, this sprightly quartet make the sounds of a symphony, utilizing a range of synthesizer effects and showcasing an ability to play tightly and enthusiastically on songs of difficult composition.'[134]

Walrus!, a US music industry magazine, was a little less effusive, suggesting that this iteration of Colosseum was not an improvement on the original. 'They are commanding instrumentally', *Walrus!* opined, 'yet, only fair writers. When their melodies catch up to their techniques Colosseum II approaches importance.'[135]

The only single released from the album, 'Lament' failed to chart in the UK or USA. Music journalist Charles Shaar Murray gave it a poor review in *New Musical Express*: 'It would be dangerous to play it on the radio, as it would cause motorists to fall asleep at the wheel.'[136]

Colosseum II's third and final album, entitled *Wardance*, was very much a continuation of the direction the band followed with *Electric Savage*. It was recorded once more in Morgan Studios with the same line-up, only nine months after the previous album's December 1976 recording session, and once more was recorded while the band played together live in the studio, rather than record individual instruments separately.

As a result, *Wardance* feels very much like a continuation of *Electric Savage*. One song is even entitled 'Put It That Way', in comparison to the preceding album's opening track, 'Put It This Way'. Like *Electric Savage*, *Wardance* is almost entirely without vocals, except for the song 'Castles', which was sung by Moore. Six of the eight songs on the album were co-written by Moore. *Wardance* continued Colosseum II's evolution into harder jazz-rock, with intricate melodies, and virtuoso playing. In general, the album's dynamics come from the interplay between Moore and Airey, underpinned by Hiseman's energetic and precise drumming.

The opening song, 'War Dance', is pure prog rock and is reminiscent of side one of Canadian prog rock band Rush's 1976 album, *2112*. A two-minute introduction features some heavy power chords from Moore, and the remainder of the song is driven along by chunky guitar riffs. 'Major Keys' features some funk-inspired playing by Moore, as well as some musical dialogue between Moore and Airey's instruments. 'Put It That Way' features harmony playing by Moore and Airey that hints at Thin Lizzy's dual guitar harmonies, but with more sophistication. Moore's solo break is spiky and edgy.

Side one's final track, 'Castles', is pure piano bar schmaltz, although that probably wasn't the effect the band hoped to achieve. It features Moore on vocals, and while he hits some accomplished high notes, it's clear that his vocals are still in development and not yet the finished article. Double tracking his vocals at one point likely shows how much Moore had learned from time spent in the studio with Lynott.

Opening side two is the fierce 'Fighting Talk', which features an instrumental duel between Moore's lead guitar and Airey's Minimoog. A similar 'duel' takes place on 'The Inquisition', where Moore plays acoustic flamenco guitar. That itself is worthy of note, given how infrequently he played acoustic guitar in his professional career. 'Star Maiden / Mysterioso / Quasar' — a six-minute-plus suite in three parts — is pure prog rock, evoking a kind of cosmic journey which opens slowly then accelerates through a variety of instrumental mood music.

'Last Exit' is reminiscent of something that might have appeared on Pink Floyd's *Dark Side Of The Moon* (1973) and is probably the album's most accessible and therefore potentially commercial track. It features some effective sweep picking from Moore, as well as some space age phrases akin to the vibe Joe Satriani would later create on his album, *Surfing With The Alien* (1987).

Wardance reviewers recognised the virtuoso aspect of the Colosseum II ensemble: *Record World* claimed the line-up was 'capable of some extraordinary instrumental flights with guitarist Gary Moore and drummer Jon Hiseman providing the thrust.'

Record World noted that the group was well rounded and showed 'fine knowledge of jazz/rock stylings.'[137] In a similar vein, *Cash Box* adjudged *Wardance* 'invigorating' and the group 'technically proficient'. *Cash Box* singled out Hiseman's 'intricate, energetic drumming', and summed up the album as 'an impressive combination of innovative jazz textures and hard rock muscle.'[138]

Ironically perhaps, the biggest commercial success Colosseum II had was a collaboration with composer Andrew Lloyd Webber on his 1978 album, *Variations*, which reached number two in the UK album chart. The piece, originally 25 minutes in length, was premiered at the 1977 Sydmonton Festival, which was essentially an event held annually on the grounds of Lloyd Webber's estate at Sydmonton Court, Hampshire.

This was the third annual festival at which Lloyd Webber would premier his new musical creations. The piece was rearranged, lengthened, and recorded for an album release, on which Moore is listed as playing a Gibson Les Paul, Rickenbacker electric 12 string,

Guild acoustic, and Fender Stratocaster. MCA gave the album extensive promotion for a late January 1978 release, including press and radio advertising and 500 window displays. A feature on the recording process, together with extracts from the album, were broadcast on the arts series *The South Bank Show* on January 21, 1978, six days before the album release. An extract from the album entitled 'Theme And Variations 1-4', was selected as the theme music for this television series, and was released as a single a week before the album was available.

An album launch took place on January 24 at Greenwood Theatre, London, which included a full live performance by all the musicians who participated in the album, including Moore, Hiseman, Airey and Mole.[139] The gig was reviewed by Terri Anderson of *Music Week*, who noted the ability of classical celloist Julian Lloyd Webber to hold his own with a rock band, but also that the reverse was true, 'the impressive rock back line of Rod Argent, Jon Hiseman, Gary Moore, Barbara Thompson, Don Airey and John Mole, had plenty of opportunity to show its collective virtuosity, and obviously greatly enjoyed doing so.'[140]

Variations was also premiered in the United States, with performances at the Roxy in Los Angeles on April 23, followed by two performances at the Newman Theatre, in New York. A further concert to promote *Variations* took place in July in London at the Royal Festival Hall. This was part of the Capital Summer concerts series, supported by Capital Radio. This gig was reviewed by Chris White for *Music Week*, who thought highly of the rock-classical concept, and praised the musicians involved for their 'brilliant playing'. White ended the review wishing the concert would be repeated 'several times over.'[141] Little did he know that Colosseum II would effectively disband less than a month later.

It was no surprise with extensive promotion from MCA, as well as Colosseum II's willingness to perform live to promote the album, that *Variations* sold well. In March 1978, MCA awarded gold and silver discs to the musicians involved in *Variations*, which surely demonstrated to Moore and Hiseman the benefits of their record company getting fully behind a release by putting together a professional marketing campaign, something MCA had yet to do for Colosseum II.[142]

As it happened, Colosseum II did not benefit substantially from their involvement with Lloyd Webber's project: *The South Bank Show* appearances and its catchy theme should have been their biggest exposure to date, yet in those pre-internet days hardly anyone listening to the weekly theme music knew that Colosseum II was involved. While trade adverts for the album listed the musicians individually, the name Colosseum II was absent. It remains open to speculation if Colosseum II would have been more successful with more support and promotion from their record label.

At the time, Colosseum II received more critical acceptance as a live band than for their studio recordings. From the start, they were determined to hone their skills playing live: for example, in February 1975, Moore told *Sounds* magazine: 'We're not going to record an album until we've been on the road for at least three months cause that's when it's peaking.'[143]

To some extent, their visibility and popularity can be gleaned by noting the venues they played and who they supported. For example, in late 1975 and early 1976, Colosseum II played warm-up gigs in England before embarking on an extensive two-month tour beginning February 14. Some of these were at small halls, nightclub or university venues, for example at Lanchester Polytechnic, Coventry, at Quaintways, Chester, Johnson Hall, Yeovil, Reading and Loughborough Universities, and at the Twickenham Winning Post. However, in December 1975, Colosseum II supported the Electric Light Orchestra at more prestigious venues such as the New Victoria Theatre, London, and the Odeon Theatre, Birmingham.

It's unlikely Colosseum II would have had the drawing power to fill even these medium-sized venues if they were not supporting the popular Electric Light Orchestra, whose previous two albums *Eldorado* (1974) and *Face the Music* (1975) had achieved gold disc level sales in the UK.

Colosseum II's appearance at the Reading Festival, 27-29 August 1976, also indicates their status at the time. They were big enough to be invited and to play on the second of the three days but not big enough to be among the headline acts. Ahead of them on the bill that day were the Rory Gallagher Band, Camel, The Phil Manzanera Band featuring Eno, Manfred Mann's Earth Band, and Van Der Graaf Generator. Below them were relatively unknown acts such as Sadista Sisters, Moon, Sassafras, Eddie and the Hot Rods, and Nick Pickett.

For Moore though, this must have been a special occasion to appear on the same bill as one of his early guitar heroes, Rory Gallagher.

(The bill on Sunday was headlined by Black Oak Arkansas, a hugely successful live act at that time, with the likes of Ted Nugent, Sutherland Brothers and Quiver, the Pat Travers Band, and AC/DC. Also on the line-up was Brand X featuring Phil Collins, a jazz-fusion band with which Colosseum II is often compared.) Nevertheless, when the band undertook a short UK tour in November 1977 to promote *Wardance*, the majority of venues booked were small halls and university rooms, which indicates that Colosseum II hadn't grown their live audience and were still struggling to make an impact.[144]

In addition, Colosseum II made some high-profile media appearances. As well as the aforementioned BBC in Concert radio performance, on August 15, 1977 the band recorded a live session for John Peel's Radio One show, which was broadcast later that month; and the BBC recorded a Colosseum II concert for their *Sight and Sound in Concert* programme, which was broadcast in January 1978.

As can be seen and heard in these media appearances, Colosseum II was a tight, dynamic live band, which had little difficulty replicating the complexity of its studio performances. Moore, in particular, was an eye-catching presence on stage, and his animated playing seemed to reflect the dynamism of the band — something *Music Week*'s reviewer noted about Moore's performance at the band's gig at Victoria Palace, London on November 20, 1977: 'it is guitarist Gary Moore who dominates the stage', *Music Week* wrote. 'His antics are pure rock theatre: all slashed sleeves, sequined pants, athletic leaps and facial grimaces, his energy to all appearances boundless. His playing was in every way impressive: fluent and fast, full of drama and humour. An endless variety of tones seemed to be at his disposal, his Les Paul sounding at one moment like Robert Fripp's most experimental work, at the next as pure as a Spanish guitar. His high spot was a solo welding together scraps of this and that, assorted scale exercises, and other demonstrations of technical expertise, all thrown off with panache and played entirely for laughs.' The review also evokes a sense of the band's overall live presence: 'emphasis was firmly on entertainment. Noise and spectacle were the ingredients: ferocious rock on the one hand; dry ice, thunder flashes and rotating mirrors on the other. The quality of the music — advanced yet gutsy — was faultless, the commitment of the players total, and the end result a really exhilarating concert.'[145]

In mid-1975, before Colosseum II had even signed its first record deal, Hiseman sounded a note of caution about the band's prospects.

He explained to *Melody Maker*, 'if a band gets together now with people who have been successful before, the public expects them to be as good as the old band right away. But it takes a band three years to reach a standard. Audiences will have to be more patient.'[146]

Three years on from Hiseman's observations, it was clear that Colosseum II had made rapid improvement in the overall quality of their studio work, while remaining a killer live band. The musicianship had always been there, but Hiseman was correct in his assessment that a band such as this needed time to build a fanbase. Unfortunately, while the critical reaction to their final album was positive, like the previous albums it was a commercial failure. As journalist Mick Wall put it, Colosseum II produced three 'very thought provoking albums', which were nevertheless 'three stiffs', and when the band broke up Moore felt justified in, as he put it, 'putting his feet up for a while in Thin Lizzy.'[147]

Looking back on his Colosseum II experiences eight years later Moore, reflected: 'we did a sort of British version of what Chick Corea and John McLaughlin were doing, just showing off on our instruments. It didn't really amount to anything commercially; it was just something we wanted to do at the time. I don't think that kind of music will occupy a large place in the history of Rock.'[148]

Yet, Moore did appreciate Colosseum II's band dynamics. For example, in 1988, he told *Metal Hammer*: 'I was proud of what I did with Jon Hiseman and it was a good band with none of the back stabbing that goes on in rock groups and dissension over who gets paid the most. That band was very above board and everyone was treated with respect.'[149]

In retrospect, Hiseman thought that the concept he envisaged with Colosseum II had already missed a window of opportunity for success. 'I had split up my previous band Tempest', he revealed, because 'the time for that sort of music had gone but then I got Colosseum II together, and really we were five years too late!'[150]

If Colosseum II had been around just a few years earlier it would have avoided the punk, disco, and new wave musical genres that increasingly dominated the music charts in the late 1970s. Almost by itself, punk put a knife through the heart of the jazz-rock and prog-rock bands that the punks condemned as pompous and aloof. Many music journalists jumped on the punk bandwagon, and record companies, eager to exploit punk for a quick profit, followed suit. Complexity and virtuosity were out: simplicity and a more direct connection with the audience was now in vogue.

Moore picked up on that quickly and left to re-join Thin Lizzy, a rock band with a punk attitude that was well-situated to ride the punk wave until it eventually dissipated. His departure was a huge blow to Colosseum II, but Hiseman soldiered on for a time before he too realised how the wind was blowing. Eventually, he returned to playing pure jazz, with little commercial appeal; however, Airey and Mole worked with Moore on his solo album, *Back On The Streets*, which would feature a blend of the styles Moore utilised in Colosseum II and Thin Lizzy, but with some of punk's anti-authority attitude.

Back On The Streets (1978)

As *Grinding Stone* was credited to the Gary Moore Band, *Back On The Streets* is often thought of as Moore's first solo album. Unlike *Grinding Stone*, *Back On The Streets* was a family affair, with Moore relying on bandmates from both Thin Lizzy and Colosseum II to provide studio support. Given that Lizzy was the higher profile act, promotional advertising for the album in the UK made the most of Moore's connection to Lizzy.

For example, a full-page advert in *New Musical Express* featured a picture of Moore in dynamic pose, standing beside Phil Lynott as the band played live at the Sydney Opera House during Lizzy's short tour of Australia a few months previously. The advert even refers to *Back On The Streets* as the debut album from 'Thin Lizzy's ace guitarist', and Lynott and Brian Downey are given top billing as featured artists, above drummer Simon Phillips, Mole and Airey.[151]

Promotional adverts in the United States took a slightly different approach because by the time the album had been released there, Moore and Lizzy had parted company. The promotional picture used in *Cash Box* featured only Moore, while omitting Lynott entirely. The advert avoided making any reference to Thin Lizzy and instead made a virtue of Moore's solo efforts, proclaiming: 'The air is alive with the sound of Gary Moore. "Back On The Streets" for the first time, in his solo debut. New dimensions in guitarism'.[152]

In addition, the American album featured a different cover image to that used for the UK release. On the cover is a close-up picture of Moore with long hair, wearing sunglasses, a black leather jacket, and plain red t-shirt. He bears a striking resemblance to the publicity imagery of the American punk band The Ramones, and with punk just beginning to make an impact in the States at this time, it's likely the resemblance was not a coincidence.

Lynott provided lead vocals on 'Parisienne Walkways', and shared lead vocals with Moore on 'Don't Believe A Word', as well as backing vocals on two other tracks. He also played bass and acoustic guitar on three tracks. Brian Downey provided his percussion skills on the same three tracks on which Lynott featured. Don Airey played keyboard, organ and piano on five of the album's eight tracks, while John Mole played bass on four. Ex-Judas Priest drummer Simon Phillips provided main drumming duties on the album, performing on five tracks. Moore played guitars on all tracks, and lead vocals on those tracks not sung by Lynott. He also played bass on the title track, as well as guitar synthesizer, mandolin and accordion on 'Parisienne Walkways'.

Moore is given sole writing credit on five of the album's eight tracks and he co-wrote one.[153] Several tracks originated while Moore still had a foot in both Lizzy and Colosseum II. In January and February 1978, for example, he worked with Lynott on demos of 'Don't Believe A Word', 'Fanatical Fascists', and 'Parisienne Walkways'. They also collaborated on a co-written song called 'Spanish Guitar', which wouldn't appear on *Back On The Streets* but was, in fact, released as a Moore solo single in late 1979. After Moore departed Thin Lizzy in acrimonious circumstances, he replaced Lynott's original vocals with his own, although Lynott's bass playing remained on the track.

'Parisienne Walkways' is a Moore/Lynott co-write, while Lynott alone is credited with 'Fanatical Fascists and 'Don't Believe A Word,' the latter being the *Johnny the Fox* track but played here at a slower tempo and in a more blues-influenced style. Moore revealed the song was originally written with a slow tempo, 'like a hand-me-down from Peter Green.' In fact, Peter Green was in the studio at the time and when Moore played him the track, Green said: 'I really like it, it sounds like something Fleetwood Mac would have done', to which Moore replied, 'Where do you think we got it from?'[154]

Moore considered 'Fanatical Fascists' to be Lynott's 'version of punk'. Lynott was constantly aware of new musical trends, and he didn't want Lizzy to be a victim of the scorched earth effect that punk left on the musical landscape. He hung out, for example, with the likes of Bob Geldof, Steve Jones and Paul Cook. And as punk gave way to New Wave, Phil befriended Midge Ure and Sting. Ironically, Moore's rendition of 'Fanatical Fascists' has more bite and more of a punk vibe than the version recorded at Good Earth studios with Lynott on vocals, which demonstrates that Moore too had an eye for current trends.

The origin of 'Parisienne Walkways' was an informal jam session between Moore and Lynott in the latter's apartment in West Hampstead, London. Previously, Moore had rehearsed it with Colosseum II as an instrumental, but it didn't fit with the band's style of music.[155] Moore played the chord structure on acoustic guitar, and Lynott added lyrics. Fans know the famous opening line refers to Lynott's father Cecil Parris and Lynott's birth year of 1949, but of course its face-value meaning makes it more accessible to a wider audience. When the song was recorded for Moore's album, Brian Downey played drums and Lynott played fretless bass.[156]

Moore and Lynott featured in an atmospheric promotional video, which helped the song reach the top ten in the UK singles chart in May 1979, about a month after its release. Moore was then in the unusual and happy position of having two concurrent hit singles, one credited to he and Lynott, and 'Waiting For An Alibi' with Thin Lizzy, which also made it into the UK top ten singles chart. Judging by single releases alone, this was the most commercially successful period of Moore's career thus far.

The songs written solely by Moore on this album are an eclectic mix of jazz-fusion, rock, and blues. The title track begins like a Colosseum II arrangement, with Moore playing a repeating fast guitar run before the song transforms into hard rock in the vein of early 1970s Deep Purple. Lynott provides backing vocals. 'Flight Of The Snow Moose' is an instrumental track featuring Moore, Mole, Airey and Phillips. It could easily be a Colosseum II track: Moore wrote many of that band's tunes, and of course after their debut album, Colosseum II played mainly instrumental tracks to showcase their virtuoso musicianship.

If 'Fanatical Fascists' was a nod to the punk movement, 'Flight Of The Snow Moose' is dismissive of punk's back to basics, anti-virtuoso approach. It begins with gentle yet dramatic acoustic guitar from Moore and keyboards from Airey, before picking up pace as it develops into a speedy jazz-fusion rocker. The track is somewhat reminiscent of the prog rock of Rush in that era, but with guitar more in the foreground than keyboards, and with Moore out-shredding Alex Lifeson to keep his rock audience happy.

'Flight Of The Snow Moose' ended side one of the original vinyl release and the pace is unrelenting as another fast paced jazz-rock fusion instrumental track, aptly entitled 'Hurricane', opens side two. Simon Phillips is tremendous on this track, keeping a fast tempo and playing intricate fills, and it's no surprise that the following year he would go on to work with virtuoso guitarist Jeff Beck on Beck's jazz-rock fusion album *There & Back* (1980), nor that Moore would again seek out Phillips' services a decade later for his *After the War* (1989) album.

Nevertheless, despite Phillips' drumming, and some interesting interplay between guitar and keyboards, 'Hurricane' is little more than a vehicle for Moore to showcase his fast tempo lead guitar breaks. 'Song For Donna' — possibly a reference to Moore's friend, Donna Campbell — is a soulful jazz-funk ballad with Moore providing lead vocals mainly in his higher register. As such, it is reminiscent of the Colosseum II track 'Rivers', from the band's 1977 *Electric Savage* album.

Another lengthy instrumental track entitled 'What Would You Rather Bee Or A Wasp' follows. This is a funk-soul track, that veers at times towards the kind of disco vibe that would soon take over the airwaves. To put that in context, 1978 was also the year that the Rolling Stones had a massive hit in the United States with their disco-inspired track 'Miss You'. The following year, Van Halen had a top twenty hit with 'Dance The Night Away', a song influenced by the light tone of that era's chart music. Also in 1979, rock band Kiss released a disco single, 'I Was Made For Lovin' You', which became a top twenty hit.

Moore, however, could not resist adding some fast guitar solos that undermine the disco mood somewhat; in retrospect, this track predates the soul-funk-rock stylings of Extreme and guitar maestro Nuno Bettencourt's popular hit 'Get The Funk Out' by a full two decades. The song's title also evokes thoughts of Bettencourt's signature guitar piece, 'Flight Of The Wounded Bumblebee', although it bears little musical resemblance to Moore's track. It's also the second track on the album with a flight or flying theme, which in literature is often symbolic of the themes of freedom or escape, and may therefore hint at Moore's state of mind at being free to explore his musical ideas on this new solo album.

Back On The Streets is then an eclectic album, featuring two distinctive lead vocalists, and tracks with a diverse mixture of musical styles. Possibly for this reason, reviewers found it difficult to categorise. Nick Kent of *New Musical Express* was dismissive, saying: 'Moore himself isn't really adequate solo material, a fact nailed home with a vengeance in the clumsy juxtaposition of styles from track to track. But saving graces are provided by Lynott, whose three or so originals give Moore actual songs to work on. Inevitably, they sound like Lizzy out-takes.'[157]

Australia's *The Age* newspaper also noted the Lizzy influence, but without Kent's negativity. Reviewer Mike Daly opined: 'While numbers like the title track have the same driving fury you expect from Thin Lizzy, the more bluesy Don't Believe A Word, the jazz-rock of Hurricane and Flight Of The Snow Moose (the latter having an Al Dimeola influence) are a different proposition.' Overall, Daly viewed the album mainly as an opportunity for Moore to 'air his guitar talents'.[158]

The US music industry magazine *Walrus!* reviewed the album positively, saying: 'The three jazz/rock/fusion tunes are well done. The two bluesy tunes aren't filler. Neither is the George Benson-ish 'Song For Donna'. The other two tracks are blitzkrieg rockers.'[159]

Cash Box was more effusive with its praise of Moore and the album: calling Moore 'Ireland's best kept secret', and a man who 'knows and fully exploits the bottomless potential of the guitar', *Cash Box* said the new album featured 'Lizzyesque rockers [which] segue with soulful balladeering and the odd foray into the world of jazz -tinged progressive music thrown in to make this one of the more listenable efforts this year.'[160]

Harry Doherty of *Melody Maker* had mixed feelings about the album. He praised Moore's guitar skills, but thought they worked best in the context of a strong song. Predictably, Lizzy fan Doherty thought the strongest tracks were those with the strongest Lizzy connection. On those particular songs, he wrote, 'Moore shows that, given the solid base of a good song, his imagination on guitar can run wonderfully free, creating a powerful force that enhances the song.' On the other hand, Doherty thought Moore's own songs relied too heavily on his guitar skills. On these, Doherty wrote, 'it's obvious that his writing isn't quite up to it.'

Somewhat contradictorily, Doherty also praised Moore's two instrumental as examples of the scope of Moore's musical vision, and as vehicles for Moore to display his virtuoso guitar skills. A particular highlight for Doherty was 'Don't Believe A Word', which he compared to Fleetwood Mac's 'Black Magic Woman'. Doherty cited this as an example of Moore not having 'lost his feeling for the blues.' Doherty's opinions on *Back On The Streets* are, then, somewhat ambivalent, but leaning more toward positive than negative. He concluded that *Back On The Streets* was: 'Not a great album, then, but the odds are that if you like Gary Moore, either as jazz-rocker or hard-rocker, you'll like this. There's something for both sets of fans.'[161]

A retrospective review by *Creem*, a US hard rock magazine, was, however, particularly scathing about Moore and the album, saying: 'The ex-Thin Lizzy guitarist and no-show is a rare case of an artist saving all his worst material for his solo LP. This is the guy who went back and removed all of Phil Lynott's guest vocals, no doubt because they showed up his own cruddy voice.'[162]

Aside from being unnecessarily vindictive, this is also an inaccurate assessment of *Back On The Streets*, since Lynott's vocals are clearly heard on the album. One wonders then if the reviewer even listened to it and therefore if the views expressed can be dismissed as any indicator of Moore's standing in the US at that time. In any event, *Creem*'s viewpoint was an outlier, and not indicative of the general tone of reviews.

There is a lot to like on *Back On The Streets*, which features a blend of commercial pop hits, a slow blues track, and songs with more complex arrangements. At various points it is of its time, but also ahead and behind then-current trends. As such, it was difficult for reviewers to make sense of the variety of musical styles on offer. In retrospect, it is a fascinating album that showcases some of Moore's best early guitar and vocal performances.

The title track was released as a single in the UK in November 1978, with the non-album song 'Track 9' on the B-side. Regrettably for Moore, it failed to chart. *Record Mirror* called the title track a 'statement of intent' from Moore, with 'great guitar playing and an incessant repetition of the title hook'. However, *Record Mirror* found the song disappointing overall, concluding that 'even the man who was described by Phil Lynott as being the world's greatest guitarist can't drag this out of its mediocre mire. A shame.'[163]

A year later, when the track was released as a single in the United States, it was reviewed more favourably. *Cash Box*, for instance, wrote: 'Moore… attacks the title track from his current solo LP with all of the fury that six guitar strings could possibly inflict on a song.

Though the onslaught is relentless, the tune is catchy enough for most AOR [Adult Orientated Rock] lists.'[164]

Despite such positivity, the 'Back On The Streets' single also failed to chart in the US. This would be the first of many disappointments for Moore on that side of the Atlantic: no matter how well he did in the rest of the world, whatever combination of talent, promotion, timing, and luck it takes to be a successful recording artist in the US would always elude Moore.

G-Force, a pop-metal experiment

Moore's departure from Thin Lizzy coincided with other events that would lead to him setting up a new band, and the release of an album of new material. Adrift and virtually alone in the United States, Moore turned to ex-Deep Purple bassist and vocalist Glenn Hughes for help.

Hughes had allowed Moore to stay at his home in Los Angeles while Lizzy management frantically tried to contact him. Naturally, Moore and Hughes began to discuss a musical collaboration. The other pertinent event was that Sharon Arden, daughter of Don Arden, who was head of Jet Records, began working for the company and took an interest in Moore. Moore signed to Jet as a recording artist, and Sharon convinced him to let her manage his business.

They both needed each other: Moore was musically ambitious, but he also needed some commercial success to ensure financial security. The chart success of 'Parisienne Walkways' gave him hope that lightning might strike twice, and this time he wouldn't have to share royalties with Lynott.

From Sharon Arden's perspective, Moore offered her an opportunity to make a mark in the music business. Moore's main selling point was his guitar prowess in an era when Eddie Van Halen had almost singlehandedly reinvented the idea of the 'guitar hero'; moreover, Van Halen had demonstrated that an innovative guitarist could achieve commercial success, albeit within the structure of a talented band. Moreover, Moore had already shown with the success of 'Parisienne Walkways', and to a lesser extent with Thin Lizzy's 'Sarah', which Moore had co-written, that a catchy pop song with a memorable guitar sound could produce a chart hit, and that was normally the holy grail formula for selling albums.

Moore soon recruited drummer Mark Nauseef, whom he knew from when Nauseef stood in for Brian Downey on Lizzy's 1978 US and Australian tours. Nauseef revealed recently that he had high hopes for this power trio. They rehearsed and wrote every day, before using Record Plant studios to record some demos.[165]

However, Hughes had a drug problem and became unreliable. After a particularly rowdy party in August 1979 at a restaurant on Sunset Boulevard to celebrate Hughes' 28th birthday, Sharon Arden lost patience with him and he was cut loose from the group.[166]

Losing someone as talented as Hughes, who was a fine bass player and had a powerful singing voice, was a setback but such was Arden's faith in Moore that they immediately began a search for two replacements for Hughes. As a result, vocalist Willie Dee was brought in, as was bassist Tony Newton.

The group worked on demos at Cherokee Studios in Los Angeles. These included tracks that originated from the *Back On The Streets* period, and some from Moore's creative collaboration with Hughes. Released in May 1980, Moore claimed writing credits on eight of the nine songs on the *G-Force* album and is sole writer of four tracks. Like all of Moore's earlier work, and as with most of his albums in the decade to follow, *G-Force* features a mix of hard rock and lighter, more pop-orientated tracks. This 'pop-rock' approach seemed to give the album the best opportunity for commercial success.

One thing it is not, however, is a heavy metal album, so it would be an error to categorise it with the likes of New Wave of British Heavy Metal (NWOBHM) bands such as Motörhead and Iron Maiden. It is, in fact, more akin to Van Halen's melodic, guitar driven rock than to the music of any British heavy metal band in that era.

The album's opening track, simply titled 'You', was written by Moore, and is a melodic soft rock tune. It sets the tone for the rest of the album, with a very American adult-orientated rock (AOR) sound, reminiscent of Journey, with whom Moore was familiar as Lizzy had supported that band on a previous American tour.

Moore plays arpeggiated chords in the chorus, adding some tunefulness to the melody. Although competently handled, the guitar solo is a little uninspired, with Moore playing the same repeating phrase on a descending run down the fretboard. Furthermore, the guitar on the solo sounds very processed.

For this album Moore tried to replicate the guitar tone he had achieved with Lizzy's 'Sarah'. Perhaps if he had used his beloved Gibsons that might have transpired but instead he used a new Charvel guitar on this album, and the result was a fuzzy, trebly tone that sometimes feels isolated from the rest of the mix.

Dee sings the lead vocal on 'You', while Moore provides backing vocals. A live performance of the song can be heard on Moore's 1983 album *Live At The Marquee*, albeit recorded on that occasion with a different collection of musicians. Moore's guitar sound on that live release is much cleaner than on the *G-Force* album, likely because it was plugged into amplifiers and not run straight through a mixing desk as it was on the album. Keyboards are more prominent on the live version, taking over some of the rhythm parts, and substituting for a guitar during an instrumental harmony section.

'White Knuckles / Rockin' And Rollin'' is really two songs merged into one, with the former being a guitar instrumental written by Moore, and the latter a hard rock track written by Nauseef. 'White Knuckles' is Moore's answer to Eddie Van Halen's game changing guitar solo entitled 'Eruption'. While not the first song to demonstrate Van Halen's 'tapping' technique, it is an early, and possibly the best example of Van Halen's trademark technique.

Just as 'Eruption' segues into a cover of The Kinks song, 'You Really Got Me' on Van Halen's 1978 debut album, 'White Knuckles' merges into 'Rockin' and Rollin''. While Moore knew already how to use the two-handed tapping technique, he didn't try to emulate Van Halen. Instead, he used the track to demonstrate his fast, accurate picking, while also utilising a number of techniques such as dive bombs and pinch harmonics that would soon become the stock in trade of heavy metal guitarists worldwide.

'White Knuckles' is the album's heaviest track, and a further example of Moore's dexterity and skill. 'Rockin' and Rollin' uses the main riff from 'White Knuckles' as the backbone for three minutes of head-banging rock.

'She's Got You', co-written by Moore and Nauseef, is a mid-tempo, dramatic hard rock track in which Moore surprises by mixing in some reggae riffs. Dee and Moore share lead vocals. The track bears some similarities to a song written many years later, Skunk Anansie's 'Weak'. The chord structure is very similar, as is the shift in vocal intensity from mellow to intense. Interestingly, Richard 'Cass' Lewis of Skunk Anansie worked with Moore a few years after 'Weak' on Moore's Scars project. 'She's Got You' ends with some Van Halen-like fast soloing from Moore. A live version of the track appeared on *Live*

At The Marquee (1983).

The third and final track on side one is 'I Look At You'. Written by Moore, it is a somewhat overwrought power ballad, with Dee providing insipid lead vocals. A song very much of its time, it could be mistaken for something from the catalogue of Supertramp, Chicago or even Barry Manilow. Keyboards and strings join in as the song builds to a climax, and then Moore lays down a classy guitar solo over the top. Nevertheless, the guitar mix is underwhelming, making the instrument sound at times fuzzy and distant.

The opening track on side two, 'Because Of Your Love' is the only one on the album on which Moore does not receive a writing credit. A busy song, it features catchy riffs, with lots of neat guitar fills and a blistering solo. Despite the wider musical context being the emergence of the NWOBHM, this is very much in the vein of 1980s AOR, like an up-tempo offering from Ritchie Blackmore's Rainbow. 'You Kissed Me Sweetly', composed by Newton, Dee and Moore, is a mid-pace rocker with a string arrangement that evokes the Electric Light Orchestra, who not only were also on the Jet label with Moore, but were also a band that Colosseum II had supported just a few years previously. Moore's tasteful use of pinch harmonics is a treat, but one can only speculate how good this track would have sounded with the clean and rich tone of Moore's Gibson Les Paul rather than the scratchy, trebly sound heard here.

Moore's 'Hot Gossip' is pure three-minute pop. In a somewhat calculated attempt to obtain chart success, it was the first single released from the album, complete with a promotional video that was broadcast on MTV. Lead vocals are by Moore, who plays delicate, arpeggiated chords and a light, harmonious guitar solo. It bears some similarities to Rick Springfield's hit song, 'Jessie's Girl' (1981), which is not to suggest that Springfield was influenced by 'Hot Gossip', just that this was one of the styles of music that was finding chart success at the time.

'The Woman's In Love', is another of Moore's pop tunes, and he shares lead vocals with Dee on the track. It begins in similar fashion to Randy Newman's 1983 hit, 'I Love L. A.' but then develops into AOR in the vein of Elvis Costello or Toto. If the Electric Light Orchestra wasn't on the same label, Jeff Lynne might have sued G-Force for stealing the string section from his song, 'Evil Woman'. To cover all pop bases, the song also features two saxophone breaks.

'Dancin'', credited to all four members of G-Force, is a frenetic rocker on which Dee sounds remarkably like Australian rock vocalist Jimmy Barnes. It features a sizzling guitar break from Moore, and Nauseef adds a short drum solo. Some synth background fills imitate the soundtrack of the popular space invaders video arcade game. Don Airey makes a valiant attempt to add some colour to the track with some keyboard special effects. In total, however, it adds up to a hot mess, part rocker, part train wreck, predating by a few years some of the worst excesses of mid-1980s hair-metal.

A non-album track entitled 'Trust Your Lovin'' ended up as the B-side of the album's second single release, with the A-side being 'You'. It's a mid-tempo rocker with some funky slap-bass playing from Newton, and another spicy solo from Moore. The track features guitar orchestration and harmonising throughout, which is as close to the 'Sarah' guitar sound that Moore would get with G-Force.

The album was widely advertised in the British music press with the text 'Moore for your money: a tremendous new heavy metal album'. The album cover featured a striking, blue-tinted front cover image of the band. Moore has shorter hair than on the promotional pictures for *Back On The Streets* and wears a bomber jacket in contrast to his usual leather jacket or the New Wave look he adopted in later media appearances with Thin Lizzy.

To boost sales, a picture disc version was released alongside the usual black vinyl and cassette mediums, with the aim of encouraging fans to buy the album multiple times. As a further part of the marketing campaign, the initial batch of vinyl came with a sew-on patch and a chance to win one of Moore's guitars.[167]

Three singles were also released, the first — 'Hot Gossip' — scheduled for May 31, the same date as the album release. The image used for the single was the same as the album cover, but unlike the album it was advertised as by 'G-Force featuring Gary Moore'. Since it was Jet who insisted that the band be called G-Force, without having Moore's name in the title, this inclusion might have been an undeclared admission from Jet that their original decision was a marketing error. Moore recorded a promotional video for this pop song, which was an unashamed attempt to garner some chart success, and therefore to boost album sales. Unlike the album cover image, in the video Moore wears a leather jacket. He plays two different guitars, which were probably the newest Charvel models.

Two more singles were released: in July, 'You' was coupled with 'Trust Your Lovin''; and in November, 'White Knuckles / Rockin' And Rollin' was released, with 'I Look At You' on the B-side, but neither made an impact on the singles charts in either the UK or USA. Interestingly, the image on the cover of the final single, which was released after G-Force disbanded, features three images of Moore and none of the other band members. It was advertised as G-Force featuring Gary Moore, which suggests Jet had belatedly come to understand that Moore had enough name recognition that his 'brand' could help sell the single.

There were mixed reviews of the album. *Music Week* wrote that it featured 'powerful rock music', whereas *Record Mirror*'s Ronnie Gurr took issue with Moore's complex guitar solos: 'We all know', Gurr said, 'that Moore is a great, great guitar virtuoso. so quite why he should feel the need to gratuitously plaster this album with technical brilliance, that is pure bloated excess, is beyond me.'

Yet, Gurr liked some songs on the album, calling 'Hot Gossip' a 'gem' among other 'classy' tracks. Gurr's issue seemed to be the album's mix of styles, which, likely reflected Moore's own indecision about where his musical focus should lay. Gurr said: 'Perhaps the direction is lacking here. G-Force don't seem to know quite where they are heading. Here you get the omnipresent Moore Jazz-undercurrent, cantering a quasi-punk on Dancin', hard heavy metal and pop excellence. Gurr predicted that Moore would be huge when he 'gets over the problem of letting his brain control his flighty digits and buckles under to write more great rock tunes, and when he gets a producer to assure him he's a guitar genius then gives him a swift foot in the pants he'll be huge.'[168]

At heart, Moore was drawn to blues-based rock, and the burgeoning success of NWOBHM artists suggested there was a market for guitar-based rock, including power ballads. Furthermore, Van Halen showed there was a market for guitar virtuosity, especially within a band framework. But the evidence of the past few years also suggested that New Wave music was successful in the pop charts. If G-Force had an identity crisis, it was a reflection of Moore's hesitancy at this time to commit entirely to a single musical style.

Record Mirror reviewed G-Force's 'Hot Gossip' single on two occasions, the first at the end of May, and then once more three weeks later. Presumably the first review was of an advance promotional copy and then after the single's release it was reviewed again. The reviews are at opposite ends of the spectrum, with the first being very positive and the second much less so. The first reviewer wrote: 'Gary Moore at last comes in from the cold, signing a lucrative deal with Jet and recruiting a new band. Not averse to stealing the odd idea from Lizzy, Gary hacks out a song that's almost stunning. It's lovingly put together with some quirky keyboards, and G Force look destined for the same type of success as Wild Horses.'[169]

Chris Westwood's review three weeks later was, in contrast, overwhelmingly negative, barely speaking about the music and instead speculating in a negative fashion about Moore's motives and personality. He wrote: a monicker [sic] like G-Force and a song like 'Hot Gossip' is a pretty damp squib start for anyone. But it actually is as bad as that. In fact, if Gary Moore would stop trying to make Thin Lizzy jealous and prove what a diz bustin' [sic] guitarist he still is, and instead get on with making relevant rock music to replace this farty wall of sound whitewash I might have a modicum of time for his egocentric little rockstar world. In fact, on second thoughts perhaps I might not, either.'

While Westwood didn't have much positive to say about any of that week's batch of review singles, which included releases by Saxon, The Human League, and Frank Zappa, this type of personal animosity towards Moore would, sadly be a recurring trait of reviewers through the remainder of Moore's career.[170]

At this point it seemed to be Moore leaving Lizzy that was a bone of contention, but in later years as that event drifted off into the mists of time, it would be Moore having the audacity to play the blues and supposedly overshadowing black blues players. Sadly, there would also be personal attacks on his appearance, particularly his facial scars and his weight, comments that need not be repeated here.

G-Force was booked for a 16-date tour of the UK in June 1980 in support of British blues-rock band, Whitesnake. Whitesnake was led by ex-Deep Purple vocalist David Coverdale, a man, unlike Moore, whose talents never threatened to exceed his ego. While Whitesnake had not yet achieved major chart success, Coverdale had a loyal following and his connection to Deep Purple ensured ongoing interest from the music press.

This tour was, therefore, a profile-raising opportunity for G-Force. The band played a handful of warm-up gigs in late May at Grangemouth

Town Hall (26), Dundee Barracuda Club (27), Glasgow College of Technology (28) and Edinburgh Playhouse Nite Club (29), before the tour began on June 1 at the Liverpool Empire Theatre. It was scheduled to end with two consecutive nights at London's Hammersmith Odeon on 23-24 June. The tour took G-Force throughout England and Scotland, with gigs in Leicester, Southampton, Bristol, Edinburgh, Glasgow, Hanley, Birmingham, Manchester, Preston, Bradford, Sheffield, and two dates in Newcastle at the City Hall. They were booked into medium sized halls and theatres, with capacities of up to around 3,000 fans.[171]

It's unclear if G-Force supported Whitesnake at two further gigs in early July at Sheffield City Hall, and Bradford St. George's Hall as these gigs weren't listed on the original tour itinerary adverts from the time, and no reviews or bootlegs are available. These gigs were probably added due to popular demand and it's possible that G-Force provided support. G-Force was also scheduled to play at the Reading Festival on Sunday August 24. Whitesnake was top of bill that day, followed by Def Leppard and then, somewhat surprisingly, G-Force (billed as 'Gary Moore's G-Force'), who were third on the bill, above the likes of Magnum, Budgie, and Tygers of Pan Tang. However, G-Force was one of two bands to cancel their appearance, the other being Ozzy Osbourne's Blizzard of Oz, to be replaced on the bill by Slade.

While a setback for G-Force, it is an indicator of Moore's status at the time, firstly that his band had third billing at Reading, secondly that he was named on concert adverts, which again suggests that promoters believed he had significant name recognition, and finally that popular crowd pleasers Slade were asked to fill the holes left by both Ozzy and G-Force's non-appearances.

Bootlegs of the tour are rare but those that have surfaced indicate an interesting set list that focuses on new G-Force material, but also includes 'Back On The Streets' and 'Parisienne Walkways' from Moore's previous solo album, as well as one Thin Lizzy track, 'Toughest Street in Town', which Moore co-wrote. The set list from the gig supporting Whitesnake on June 15 at the Preston Guildhall features those two solo tracks plus the Thin Lizzy track, plus the G-Force tracks 'Because Of Your Love', 'Dancin'', 'You Kissed Me Sweetly', 'You', 'White Knuckles' and 'Rockin And Rollin''. Bootlegs of further gigs on the tour, including Hammersmith Odeon and The Venue, London, confirm almost identical set lists, with the only addition being 'She's Got You', and some variation in the order of songs played.

A footnote to the G-Force project is fuel for speculation as to how successful the band might have become. One enduring story is that G-Force almost became Ozzy Osbourne's backing band. This supposedly came about because Sharon Arden managed both Osbourne and Moore. After Ozzy left Black Sabbath, she invited him to Los Angeles to rehearse some of his songs with G-Force, which at that point still featured Glenn Hughes.

Sharon and Ozzy were particularly interested in recruiting Moore into a new music combo that Ozzy would lead. However, Moore was committed to his solo career and likely thought that joining Ozzy after leaving Lizzy due to Lynott's increasingly erratic, drug-fuelled behaviour, would be a case of out of the frying pan into the fire. Osbourne later reflected: 'Gary is such a phenomenal guitar player. I mean he's really brilliant. He would have been great to work with but he wanted to get his own band together and I wanted to get mine. I don't think our ideas were quite the same so it didn't really work out. I think he was a bit too good for me, to be honest.'[172]

G-Force broke up soon after the Whitesnake tour ended. By that stage, Moore had run out of patience with frontman Willie Dee. Years later he revealed: 'Dee, was a disaster on stage. He'd trip over the monitors and make a total prat of himself every night; it was so funny, except my career was going down the drain because of this guy. Whitesnake fans were tearing up our album sleeves and throwing them on to the stage!'[173]

Furthermore, the album hadn't sold well, and Sharon Arden became distracted from G-Force when she began to focus on managing and developing Ozzy Osbourne's solo career, a development that would soon lead to a romantic relationship between manager and artist.

Having put their energies into supporting Moore rather than G-Force, Jet stopped paying Newton, Nauseef and Dee, and the band dissolved more through entropy than anger. A comment made my Arden about Osbourne's new band, Blizzard of Oz, may also shed some light on the triangular relationship between Jet, Moore, and the other members of G-Force: '[Osbourne's] the only member of Blizzard of Ozz I actually manage', she said. 'I represent the rest of the guys in so far as they're part of the touring or recording operation, but beyond that they're free to come and go as they please. They're all great musicians but I don't think they'll ever be stars in their own right. So I'm not interested.'[174]

Subsequent accusations by musicians Bob Daisley and Jake E. Lee, both of whom worked with Ozzy, that Sharon denied them song-writing credits might suggest that it was a blessing in disguise when Moore's relationship with Jet and Arden ran its course and wasn't renewed.

Nevertheless, material from the G-Force album would continue to get an airing in late 1980 when Moore put together a new line up for some live gigs. Moore recruited Kenny Driscoll to help with vocals, Andy Pyle to play bass, Tommy Aldridge on drums, and his old Colosseum II bandmate Don Airey on keyboards.

The first of these gigs was billed as 'Gary Moore and Friends', and took place at the Stour Centre, Ashford, Kent on November 1, 1980. A bootleg of this gig indicates a similar set list to the Whitesnake tour, but Moore also performed some newer material such as 'Nuclear Attack', 'Dallas Warhead', and 'Run To Your Mama', each of which was played live here for the first time. The G-Force song 'I Look At You' was also given its first live rendition, possibly because it was the B-side of Moore's new single, due for release that week. This line-up of the band also played three further gigs from November 5-7 at the Marquee Club in London, supported by English rock newcomers, Diamond Head. These gigs were recorded, and an extended play single was planned for release in early 1981. The full concert, made up of songs from two nights, would later appear on the Jet release *Gary Moore Live* aka *Live At The Marquee* (1983).

While it's unclear when G-Force legally and officially ceased to exist, the band's non-appearance at the Reading Festival in August suggests it occurred before then, probably immediately after the Whitesnake tour ended.

That Moore put together a different line-up for these November gigs was confirmation, however, that G-Force was over and done with, and also that, in future, Moore was going to be billed as a solo artist, having his name prominently displayed on the covers of album and single releases, as well as on all promotional material. In retrospect, Moore spoke of G-Force as 'a good band', but a 'disaster' when playing live. 'Anything I've done since then was better than G-Force!', Moore declared, obviously keen to consign it to history as a failed experiment.[175]

Dirty Fingers (1983) — the forgotten album

Following the break-up of G-Force, Moore put his energy into recording new material with other musicians. The full results of these sessions weren't made available until 1983 when Jet released an album in Japan only, which was entitled *Dirty Fingers* probably in reference to the powerful Gibson 'Dirty Fingers' guitar pick-ups that became commercially available in the late 1970s.

The album was released in Europe in 1984 and by that time, Moore had split from Jet and was with the Virgin label. In 1982, his *Corridors Of Power* album was well-received, which encouraged Jet to release those tracks by Moore that Jet still had rights to. The label anticipated making a quick and easy profit. Moore wasn't happy with the *Dirty Fingers* release, though, claiming that the tracks hadn't been finished. It's likely, however, that Moore simply didn't want older material available that could deflect attention away from music on the new label.

Jet also had the rights to Moore's live performances at the Marquee from 1980, which they also released in 1983. To complicate matters further that year, Virgin, released a Japan-only live album entitled *Rockin' Every Night – Live In Japan,* which was a record of Moore's *Corridors Of Power* tour. And then in January 1984, another new Moore studio album appeared, entitled *Victims Of The Future.*

Later that year, Virgin released a further live album, which was entitled *We Want Moore!* So within the space of three years from 1982 to 1984, Moore had three studio albums (*Corridors Of Power, Victims Of The Future* and *Dirty Fingers*) and three live albums (*Gary Moore Live, Rockin' Every Night*, and *We Want Moore!*) on the market, which raised concerns from Moore about possible over-exposure.

It's likely, therefore that it was mainly for this reason that Moore was unhappy especially with the release of *Dirty Fingers*. 'Talk about overplaying yourself', Moore told *Kerrang!* magazine just before the release of *Victims Of The Future* in January 1984. 'I'm really pissed off... I was pleased with the songs on [*Dirty Fingers*], but I would have liked to have finished the mixes before letting people hear it.'[176]

While full details are scarce, mainly because Moore declined to endorse that album and rarely spoke about it, we know *Dirty Fingers* was recorded in January and February 1981. Moore was assisted once more by Don Airey and Tommy Aldridge, with Jimmy Bain on bass, and former Ted Nugent singer Charlie Huhn on lead vocals for every song except 'Rest In Peace', for which Moore provided vocals. Nine of the album's ten tracks were written by Moore, and the other was a cover of the 1960s song 'Don't Let Me Be Misunderstood', which was a hit back then first for Nina Simone, and then for The Animals.

The album's opening track, 'Hiroshima' is four-and-a-half minutes of fast paced, melodic rock. 'Hiroshima' features heavy power-chord riffing reminiscent of Black Sabbath's Tony Iommi, and a short, fiery solo by Moore. Perhaps Moore had been listening to Sabbath's *Heaven and Hell* (1980) as inspiration.

One downside is that 'Hiroshima' features the cliched 'oriental riff' to evoke images of Japan. Alex Lifeson had a similar moment of ill-judgement when he played the riff on the track 'A Passage To Bangkok' from Rush's 1976 prog rock album *2112*. Yet 'A Passage To Bangkok' was meant to inject some humour into an otherwise thematically dour concept album, whereas Moore appears to play it straight here.

Nevertheless, it is immediately clear that *Dirty Fingers* was more in step than was *G-Force* with the melodic metal that was popular in the early 1980s. Yet the album is also a linear progression from 1970s rock stylings rather than an embrace of new metal.

For instance, Moore avoids typical lyrical themes of 1980s heavy metal such as those identified by popular music scholar Alan F. Moore: 'madness, violence and the occult'.[177] Yet neither are there any fantasy tales of goblins and dragons — a feature of many 1970s rock bands. Nor does the album artwork reflect this imagery and, to Moore's credit, there is none of the rampant misogyny that often featured in 1970s rock music and 1980s metal. Instead, his lyrical themes are mainly personal, social, historical and political in nature.[178]

Moore told *Kerrang!*'s Malcolm Dome, 'I try to say something in my songs that goes beyond the sex 'n' drugs thing. Firstly, there are more important events/attitudes to write about, and secondly other people sing about that sort of thing far better than I could.'[179]

Allan F. Moore noted also hard rock's 'crucial connotations of rootlessness and individual autonomy', themes that feature in both Moore's peripatetic musical career, and in his lyrics. Moreover, despite Dee's undoubted talent, Huhn's vocals were a better fit for this style of music. In particular, he had mastered the 'metal scream' that was part of the armoury of metal vocalists such as Bruce Dickinson of Iron

Maiden or Rob Halford of Judas Priest. What is also noticeable on this opening track is how natural, clean and unprocessed Moore's guitar sounds compared to the *G-Force* album.

'Dirty Fingers' is a short instrumental guitar track, on which Moore throws down a challenge to Eddie Van Halen as to who is the fastest guitarist around. Indeed, some thought Moore left Van Halen in his wake. Chris Welch of *Kerrang!* wrote, for example, that this solo 'runs clean round all the opposition. Eddie Van Halen may be fast, but Gary has speed and imagination.'[180]

'Dirty Fingers' leads into 'Bad News', a mid-tempo rocker that predates the similar-sounding Motley Crüe song 'Wild Side' by around six years.

A punchy, precise cover of 'Don't Let Me Be Misunderstood' follows, with some great vocals by Huhn and a slick solo from Moore. It retains the charm of earlier versions, but the electric guitar updates the sound for the 1980s.

Side one ends with 'Run To Your Mama', a fast-paced rocker with a catchy chorus reminiscent of some of UFO's poppier numbers. It features a keyboard-guitar duel between Airey and Moore, which resolves into some harmonising before the vocals re-emerge to end the track. It is a tough, gritty song about self-reliance, and it's not much of a stretch to believe it may refer to Moore's experiences in the music business.

The opening track on side two is 'Nuclear Attack, which begins with a riff very similar in composition and tempo to that of the Rainbow song 'All Night Long'. The lyrics were topical, with fears of a nuclear war between the West and the Soviet Union having been raised by the election of President Ronald Reagan and subsequent nuclear arms race, the resurgence in popularity and activity of the Campaign for Nuclear Disarmament in the UK, and the Greenham Common peace protests. This climate of fear led to a number of topical music releases such as Nena's '99 Red Balloons' (1983), Frankie Goes To Hollywood's 'Two Tribes' (1984), Rush's 'Distant Early Warning' (1984), and Ozzy Osbourne's 'Thank God For The Bomb' (1986), all of which were predated by Moore's 'Nuclear Attack'.

By 1983, when *Dirty Fingers* got its initial Japanese release, 'Nuclear Attack' had already appeared on Greg Lake's eponymous 1981 debut album, which was a collaboration between Lake and Moore. As the album begins with 'Hiroshima', the placement of 'Nuclear Attack' as the opening track of side two of the original vinyl release adds some balance to the album's track list and suggests a possible apocalyptic theme that was abandoned at some point in the album's composition.

'Kidnapped' takes Moore into the pop-rock territory that was, at the time, dominated by the likes of Foreigner, Scorpions and Journey. Moore plays powerful but restrained rhythm guitar with a short, tuneful solo. At just under four minutes in length, it was radio-friendly and likely would have been a single if the album had been released in 1981.

'Really Gonna Rock Tonight' sits somewhere between the gaudy brashness of a Kiss song and the hard driving beat of Judas Priest. Thankfully, Moore's solo leans towards the latter band's style, and it's another sizzler. Soon after, there is a musical dialogue between Huhn's vocals and Moore's guitar, which drives the song towards its climax. 'Lonely Nights' is another Foreigner-style work out, with a catchy chorus and some tasteful fills by Moore. If things had turned out differently, it might have competed with 'Kidnapped' as the choice for first single from the album. The final track, 'Rest In Peace' is slow and mournful, with sad lyrics about a deceased lover who the protagonist is unable to forget. Huhn handles his vocal duties competently, but the lyrics are rather bland, and the song is rescued only by a duo of tasteful Moore solos.

Jet released three songs from *Dirty Fingers* as an EP in the UK. These tracks were 'Nuclear Attack', 'Run To Your Mama', and 'Don't Let Me Be Misunderstood'. Without Moore's support in promoting the EP, it failed to make an impact on the charts.

Moore had left his Jet days behind but some bitterness remained. In an interview he gave to *Kerrang!* to promote *Victims Of The Future*, Moore bemoaned Jet's release of his older recordings, calling the company, 'thieving bastards'. He continued: 'they work pretty quick those Jet people — except when you wanna get some money off them! That's just the way they are, nothing I can do about it.'[181]

Nevertheless, *Dirty Fingers* was a raw, exciting album that got some appreciation at time of release. For example, Chris Welch of *Kerrang!* wrote that it was 'packed full of good songs and superb playing', and that Gary was 'master of the exciting break, with a succession of witty mind blowers'.

Welch hoped the album might open a few eyes as to Moore's talent, and that the rock world might now 'stop taking him for granted.'[182] As it turned out, Welch would get his wish, but it took Moore most of the decade to gain commercial success and critical approval.

1980s: The Hard Rock Years

The musical climate of the early 1980s seemed ideal for Moore: in 1979, *Sounds* journalist Geoff Barton coined the phrase 'New Wave of British Heavy Metal' to describe the emergence of late 1970s rock bands that owed a debt to their forerunners in the 1960s, but were also influenced to a greater or lesser extent by the back-to-basics aesthetic of the punk movement.

By giving it a name, Barton provided these bands with a marketing opportunity that soon brought to the fore the likes of Iron Maiden, Def Leppard, Motörhead and Saxon. The success of these bands also raised the profile of rock bands from the 1970s who had struggled when disco emerged, and the likes of Judas Priest, Scorpions, UFO, and Rush re-emerged in the 1980s with a stripped-down sound and new commercial appeal. Even Lizzy reinvented itself, bringing in guitarist John Sykes to provide a heavier, more metallic guitar sound as evidenced on Lizzy's 1983 album *Thunder and Lightning*.

So, in late 1979, with all of this just visible on the horizon, guitar hero Moore's particular talents gave him grounds to believe he had good prospects for success. However, his experiences with Jet, especially Jet's marketing decisions, left Moore a little disillusioned, but also even more determined to forge his own path. His move to Virgin seemed like a good start, but now, having finally — it appeared — gained control over his music and image, as well as deciding to take a more prominent role as a singer, song-writer, and frontman, he needed to produce the goods, and his new album for Virgin, *Corridors of Power*, was the first concrete example that his choices might lead to some commercial success and musical gratification.

Corridors Of Power (1982)
While Moore considers *Corridors Of Power* to be his first 'proper' solo album of the 1980s, the tracks from *Dirty Fingers* precede that

album by around a year. However, whereas Huhn sang lead vocals on almost all the tracks on *Dirty Fingers*, on *Corridors Of Power* Moore took on that responsibility, so it could be argued that the latter album at the very least marked Moore's introduction to the decade as a singer-songwriter rather than just a guitar virtuoso.

A few years earlier, in reviewing Moore's *Back On The Streets* album, Harry Doherty wrote: 'Gary's singing and writing comes a poor second to his playing.'[183] To use the informal lexicon of music journalism, Moore already had the musical 'chops', but when his ability as a singer-song writer became evident with *Corridors Of Power* it became clear Moore had evolved into a significant figure in the music business.

Indeed, a few years later Moore revealed that his aim in the 1980s was not necessarily to be known as a great guitar player, but to be accepted as a singer-song writer-instrumentalist, in other words, the full package of musicianship. Moore said, 'if you want to set yourself apart from every other rock Guitar Hero — so called — in the world, one way of doing it [is] to set yourself up as an identity, and that to me means being a singer and a songwriter as well... I want to be a singer, songwriter and guitarist, and achieve a good balance of all three.'[184] But would the hits come along with that?

For this album, Moore put together a band consisting of ex-Deep Purple drummer Ian Paice, former Colosseum II bassist Neil Murray, and Tommy Eyre on keyboards. (Moore knew Eyre from their recent collaboration with Greg Lake.) In addition, Cream's Jack Bruce shared lead vocals with Moore on the track 'End Of The World', and John Sloman, formerly of Uriah Heep, provided backing vocals on several tracks.

Corridors Of Power is evidence both of how prolific Moore was in this time period, but also of his continuing desire for commercial success. From September 1977 until September 1982, Moore had written most of the tracks on Colosseum II's *Wardance*, on G-Force's eponymous album, and on his solo albums *Back On The Streets* and *Corridors Of Power*. In addition, he had written and recorded all of what was to become *Dirty Fingers*, and had toured, written, and recorded with Thin Lizzy. This was a remarkable period of creativity and is evidence by itself of Moore's drive to succeed.

Furthermore, on each of these albums, even on Colosseum II's somewhat impenetrable *Wardance*, there is at least one track composed with a possible single release in mind, in the hope of obtaining some popular chart success. Not only did this ratio increase on Moore's 1980s' albums, from *Corridors Of Power* onwards, these albums also featured more cover versions and guest appearances, occurrences that would potentially make his music more radio friendly, generate media interest, and provide further potential for chart success.

Moore was particularly attentive to the brand of melodic rock music that American audiences favoured. His goal on *Corridors Of Power* was therefore to create music that was 'slower but heavier' and 'more melodic' than his previous work, an album, Moore would later admit, that was 'aimed more at the American market' than the UK.[185]

The opening track, 'Don't Take Me For A Loser', sets the tone for the rest of the album, being a mid-paced, radio-friendly piece of pop metal with a repetitive chorus likely to stick in the memory.

The following track, 'Always Gonna Love You', is a piano-based power ballad, with some chunky guitar riffs, a melodic and passionate guitar solo, and soaring vocal chorus. Uncharacteristically, Moore also plays a Takamine acoustic guitar on this track, although it is difficult to discern as it is low in the mix. Moore chose 'Always Gonna Love You' as the first single from the album.

Up next is Moore's cover of the Free classic, 'Wishing Well', which mostly remains faithful to the original, updated only with a few metallic guitar flourishes. Given that Free vocalist Paul Rodgers had one of the great blues-rock voices of the 1970s, Moore's vocals hold up well in comparison.[186]

'Gonna Break My Heart Again' is three minutes-plus of power pop, undistinguishable from most of that era's radio-friendly, American AOR. Moore's short solo is sizzling hot, however, with the kind of sharp, distinctive playing that made him stand out from that era's many metal guitar clones.

The final track on side one is 'Falling In Love With You', a slow, tasteful love song. It was chosen as the second and final single from the album and would be Moore's first 12-inch vinyl single release.

If side one was a statement for radio stations that Moore was on safe AOR territory, side two began with Moore putting new metal guitarists to the sword on 'End Of The World', which features nearly seven minutes of blistering hard rock. Written in the key of A minor, the track begins with some delicate picking from Moore, and a few atmospheric bends, before Moore launches into a devastating guitar solo reminiscent of Michael Schenker at his best, and more than a little of the title track from *Dirty Fingers*.

Moore then lays down some apocalyptic heavy riffing. And when guest vocalist Jack Bruce joins Moore for some vocal acrobatics, one wonders why this track didn't encourage Moore to reconsider his pop-leanings. A short but no less impactful solo sees Moore wring some tortured, Hendrix-like sounds from his Stratocaster.

'End Of The World's lyrics about nuclear war are in the same vein as those of 'Hiroshima' and 'Nuclear Attack', from the still-to-be-released *Dirty Fingers* album, so Moore was either tuned into current events in international affairs, or possibly he believed and hoped those earlier tracks would not see the light of day.

Certainly, the album title suggests that Moore was paying particular attention to ongoing nuclear weapons tensions. If Moore didn't base it directly on C. P. Snow's 1964 book of the same name, a book whose plot is concerned with the UK's nuclear weapons policy in the 1950s, it was likely based on the phrase 'corridors of power', which, because of the book's popularity, became a commonly-used metaphor to describe where power lay in the country.

There is no let-up in pace with 'Rockin' Every Night', a short good-times rocker co-written by Moore and Paice. It is reminiscent of the early Queen track, 'Modern Times Rock 'n' Roll', which was also written by that band's drummer, and like that track it probably began as drummer-led studio jam which then developed into a full-blown song. If the cliché 'drummers have more fun' is true, then this song is evidence of that.

The following track, 'Cold Hearted', is as close to the ground covered by Whitesnake as Moore gets on this album, including just a hint of the 'woman as sex object' trope that was often a feature of the genre. Because of that, it is rather generic and forgettable. Even Moore's short solo, and lengthier play-out solo can't rescue it from its blandness.

An album's closing track is usually a statement of some sort because it is the one that remains fresh in the listener (or reviewer's) memory. In this case, Moore chose 'I Can't Wait Until Tomorrow', a lengthy soul work-out with tasteful vocals from Moore, but with somewhat impenetrable lyrics. Choosing this song to end the album reinforces the idea that Moore didn't just want to be known for his pyrotechnical guitar displays, and instead wanted to be considered more of an all-round musician and songwriter.

Contemporary reviews of the album were mainly positive, and comments from American reviewers suggest Moore's strategy of aiming at the American market did make some headway. For example, *Billboard* predicted that hard rockers would 'rejoice' at the prospect of a Moore and Paice team-up, with side one being 'pop-orientated', whereas as side two, and in particular the tracks 'End Of The World' and 'I Can't Wait Until Tomorrow' being the selections 'where all the musicians can show their stuff.'[187]

The Connecticut newspaper *Record-Journal* adjudged *Corridors Of Power* 'one of the best solo albums by a guitarist since Phil Manzanara's *Diamond Head* and Steve Hunter's *Swept Away*', while praising the album's 'fluent, majestic guitar' and 'style that is highly reminiscent of the British bands of the early 70s.' Moore would have been happy to hear praise for his vocals and compositions: 'Moore is in top vocal and instrumental form… but what distinguishes this LP from so many others in the genre is [his] fine song writing'.[188]

Creem's Michael Davis also praised Moore's singer-songwriter talents: 'I never really listened to journeyman guitar hero Moore singing before', wrote Davis, 'so imagine my surprise when it turned out sounding a lot like Boston's Brad Delp. He might have noticed it too since he's put together an album of polished, layered hard rock'. Given Delp's reputation as one of the great American rock vocalists, that was high praise indeed. Davis's final analysis, though, was that despite 'moments of erratic inspiration', the album 'comes off too controlled to be very inspiring.'[189]

In the UK, the ever-supportive Chris Welch of *Kerrang!* magazine called the album 'five star', 'marvellous', and 'the finest of his career.' Welch thought the band's performances were spontaneous and fresh, but singled out Moore's virtuoso playing, specifically the 'unexpected leaps, twists and spirals' and the way Moore expressed himself through his guitar playing that Welch said had been absent since the days of Hendrix.

Yet *Corridors Of Power* was not a display of long, indulgent guitar solos; instead, Welch noted how Moore's playing served the song through 'well-constructed and meaningful breaks and fills… which bring colour and excitement to everything.' Like other reviewers, Welch praised Moore's vocal skills, which were 'unpretentious, soulful and as passionate as his guitar work.'[190]

In contrast, the most negative review from a British music magazine came from *Smash Hits*, whose reviewer, Peter Stockton, wrote that Moore's lyrics 'bristle with empty posturing, apart from "End Of The World" in which he trots out a few cliches about the Eastern threat. At least the words rhyme even if they don't make sense.' Stockton gave the album two out of ten.[191]

Of course, *Smash Hits* readers weren't Moore's natural constituency, but one of the consequences of writing a pop-rock album was that it would attract the attention of lightweight pop magazine reviewers. The road to success is paved not just with setbacks and mistakes, but also with superficial reviews from fluff publications. Moreover, searching for a new pop audience risked alienating rock fans.

Nevertheless, when Moore made these artistic compromises to chase popular success, he was following in the footsteps of guitarists such as Robert Johnson, Eric Clapton, and Keith Richards, not quite doing a midnight deal with the Devil at the crossroads in return for fame and fortune, but still, in Moore's case, making a concession to commercial ambition. As a result, Moore would be pursued by *Smash Hits* reviewers rather than Satanic Hellhounds.

Nevertheless, the music business is unforgiving: when Peter Green told Moore he was quitting Fleetwood Mac, it was, Moore reflected, because 'he was pissed off with the band, the music business, the whole thing.' Or as Green said himself, 'The Green Manalishi is the wad of notes; the devil is green and he was after me.'[192] Eventually, Moore would feel the pressure of artistic compromise too.

That Moore chose two slow love songs as the singles to represent the album shows where his mind was at the time. He was maturing as an artist, and having already proven himself on guitar, he was now determined to be taken seriously as a singer and songwriter; moreover, he hoped for that one big hit song to emulate the popularity and chart success of 'Parisienne Walkways'. Thus, 'Always Gonna Love You' was released in the UK concurrently with the album, in 7-inch vinyl single format with a picture sleeve featuring only Moore, and as a 7-inch picture disc again featuring just Moore. To give it the best chance of success, a performance-based promotional video was recorded. In this video, Moore is dressed in jeans and brown leather jacket, and he plays a red Fender Stratocaster, his guitar of choice on *Corridors Of Power* and for a few years afterwards.

A *Cash Box* review praised Moore's singing and noted astutely the single's potential audience: 'Newcomer Gary Moore sets his sites on AOR with this debut single. Traversing the musical spectrum from the delicate to the brash, Moore proves himself the possessor of a strong set of pipes and finely honed ears. Expect to hear Moore.'[193]

'Falling In Love With You' was released five months later, while the band was on tour in the States supporting Def Leppard. It was released in multiple formats including 7-inch and 12-inch vinyl, and a 7-inch picture disc. Once more, only images of Moore appeared on the picture sleeves of the vinyl releases and also on the picture disc, suggesting that Virgin Records considered Moore's 'brand' to be the music's key selling point. Moore revealed in a contemporary interview that it was re-recorded for this release, and produced on this occasion by Steve Levine, who was known for his work with pop band Culture Club.[194]

Cash Box again reviewed the single, writing: 'Moore follows in the footsteps of Foreigner and Journey as a rock 'n' roller with a soft side. This Santana-influenced single… is an impressive love ballad that's sure to garner pop airplay.'[195]

In contrast, UK rock magazine *Kerrang!* compared the song to 'Parisienne Walkways' but bemoaned Moore's vocals as more like 'lush Lionel Richie than... Thin Lizzy'. Because of this, *Kerrang!* preferred the instrumental B-side version to the sung version.[196]

Corridors Of Power was originally released on album and cassette formats. To boost sales, the first vinyl release came with a three-track live EP, featuring live performances of 'Back On The Streets', 'Parisienne Walkways' and 'Rockin' Every Night', which were recorded at the Marquee in August 1982.

Moore came up with the cover design concept, a striking black and white image of the guitarist standing in a dead-end corridor of a building that appears to be made from parts of a giant guitar. There are over-sized pick-ups and volume knobs on the wall, the floor is a colossal fretboard, and the far wall is comprised of massive tuners. Despite the effort that went into this design, Mirage released the US version of the album with a simpler, full-colour cover depicting Moore on stage emerging from a cloud of smoke. It is tempting to declare that Moore's concept makes for the better cover, but the US version is also striking, if perhaps not quite as innovative. Interestingly, it also features a version of the inverted triangle 'Gary Moore' logo that would feature on the UK release of Moore's next album, *Victims Of The Future,* but was missing on that album's US release.

Corridors Of Power did not give Moore the breakthrough chart success that he was hoping for, just creeping into the UK top thirty album chart. In addition, neither of the singles made an impression on the charts. The follow-up album with Virgin was therefore, either going to be a radical change of direction or a case of 'If at first you don't succeed…' Moore chose the latter approach.

Victims Of The Future (1984)

While Moore always kept an eye on trends, after the relative commercial failure of *Corridors Of Power* one critic took stock of his situation. Steven Rosen, of *Guitar World*, wrote: 'His struggle for success has been long and arduous; in this country [USA] he has yet to break into the commercial inner circles (where lie the likes of Van Halen, AC/DC, Judas Priest, et al) although in Europe and Japan he constantly reaches the Top Twenty with album releases.'[197]

However, Moore told journalist Neil Jeffries he was content with the decisions he had made; 'Five, ten years ago I wouldn't have had the confidence to handle the pressures, but now I've taken my time finding the right band, the right manager, the right record company etc. So, everything fits together properly.'[198] Nevertheless, whether through design or not, change did come between albums.

In an interview with Chris Welch of *Kerrang!* magazine in the summer of 1982, Moore revealed that the impressive group of musicians he put together for *Corridors Of Power* was not meant to last: 'It's not permanent, I've just put this line-up together for an album', he explained.[199]

However, when it came to putting together a touring band to promote the album, Moore hoped to keep the core of the group together, but admitted circumstances were beyond his control: 'We have to see how everyone is fixed and check out their availability', he explained. 'I don't know what's happening with Whitesnake at the moment. Ian and Neil have to find out about their position with David Coverdale... We're just gonna keep going as long as we can and enjoy playing together.'

Initially, the touring group featured Murray, Paice, and long-term musical collaborator Don Airey, who was recruited just a week before the tour began. 'Gary gave me the LP and said, "Learn this!"', Airey recalled.[200]

Moore told Welch that Charlie Huhn would be handling vocal duties on tour so that Moore could concentrate on playing guitar. Huhn had performed with Moore at the Reading festival earlier in the year in a set that was plagued by sound problems.[201] In the end, however, Moore asked John Sloman to tour instead of Huhn.

This line-up began gigging in November 1982, with Moore and Sloman sharing lead vocal duties. Chris Welch, who reviewed the band's first tour date at Surrey University, Guildford, praised Sloman's performance, calling him 'the master of high note hollering and vocal pyrotechnics.'[202]

However, after a tour of Japan, Sloman quit, according to Moore to focus on his solo career. Along with 'musical differences' and 'spend time with his family', 'focus on solo career' was the kind of public relations terminology often deployed to explain away the sudden departure of a band member whose behaviour or performance had become problematic. In June that year, *Kerrang!* reported that Sloman left to form his own band and had, in fact, recorded some demos with Moore for that band. This suggests his departure was amicable.[203]

Moore later revealed more details of Sloman's departure, claiming that during the tour of Japan in early 1983, Moore decided that Sloman wasn't performing the songs any better than he could do it himself. In addition, it was awkward having two singers on stage because when Moore took over vocal duties for some songs, Sloman wasn't comfortable being on the side lines.

Finally, Moore wanted songs he had written to be sung as he imagined them, and he believed only he could do that. For these reasons, Moore decided not to bring in a replacement and instead, he would now perform lead vocals at live gigs. This would be a challenge, Moore admitted, as he was more comfortable as a studio vocalist, but he was determined to overcome it. He told *Kerrang!*'s Neil Jeffries, 'I think that's what keeps me going at *anything*. If there's a challenge, I'll always try to rise to it as opposed to backing away!'[204]

With the touring band now reduced to a four-piece, Don Airey then decided to join Ozzy Osbourne's band, so Moore hired former UFO keyboard player and guitarist Neil Carter to replace Airey for the band's US Tour, scheduled for June and July 1983. In October, this line-up entered the Sarm West Studios in London to begin work on a new album, which would soon be named *Victims Of The Future*.

In November, however, Murray left to re-join Whitesnake, so Moore brought in Ozzy Osbourne bassist Bob Daisley and respected session player Mo Foster to replace him.

With British and Irish tour dates planned to promote the album, former Rainbow and Elf bassist Craig Gruber was also drafted in. Due to illness, Ian Paice played on only four of the album's eight tracks, and while Paice took part in the British tour as well as some gigs in Japan, he quit in April to re-join the reformed Deep Purple. American Bobby Chouinard, who had featured on one track on *Corridors Of Power*, filled in for Paice on *Victims Of The Future*, and took his place for the American leg of that album's 1984 promotional tour.

There were, therefore, unplanned personnel changes before and after the studio sessions for *Victims Of The Future*. In less than a year, the band Moore formed to tour *Corridors Of Power*, which was, according to journalist Chris Welch, 'hatched in the shadow of Whitesnake' and had potential to 'blast all other groups to oblivion', had drifted apart.[205]

Nevertheless, Moore had a clear direction in mind and was resolved to follow it. He told Jeffries that he was determined to avoid some of the pitfalls of the previous album: 'I've managed to stay away from the "lovey-dovey" type songs this time… Although I like playing slower stuff, I think on the last album there was a little bit too much of it. This time around it's going to be a much harder sounding record. It's going to be a lot more moody! Even if the subject of love comes up, it's dealt with in a much darker way... bluesier and lonely'.

The result of this, Moore hoped, was that the material on the new album was 'potentially a lot stronger than that on *Corridors Of Power*.'[206] Additionally, Moore gave the album every chance of commercial radio success by recording a version of the Yardbird's 'Shapes Of Things', and by asking a famed guest vocalist, Slade's Noddy Holder, to provide backing vocals on the track.

The album's opening track is also the title track. Credited to Moore, Carter, Paice and Murray, it is another apocalyptic song, with a pessimistic theme about politicians leading people towards nuclear destruction. 'Victims Of The Future' is a riff-driven slice of pop-metal, with a punchy solo by Moore, played, as was most of the album, with a Gibson Les Paul Junior.

The next track, 'Teenage Idol', could be an autobiographical story of a young lad who aspired to be a famous guitarist, so he quit school, walked out of work, and sold his car to fund the purchase of a 'hot guitar'. The story moves on to a time when the man is successful, famous, and 'out of control', without filling in the blanks as to how he got to that point. As such, this must be considered a celebratory song which omits all the downsides of the music business such as the amount of practice and hard work it takes, the pitfalls of fame, being ripped off, and the dangers of substance abuse. It is as if Moore wrote it directly for those teenage boys hearing his records and aspiring to live that life.

A few years later, Moore told *Guitarist* magazine, 'the thing with the guitar is that it attracts a lot of social rejects, like me, who don't do very well at school, or people who are not popular.'[207]

'Teenage Idol' is a mid-paced rocker, with a simple, basic beat similar in theme and musical style to the Bryan Adams track, 'Kids Wanna Rock', from Adams' 1984 album, *Reckless*, or indeed any number of generic pop-rock songs celebrating teenage rebellion. If the lyrics are unoriginal, the song is lifted by Moore's playing, with some fast fills, and with Moore utilising a variety of techniques including hammer-ons and pinch harmonics.

'Shapes Of Things' is, of course, a classic anti-war track by the Yardbirds, but Moore's version is closer to Jeff Beck's solo rendition from his 1969 album, *Truth*. The original Yardbirds' version saw Beck use feedback and a fuzz box to create an Eastern raga rock sound. Beck's solo version is, however, heavier and purposefully more chaotic.

Moore imposes the original structure back on the song, but records a much heavier version, complete with power chords, and a 'power slide' down the neck, a technique which involves placing his non-picking hand high on the neck before sliding down into the chord. Moore plays the solo very differently to both earlier versions, adding his own very fast phrases, and at one point using a one-handed hammer-on technique.

Moore told Rosen how he composed the solo: 'Sometimes I work the solos out but not in terms of scales. I work them out in terms of what fits the song. In that song I started out playing it right across the whole solo section in one go and then I decided to split it up into three sections. There is the high singing guitar in the first section and then the fast staccato picking over the breaks. And then there was the slide section (an uncommon practice) after that. I thought it would be more colourful to do that than just play a guitar solo over all of it. You get three different feels the way I did it.'[208]

In addition, this track is particularly suited to Moore's vocal style; in this instance, Moore substitutes an anguished style of delivery for the smoother Keith Relf style he adopted previously. On February 17, 1984, Moore appeared on Channel 4's music flagship show *The Tube* to promote the March release of 'Shapes Of Things'. (Somewhat surprisingly, Moore also performed 'Rockin' Every Night', which originates from the *Corridors Of Power* album.) Moore's dynamic performance announced that there was exciting new material available, and a concert tour was underway.

The final track on side one is the emotional power ballad 'Empty Rooms', which Moore co-wrote with Carter. It is a melodic track, for which Moore composed an elegant solo. It's no surprise, given the popularity of similar songs in the pop charts, that 'Empty Rooms' was chosen as a single release.

'Murder In The Skies' is the first track on side two of the UK version of the album, and the second track on the US version. The song's topic is the Soviet Union's shooting down of Korean Air Lines Flight 007 on September 1, 1983, an incident that made international headlines.

While the lyrics narrate events in documentary fashion rather make any direct condemnation of the Soviet Union, in calling the event 'murder', referring to 'innocent victims', and making reference to 'Black September' — which is both the month in which the event occurred, but also the name of an infamous terrorist organisation — all infer that Moore accepted the West's judgement on these events rather than the Soviet Union's explanation.

The song's introduction consists of around seventy seconds of guitar pyrotechnics from Moore, before some harmonics introduce the main body of the song. Moore plays ascending and descending runs as if to illustrate the upward path of the rocket and the horrific descent of the plane.

'All I Want' Is Your Sweet Lovin'… goes the next track, a song that remains hard to categorise. It begins with some stock pop riffs before Moore surprises by adding some funk phrases. A speedy solo around the two-minute mark is a precursor to a longer solo that plays out over the song's resolution.

While the lyrics are rather bland and forgettable, Moore's playing once more raises the song above that level. The following track, 'Hold On To Love', is a Foreigner-style pop-rocker, with a catchy chorus, and melodic synthesizer lines. Its lyrics follow the theme of 'Empty Rooms' and are almost a pre-cursor to that song in warning of the dangers of losing love by not trying hard enough to keep a relationship alive.

The album's closing track is 'Law Of The Jungle'. Moore told Jeffries the track was 'corny' but was an attempt to compare 'living in the jungle and living in a modern city... it's about how dangerous it is to live in a city these days.'

While that was hardly a new topic for music lyricists, or even for Moore who co-wrote the Lizzy track 'Toughest Street In Town' a few years earlier, Moore's sub-Ozzy Osbourne vocals add some substance. In fact, in 1989 Moore revealed that Osbourne was meant to sing lead vocal on the track but 'his voice was in a real mess then', so that idea had to be abandoned.[209]

Nevertheless, others have handled this theme better — AC/DC's 1980 song 'Night Prowler', for example. 'Law Of The Jungle' ends with a repetition of the song title, which brings to mind the chorus of the previous year's Survivor hit, 'Eye Of The Tiger'. With a rather plodding pace, and some mundane lyrics, this is probably the album's weakest track and was maybe not the best choice for an album closer.

One further non-album track was recorded at this time, a song penned by Moore entitled 'Devil In Her Heart'. Being little more than a generic sub-Whitesnake rocker, complete with dubious lyrics about a duplicitous lover, it's not surprising this track was only used as a B-side to a single release in the UK.

While often spoken of as a heavy metal album, *Victims Of The Future* sits more comfortably in the heavy rock genre. For example, Allan F. Moore identified the dominant attributes of hard rock as 'deep-tuned drums and ringing cymbals... guitar riffs, power chords and boogie patterns largely from the blues-based playing of Cream... and Led Zeppelin', while slower ballads 'mix these features with ringing arpeggios.'

Author Moore identified *Victims Of The Future* as an album that features many of these characteristics.[210] Moreover, as was the case for all of Gary Moore's hard rock albums, the musician avoided the cheap Satanic imagery and lyrical themes that metal bands often turned to.

Iron Maiden's 1982 album *The Number Of The Beast* is probably the most commercially successful example of this. The band did it for their own amusement, but also in the knowledge that it would likely generate controversy and garner press coverage.

It's telling then that Moore chose a different route than the likes of Iron Maiden and their many imitators. Moore was simply too down-to-Earth to dabble in supernatural imagery; in fact, in his solo efforts he even avoided the Medieval fantasy and folklore themes that proved commercially successful for other rock bands such as Led Zeppelin, Dio and Black Sabbath, and which were a mainstay of the prog rock genre. On occasion, he made an exception when writing about Irish folk legends such as Cú Chulainn, but normally his music was grounded in real world events and human emotions.

Due to personnel changes, the album cover listed only three main band members, Moore (lead vocals and all guitars), Paice (drums), and Carter (keyboards and backing vocals). 'Special thanks' were given to Chouinard, Murray, Foster, and Daisley for their musical contributions.

Moore told Jeffries that *Victims Of The Future* had 'a very dingy sort of feel... quite doomy in places.' In keeping with that, the cover is black, featuring only the inverted triangular Gary Moore logo. For the USA release, however, Mirage once more favoured a different image, in this case a coloured illustration in silhouette of ruined buildings and a horizon on flames — possibly a depiction of post-nuclear devastation. In addition, for the American release 'Devil In Her Heart' replaced 'All I Want', although both were included on the cassette version.

Only four tracks were written solely by Moore; another two were co-written with Carter; the title track was a group effort; and one song was a cover version. Song writing credits were, therefore, shared more widely on this album than on *Corridors Of Power* possibly due to the flow of musicians in and out of the recording studio.

Moore told Jeffries: 'This time [writing] has been more of a co-operative thing. Neil Carter and I have written a couple of things together which I feel are really strong.' One of these tracks was 'Empty Rooms'. Many years later, Carter told Thin Lizzy biographer Martin Popoff the song 'paid for my house... I wrote that when I was on tour with UFO. There was quite a lot of stuff I was writing with them in mind that ended up with Gary. Because it was at that time that Gary approached me to join him and that's when I jumped ship and went off with Gary.'[211]

In general, *Victims Of The Future* received positive critical reviews, and it proved to be a commercial success, reaching number twelve in the UK album charts. It did less well in the American charts, however, not breaking the top 100 albums. Despite Moore's shift to radio-friendly pop-rock, he was finding it just as hard to conquer the American market as Thin Lizzy had. This was despite a very positive review by *Cash Box*, which insisted that *Victims Of The Future* would affirm Moore as a 'hard rock guitar hero and a top-rate songwriter.'

Cash Box suggested that the album should be 'a cinch to make AOR playlists.'[212] Jerry Spangler of the Utah newspaper *The Deseret News*, was also enthusiastic, writing that the album 'combines excellent hard rock music with likeable lyrics and vocals.' Spangler singled out the title track as the album's best song, comparing it to Kansas or Journey, and he had positive words also about 'Empty Rooms', which he said illustrates Moore's vocal abilities to good effect. Spangler also thought Moore's version of 'Shapes Of Things' at times surpassed the Yardbirds' original. Spangler's final verdict was definitive: 'For Heavy Metal fans, *Victims Of The Future* is a can't miss album.'[213]

Back the UK, *Kerrang!'s* Howard Johnson was more ambivalent. He opined: 'the actual sound of the album is the record's main strength; it feels as though Moore means it'. However, Johnson was less complimentary about the calibre of song writing, claiming that only three tracks matched the best moments on *Corridors Of Power*, with those being the title track, 'Empty Rooms', and 'Hold On To Love'. The latter two tracks, Johnson claimed, were the only ones that showed 'any real songwriting emotion, songwriting feel.'

Aside from those tracks, Johnson felt that Moore had become too clinical and while his solos were 'outrageously good', the songs that they feature on were weak. Johnson concluded that, while Moore was 'one helluva [sic] guitar player', the album wouldn't reshape Moore's career, nor be looked back on as a classic.[214]

Three singles were released from the album, all offered in multiple formats to encourage fans to buy multiple copies, all of which counted towards chart placings. 'Hold On To Love', coupled with 'Devil In Her Heart', was the first single from the album.

Music Week claimed it was an example of Moore writing 'commercial rock' with, in this instance, 'pompish overtones'. Because it ran 'briskly and infectiously', *Music Week* predicted that the single could make chart in the Top 75.'[215]

In contrast, *Smash Hits* was overwhelmingly negative, writing:

'Stupendous live sound, very well produced, well-mixed and extremely boring song. "Parisian Walkways" was a very pleasant hit and this isn't.'[216]

Evidently spelling a proper noun correctly wasn't a priority for this *Smash Hits* reviewer, but, that aside, their judgement on the sound quality of the track was accurate.

Normally *Kerrang!* magazine could be relied upon to review Moore's output favourably, but the rock magazine wasn't prone to giving softer, chart-orientated releases any leeway and the magazine didn't make an exception for 'Hold On To Love'. *Kerrang!* wrote that Moore's track made 'another stab at world domination via US airplay [but] fails to cut it with a melody which isn't inspired enough to capture the hearts of lovers of the melodic rock genre.'[217]

The second single was an edited version of 'Shapes Of Things', with a B-side called 'Blinder', which was written by Craig Gruber. While the cover of the 'Shapes Of Things' single release has a performance picture of Moore, one magazine advertisement used instead an image of a mushroom cloud.

The single was also released as a shaped picture disc, cut to depict a mushroom cloud. This fits with the song's theme, but more likely was chosen to tie in with *Victims Of The Future* generally apocalyptic imagery. Oddly though, the promotional video uses none of this artwork and instead depicts a live performance, complete with female dancers. *Kerrang!*'s Howard Johnson praised the 'excellent sound of Gary's guitar' on this track.[218]

Lastly, in search of chart success, came the almost obligatory power ballad single, 'Empty Rooms', which was re-recorded and released in 7-inch format, with a live rendition of 'Nuclear Attack' on the B-side, and in 12-inch format, which included an extended version of 'Empty Rooms'. Other enticements to buy the single included a poster and rock family tree. Moore told Neil Jeffries that while the track is slow, it wasn't a 'sweet sounding' slow song, and instead had some bite to it. This re-recorded version was produced by Peter Collins, whom Moore had sought out because he liked Collins' work with pop star Nik Kershaw. Moore thought that Jeff Glixman, who had produced *Victims Of The Future* and therefore the original studio version of 'Empty Rooms', was more of an engineer than a producer, and that Collins offered 'a balance between musicianship, individuality and modern electronic sounds.'[219]

Moore considered the album version of 'Empty Rooms' to be 'virtually a demo' and that after playing the song live on numerous occasions, eliciting a good audience response, he was now more aware of how it should be recorded and presented. In fact, although, the re-recorded version remains very similar to the original: it is shorter and has some new guitar additions that give it a Whitesnake vibe. The promotional video, shot in black and white, depicts children reminiscing about a woman, probably their mother, who is no longer around. Moore appears as a character in the video and does some basic acting to provide similar elegiac emotions. It ticks every box for cynical emotional manipulation, but even so, a scene where the children try to put together a jigsaw with an image of their mother on it, is oddly affecting.

Journalist Scott Howlett called 'Empty Rooms' the best song Moore has written, 'a beautiful lament for a love long lost and the hollow consolation of solitude.'[220]

Malcolm Dome thought it was 'hauntingly beautiful' and asserted that it had 'enough hookability [sic], accessibility and deft contemporary pop touches to guarantee chart success'.[221]

Despite such praise, however, 'Empty Rooms' was only a modest hit in the UK, and it failed to chart in the United States.

In the month previous to the release of *Victims Of The Future*, Moore spoke at length to *Kerrang!* journalist Neil Jeffries. When asked if he had 'itchy feet', jumping from band to band, session to session, Moore told Jeffries this was an exaggeration: 'It's just that I've got definite ideas about what I want to do and when I get into a situation where someone in the band, for whatever reason, isn't performing as well as they should, then I do something about it. I either get out or they do. I can't just go on when things aren't happening for me. I don't believe in wasting time — life's too short. If you really want to get something great together you've got to keep looking for it. So I'm happy now to have my own career. This is really the best thing I've ever done for myself. I'm in control of it and I'm also together enough now to be able to handle it. It's not like a big power thing. I just like to be in control in the sense that... I wouldn't like to think that somebody else who isn't qualified, was making decisions for me.'[222]

That was certainly the situation Moore faced going into *Victims Of The Future* and there is also past evidence to support Moore's self-analysis. He had issues with Phil Lynott and Scott Gorham's drug use, so he left Thin Lizzy. He began work with Glenn Hughes for *G-Force* but cut Hughes loose allegedly because of Hughes' drug use (although Hughes told a different version of events).

There were rumours that Moore and Willie Dee had a fractious relationship, something Moore confirmed many years later. John Sloman left the band because neither he nor Moore were happy sharing lead vocals. And Moore and Sharon Arden's relationship fell apart, with Moore later aiming scathing criticism at Jet, and by inference, also at Sharon. Now, however, he had the line-up, record company, and management he wanted, yet *Victims Of The Future* didn't perform as well as he had hoped. Nevertheless, Moore had begun to make a name for himself as a solo artist, and as it turned out, his next album would be a breakthrough.

Run For Cover (September 1985)

Through 1984, Moore toured extensively to promote *Victims Of The Future*. This included gigs in the UK, Japan, Europe, and the United States. Some of these performances were recorded, and a selection of songs from the UK, Japan and American tours were chosen for a live album entitled *We Want Moore!* (1984).

These tours helped cement Moore's reputation as a phenomenal guitarist and dynamic live act. However, commercial success as measured by record sales, still fell short of what he had hoped. For his next album, Moore therefore sought out the help of old friends, including, perhaps surprisingly, Lynott and Glenn Hughes, as well as a few other familiar names from Moore's immediate past. In part, this was due to unplanned line-up changes; in addition, Moore could not turn down a second opportunity to work with Hughes; finally, Moore hoped that his restored friendship with Lynott would produce some magic, and happily that turned out to be the case.

While *Run For Cover* wasn't released until September, 1985, work on it had begun early in the year when Moore and Lynott recorded some demos together. This early start meant Moore was in the fortunate position of having a single ready for release well before the album was ready. This provided a great promotional opportunity, especially with Lynott being involved, making this a Lizzy reunion of sorts. These factors gave the music press plenty to talk about and generated interest to fans of Moore, Lynott, and Lizzy.

Lynott, though, rejected any suggestion that this project was forged out of desperation after he had failed to secure a record deal for his Grand Slam project, and after Moore's previous album failed to achieve the level of commercial success he hoped for.

Lynott told *Kerrang!*'s Derek Oliver, 'If I was desperate in any way, I'd reform Thin Lizzy'.[223] Moore also downplayed the reunion: 'We decided to work together again simply because the song was suitable for his voice.'[224]

The resultant single, 'Out In The Fields', received a lot of airplay when it was released that May, and it became a top five hit in Britain and Ireland. It was, in fact, to that point the highest charting song in the UK for both Moore and Lynott. It was boosted by a striking promotional video in which Moore and Lynott adorned themselves in historical British Army uniforms set against a Northern Irish backdrop. While Moore was filmed on location at the Giant's Causeway and Dunluce Castle, for the most part the two were filmed with a green screen in the background to allow visual effects to be added in post-production.

The video also depicted gritty scenes shot in Belfast showing a so-called peace wall, derelict homes, a burnt-out church, and ordinary people going about their business during 'The Troubles'. The video, therefore, contrasts the natural beauty of the landscape with urban decay and strife. While this is a simplistic dichotomy, it does represent quite well the lyrical themes of the song. Lynott said, 'With him being from Belfast and me being from Dublin, Ireland is at the forefront, but it's just a general anti-war song. Obviously we leaned it more towards Ireland because it related more towards us, and you always talk about what you know.'[225]

The video also features a Gun Sight Aiming Point (GSAP) camera placed on the headstock of Moore's guitar and pointing up the neck to show the movement of Moore's fingers during his guitar solo.

Kerrang!'s Mick Wall called the song a 'thinly veiled attempt at star chartdom', but nevertheless championed it as 'one great hard rock single' by 'two of the finest exponents of Celtic-rock the world has ever seen'. Wall singled out Moore's contribution: 'Gary croons like a sheep-killing dog and plays his axe like the true dyed-in-the-wool genius he is'. Wall predicted that the release was 'too good' to be a hit single.[226]

A second single was released in the summer, in this case the re-recording of Moore and Carter's 'Empty Rooms'. It was released with a picture sleeve featuring a new image of Moore: the 1984 single release used a close-up image of a leather jacket and the triangular Gary Moore logo but did not feature Moore at all; in contrast, the 1985 release shows Moore leaning against a pillar in a white-washed room, dressed completely in black, and holding the white Hamer guitar he had used for most of the album.

This seemed to be belated realisation that there was more brand recognition in an image of Moore than there was in opaque metaphorical symbolism or the inverted triangular logo. When one considers the new 'Empty Rooms' imagery along with the striking picture used on the cover of the 'Out In The Fields' single of Moore and Lynott dressed in red military tunics, credit is due to the record company's marketing team for capturing some of the most provocative images of Moore thus far. 'Empty Rooms' sold well, reaching the top thirty of the UK singles chart. This marked the best period of singles chart success for Moore since his days in Thin Lizzy.

When the album was released in September it was much anticipated. The success of its singles, the 'Out In The Fields' promotional video, plus memorable television performances, ensured that *Run For Cover* was immediately popular, reaching the top ten album charts in Sweden, Norway and Finland, and ranking as high as twelve in the UK album chart.

For this album, Moore once more took on most of the song writing responsibility, with six out of nine tracks written solely by him. He was also co-writer with Carter of two tracks, 'All Messed Up' and 'Empty Rooms'. The remaining track, 'Military Man', was from Lynott's solo project, Grand Slam, and was co-written by Lynott, Laurence Archer, and Mark Stanway.

Despite Moore's previous assertion that he was best placed to vocalise songs he had written, he was happy to share vocal duties on the new album. He was the sole lead vocalist on four tracks, and shared vocals with Lynott on 'Out In The Fields'. However, Glenn Hughes provided lead vocals on three tracks, 'Reach for the Sky', 'Nothing to Lose', and 'All Messed Up', whereas Lynott sang his song, 'Military Man'.

Hughes, of course, was well-known to Moore. It was Hughes who had invited Moore as a house guest when Moore left Thin Lizzy during their 1979 American tour. Hughes was also meant to be part of Moore's G-Force project, until he fell foul of substance abuse problems and Sharon Arden.

Hughes had accomplished very little musically since those days: a promising team-up with Pat Thrall led to one studio album, which was not a commercial success; and the drug problems of both men ensured a follow-up album never got off the ground.

Despite Moore's distaste for drugs, Hughes maintained that the guitarist continued to ask him to join his band and circumstances seem to favour that when Hughes and Moore met once more in AIR studios in London, where Moore was recording *Run For Cover* and Hughes was working on a music project called Phenomena. Hughes and Moore collaborated on the tracks 'Nothing To Lose' and 'Out Of My System' whereupon Moore offered him a recording contract. Hughes accepted the offer, which he called 'financially and creatively... very lucrative', and said of Moore at the time, 'there's nobody in the world I'd rather work with'.[227]

As well as Lynott and Hughes, Moore once more called upon Daisley, Airey and Carter for help, but there were new faces too, and a new approach. Andy Richards played keyboards and synthesisers on a string of 1980s pop hits, most notably when working with chart favourites Nik Kershaw, George Michael and Frankie Goes To Hollywood. Session drummer Charlie Morgan had worked with Kate Bush, Elton John, and Nik Kershaw. Drummer Paul Thompson had a string of hits with Roxy Music. In choosing these musicians it seems Moore wanted to modernise his sound for the sake of chart success and his investment paid off as Morgan and Richards helped give 'Out In The Fields' its distinctive sound. Moreover, although he produced four tracks himself, Moore employed four other producers. 'I thought it would be good to have different producers who are known for producing different styles of songs', he explained.[228]

Lastly, Moore cut back on his guitar playing on this album, telling music writer Richard Walmsley: 'I've taken the approach that the guitar is the lead instrument only where necessary. I'm lucky enough to be able to say something in a very short space so I don't go for long guitar solos.'[229]

The aim of these changes was that in eschewing some of the more indulgent aspects of hard rock, employing musicians with a track record of chart success, and engaging with producers who knew how to get the best sound for different song styles, *Run For Cover* might attain a more contemporary sound.

The album opens with the title track, 'Run For Cover', which was written and sung by Moore, and on which — somewhat ironically, as his intent was to move away from that style of music — he successfully executes a heavy metal scream. It begins with some synthesiser patterns before Moore joins in with some heavy riffing. He explained to Walmsley that many of his riffs, including those on the tracks 'Nuclear Assault', 'Cold Hearted, and here on 'Run For Cover', are based around the third and fourth strings, where he uses 'the D and then the G strings together and just play[s] patterns around that… Playing the root and the fourth together you get a sort of block sound, slightly oriental, not a melodic sound.'

'Reach For The Sky', written by Moore, with Hughes on lead vocals, treads on ground already occupied by Whitesnake, but with the addition of a little funk. Moore plays restrained rhythm guitar, then really lets rip on his short solo and on the play out.

'Military Man' follows, beginning with a martial drum beat before Lynott's distinctive vocals kick in dramatically. Its lyrics are concerned with a familiar theme in Irish folk music, that of a cynic explaining to a new, wide-eyed Army recruit the reality of his decision. A startling change in tone and perspective then occurs as the lyrics narrate the young man's words to his mother in a letter to home, while the melody softens to an almost romantic mood.

Moore plays some interesting phrases here, and as the letter is read out, he adds some guitar sound effects to evoke falling munitions. In his review of the album for *Kerrang!*, Mark Putterford noted this 'powerfully potent two-pronged assault of heart-rending lyrics and gut-twisting rock music' was a trademark of the Moore and Lynott partnership.[230] On this occasion, the overall effect of their approach acts as a passionate anti-war statement.

As on *Victims Of The Future*, 'Empty Rooms' is the closing track on side one of the vinyl release. It is a shorter version than the original, and Moore plays some of the original keyboard lines on guitar, giving the song a harder, but still melodic feel. There are more keyboard and guitar fills than on the original, and a mid-song instrumental break was shortened, along with Moore's solo. It appears to be identical to the version that was released as a single from *Victims Of The Future*.

'Out In The Fields' is an anthemic rocker, with Lynott and Moore sharing vocals, but with Moore voicing most of the lyrics. Lynott sings the first line of a verse, then Moore the second. Moore also sings the chorus, with Lynott's vocals loud in the mix for only the first word of the title. This is reminiscent of their 1978 live performance of 'Back On The Streets' on *The Old Grey Whistle Test*, when Moore sang the whole chorus but Lynott either sung just a few words or only one word on alternating lines.

The contrast in the timbre of the two voices is harmonious, and the song features a rousing chorus. Throughout, Moore plays a repeating pattern, made memorable and distinctive due to his using the tremolo arm to bend the last note quickly up and down. At one point, the song includes the melody from 'When Johnny Comes Marching Home Again', a song written in 1863 during the American Civil War, and a popular marching tune that was embraced by both Northerners and Southerners in that conflict — a message of unity likely not lost on northerner Moore and southerner, Lynott.

'Nothing To Lose' is a mid-tempo rocker, sung by Hughes, with Lynott providing backing vocals. With its 'live fast, die young'-themed lyrics, and an anthemic chorus reminiscent of AC/DC's 'Rock 'n' Roll Ain't Noise Pollution', from their 1981 *Back In Black* album, or Def Leppard's 'Rock! Rock! (Till You Drop)', from the band's 1983 album *Pyromania*, 'Nothing To Lose' features generic lyrics that are easy to sing along to, and likely designed primarily with live audience participation in mind. Moore provides heavy rhythm guitar with short, passionate fills. He also uses a technique he informally referred to as a 'harmonic descending thing' where he would run the palm of his hand up the fretboard towards the nut to create a sound 'like water running down the drain'.[231]

'Once In A Lifetime' offers a change in tone. Written and sung by Moore, it is an upbeat piece of power pop with a catchy chorus. This is strictly radio-friendly territory using a template set by the likes of Journey or Foreigner. Moore plays a restrained solo, which begins with a power slide and features some high string bending, and his playout is tasteful, serving the song rather than demonstrating virtuoso performance.

Hughes takes over lead vocals on the Moore and Carter rocker 'All Messed Up', which offers nearly five minutes of unrelenting mid-paced hard rock. The title is a play on the axiom, 'all dressed up and no place to go', and the song contains the sole reference in Moore's lyrics to blues legend Robert Johnson with the line, 'looks like a Hell hound's on my trail'.

Moore uncharacteristically plays some slide guitar, perhaps to emphasise that blues link. The lyrics are concerned with the aftermath of a night spent in a bar, how terrible the narrator feels due to overindulgence, as well as his recklessness in driving away, and perhaps also the effect drinking has had on his relationship with his son. 'Listen To Your Heartbeat' is the album's closing track. Written and sung by Moore, it is a final piece of AOR power pop. Moore seems to be channelling Journey once more, and his solo is played in a style that fans of Journey guitarist Neal Schon would surely find familiar.

Another track completed at this time, 'Out Of My System', did not appear on the vinyl album release and instead was used as a UK B-side. It also appeared on the USA cassette version of the album. The track was written by Moore and sung by Hughes. Its lyrics are told from the point of view of a person in a broken relationship who bitterly rejects any feelers towards reconciliation. Moore puts a lot of emotion into a relatively short solo section.

Earlier in the year, Moore and Lynott worked on a new version of the Thin Lizzy song 'Still In Love With You'. There was likely no intent to include it on the album as that would have been a retrograde step for the always forward-looking Moore. Instead, it was probably just an opportunity for the two artists to reintroduce themselves to each other after their extended estrangement. Nevertheless, it was released as part of a limited edition 7-inch vinyl double pack, and it was also included on the 12-inch 'Out In The Fields' single.

On this version, Lynott retains lead vocal duties, with Moore joining in only during the chorus. This version has been updated with synthesiser effects and keyboards, and Moore re-recorded his lengthy solo pieces, at one point adding some melodic trills. Moore's playing seems effortless, despite this song having many tricky phrases. Sadly, though it is perhaps also a reminder that Moore was perhaps a better composer when he wrote this song in 1969 than he was in the early-mid 1980s, and he would only rediscover that particular magic in the decade following.

One final song, 'Crying In The Shadows', originates from *Run For Cover* sessions but wasn't released at that time.[232] It was, however, used as a B-side of 'Over The Hills and Far Away', from Moore's 1987 *Wild Frontier* album. It also appeared on the CD release of that album. Written by Moore, it has a gentle melody with prominent keyboards and tasteful guitar from Moore. It's about a broken relationship and it evokes a sense of melancholy similar to 'Empty Rooms'.

Run For Cover was, at last, a commercially successful album for Moore; it also received a degree of critical acclaim that he had not experienced before, at least from popular music magazines. On one level, this can be explained by its popularity: music critics often jump on a popular bandwagon either through personal choice or because that was the tone required from their editorial policy. In the 1970s, music reviewers usually had free reign to express their true feelings about musicians and their music; by the 1980s, however, the landscape had changed considerably, with more incentives from publishers, agents, and record companies to present what amounted to little more than celebratory press releases showing artists and their music in a positive way.

That is not to say that unfavourable reviews ceased to be published, more that less-negative reviews tended to keep fans happy and were often, therefore, the difference between a magazine being successful or it going out of business. The most negative reviews were often published when a reviewer from a speciality magazine was required to review music outside that speciality, hence consistently negative reviews of Moore from *Smash Hits*, a general pop magazine aimed at younger teens whose readers weren't necessarily interested in Moore's brand of rock music.

In contrast, in the 1980s Moore tended to get a positive reception from rock speciality magazines such as *Kerrang!*, *Metal Hammer,* and *RAW.* While there's nothing particularly startling in these observations, it is worth bearing in mind when considering the way that music was received in decades past.

It helped too if artists gave reviewers something to work with, and Moore's new approach to *Run For Cover*, as well as the relative diversity of music on the album, at least provided music journalists with opportunities to discuss it in a little more depth rather than just express opinions based on personal taste.

Walmsley stated, for example, 'although [*Run For Cover*] is cast firmly in the mould of Heavy Rock albums, it has a surprisingly wide expressive range, with passages of extreme tenderness providing a colourful contrast on tracks like 'Reach For The Sky' and Phil Lynott's 'Military Man' to the more usual bombast and bluster associated with the genre.'[233]

For *Smash Hits*, however, Moore's efforts to broaden his sound were interpreted negatively. The magazine called 'Empty Rooms' 'a pompous load of old twaddle' and 'Run For Cover' was 'ploddingly dull', with 'grinding and wailing solos'.[234]

A more supportive review came from the *Evening Times* newspaper, which deemed *Run For Cover* a 'very solid album... There are nine tracks and none of them fall into the duff category. It's a very good rock album that seems to suggest there's more to come from Mr Moore.'[235] A final indicative UK review came from the ever-loyal *Kerrang!* magazine, with Mark Putterford writing: 'in close-keeping with the sky-high standards Gary Moore has set himself, the material on display is of the highest quality.'[236]

International reviews were also mostly positive. For instance, Australian journalist Scott Howlett referred to *Run For Cover* as Moore's 'superb new album'.[237] *Courier-Mail* called the release, 'a guitarist's album and a rather loud one', and rather confusingly referred to Moore on the album cover as 'aging but still-trying-to-look-youthful'.[238]

This could, of course, be said about most people in the public eye, so it remains unclear why the reviewer thought to mention it. Moore wouldn't know for a few months how *Run For Cover* would be received in North America as his record company there, Mirage, had not planned to release it until the new year.

In the meantime, Moore took to the road to promote the album. For these tours through Britain, Japan, Scandinavia, and Europe from September through to December 1985, Moore once again had to cope with unplanned personnel changes.

First choice to play bass and provide vocal help had been Glenn Hughes. However, Hughes left for Los Angeles before the final mix of the album with all plans to tour with Moore abandoned. Hughes was suffering from health issues, which he later revealed were exacerbated by serious cocaine addiction.[239]

Bob Daisley stepped in to replace him. In addition, Moore chose session musician Gary Ferguson as his drummer. There are no official recordings from these tours, but bootlegs suggest the set list contained songs from each of Moore's solo albums, with five from *Run For Cover* — including 'Out In The Fields' but perhaps surprisingly excluding 'Empty Rooms', — three from *Victims Of The Future*, three from *Corridors Of Power*, and two from *Back On The Streets*, those being, naturally, the title track and 'Parisienne Walkways'.[240]

On October 22, after he had returned from Japan, but before embarking to Germany to begin the European leg of the *Run For Cover* tour, Moore made an appearance on the BBC's *Whistle Test* programme, performing 'Run For Cover' and 'Reach For The Sky'. After the tour ended, Moore returned home to find *Kerrang!* readers had voted him Number One Guitarist in a readers' poll, beating such luminaries as Eddie Van Halen, Steve Rothery, Jake E. Lee, Alex Lifeson, Adrian Smith, Bruce Kulick, Dave Murray, Angus Young, and Ritchie Blackmore.[241]

In the new year, 'Out In The Fields was released in the United States and the album was also made available. Reviews were very strong. *Friday Morning Quarterback* (*FMQB*), a US radio and music industry trade magazine, was particularly supportive of the new release, running positive articles in each of the first three months of the year.

In the first of these, *FMQB* wrote that 'Out In The Fields' featured a 'stunning vocal' by Lynott, and 'rapid fire guitar work' by Moore.[242]

In February, *FMQB* called 'Out In The Fields' a mainstream AOR track 'that's gonna break Gary out of his heretofore cult status.'[243] And in March, *FMQB* said, 'don't forget the rocker from Gary Moore Out In The Fields. Contrary to the way it might sound initially, it does blend nicely with old and new music. And it will keep you razor sharp.'[244]

Similarly positive views came from the high-profile *Billboard* magazine, which wrote: 'Hammering guitarist and punchy vocalist Moore leads a fine band on an uncompromising collection. Uniformly superior album still manages to have several standouts, including the title track, Once In A Lifetime and the anthemic Out In The Fields.'[245]

Cash Box was also supportive, writing: 'Moore has gained an international following on the strength of powerful playing and punchy songwriting. This new package will further his reputation.'[246]

North of the border, *Run For Cover* also garnered some support. Mike Abrams of the *Ottawa Citizen* newspaper wrote that Moore had 'struck gold with this effort... Side Two is non-stop guitar wizardry... The combination of Moore's power guitar, Phil Lynott and Glenn Hughes on bass guitars and vocals is awesome. Moore's song writing and album producing have come a long way', Abrams insisted, and he predicted that the album would 'send the blood rushing through your veins.'[247]

Despite these reviews, *Run For Cover* didn't sell well in the United

States, reaching only 146 in the *Billboard* album chart. Furthermore, 'Out In The Fields' failed to chart, despite being catchy and radio-friendly.[248] One album reviewer in the United States wrote, 'Moore is one of those artists with so much potential he almost has to try hard not to make it big. Unfortunately, he's doing a good job of maintaining his obscurity.'[249]

Nevertheless, both album and single did sell well in the UK and Ireland, as well as in Europe, Scandinavia, and the Antipodes, so Moore had cause to hope that his trajectory remained upward. Moore and Lynott kept in touch, with Lynott making a guest appearance in September, at Moore's invitation, at the Hammersmith Odeon to play bass and provide vocals. He had even discussed with Lynott an idea to collaborate once more on a new song entitled 'Wild Frontier', with plans to emulate the shared vocal approach of 'Out In The Fields'.[250]

However, Lynott fell ill before Christmas, and died early in the New Year. This affected Moore deeply, and that would show on Moore's next album, *Wild Frontier* (1987).

Wild Frontier (1987)

Moore spent around six months in 1986 writing songs for his next album. During the recording process he told *Kerrang!* that the new material was in the vein of *Run For Cover* only 'one stage further, still more towards modern music. There's a greater depth to what I'm doing these days and the lyrics are more meaningful, more convincing.'

Returning to the album a few years later he further clarified his state of mind: 'With the *Wild Frontier* stuff, I suppose it was a reflective time because it was just after Phil passed away and I shut myself in a room for a few months and started coming up with that stuff. He had a big influence on that one.'[251]

Recording took place in three stages, with a handful of summer gigs in between the first two recording sessions, and the third occurring in December. The summer gigs were few in number, but prestigious. Because Moore's band, which still consisted of Daisley, Carter and Ferguson, had not played together in public since December the previous year, the first summer gig on June 3 at Surrey University, Guildford, was a much-needed warm-up in preparation for three upcoming outdoor stadium gigs in Sweden, Germany and England.

At the first of these huge gigs on June 6, at the Raasunda Stadiuon, Stockholm, Moore was billed as special guest of the main act, the hugely popular Queen. This, of course, reunited Moore with the band he had supported a decade previously when he was part of Thin Lizzy. On June 21, in Mannheim, Moore once more supported Queen, but on this occasion was only fourth on the bill, below Marillion and Level 42.

Moore returned to England for the next gig on June 28, at the Milton Keynes Bowl, where he supported headliners Marillion and was billed above Jethro Tull, Magnum and Mama's Boys. Moore claimed not to have enjoyed this Milton Keynes appearance, mainly because the line-up of acts wasn't to his liking. It's possible the two acts he was sandwiched between, Marillion and Jethro Tull, were a little too prog-rock for Moore's tastes.

Further gigs supporting Queen and Marillion followed in July when Moore performed in Milan (17), Munich (18) and Cologne (19). In August, Moore played his final two gigs of the year at the Ruisrock Festival in Finland, and eight days later on August 10 in Oostende at the Belga Festival. At these gigs Moore gave live debuts to two new songs, 'Wild Frontier' and 'The Loner', that would appear the following year on his next album. In addition, some songs from Milton Keynes were recorded for use as future B-sides.

In the recording sessions, Moore began by using a drum machine to set out the bones of some songs. However, when Gary Ferguson started work in the studio, Moore preferred the programmed drums to Ferguson's playing, a development which, not surprisingly, caused some friction. Moore explained, 'we did have some problems to begin with; the ordinary drums weren't happening and so we ended up having to use drum machines, and programme a lot of the stuff on them.' Moore claimed that Ferguson then 'copped the needle' (got annoyed) and left Moore's band to work with Geezer Butler instead.[252]

In a further interview, Moore went into a bit more detail: 'it didn't sound perfect enough. I kept hearing these small mistakes [by Ferguson], minimal to be sure, but I couldn't endure it, and I sent the drummer home. He really felt somewhat shit upon.'[253]

This episode illustrates two things about Moore: firstly, he was a perfectionist, and if the drums (or in the case of John Sloman in early 1983, the vocals) didn't sound as he had envisioned them during the writing process, Moore would not let that situation continue; secondly, Moore could be ruthless in his treatment of those he felt didn't match his own high standards.

Using the same formula that was successful with 'Out In The Fields' and *Run For Cover*, Moore released a single in December 1986, well in advance of the album. 'Over The Hills And Far Away' was offered in a variety of formats and was an immediate success, reaching the top twenty in the UK, the top ten in Ireland, and number one in both Norway and Finland.

Indeed, at one point Moore's second single from the album, the title track 'Wild Frontier', was number one in Finland, knocking 'Over The Hills And For Away' from top spot, while at the same time the album was at number one in the country's album charts.[254]

'Wild Frontier' arrived just ahead of the album, reaching the top 40 in the UK and top 30 in Ireland. So, hopes then were high for the new album, especially as Moore considered it an improvement on the last, which he felt was 'a bit fragmented. It didn't bother me at the time', he explained, 'but when I look back at it now I think I must have been crazy having Phil (Lynott) singing on two tracks, Glenn (Hughes) singing on three, and hoping people would identify it with Gary Moore. This new one sounds more like an album than a collection of bits 'n' pieces.'[255]

There is a distinctly Irish feel to *Wild Frontier*, something Moore was happy to explain: 'I really wanted to get back to my musical roots. The impulse for this change was a trip to Ireland last year. There a lot of famous musicians appeared [at Self Aid in Dublin in May 1986] And it was suddenly clear to me how much talent cities like Dublin and Belfast have produced: people like Van Morrison, Rory Gallagher, the Chieftains, Bob Geldof and U2. I wanted to remember the music I grew up with.'[256]

Given that Moore dedicated the album to Phil Lynott (the back cover bears the dedication, 'For Philip'), it is apt that the opening track, 'Over The Hills And Far Away', is a collaboration with Irish folk musicians, The Chieftains.

Moore and The Chieftains had performed at the Self Aid concert, and it's possible the idea for a collaboration began there. Unsurprisingly, the song sounds a little like the fusion Irish folk-rock of Horslips and evokes memories of Moore's 'Black Rose' days. Paddy Moloney plays Uillean pipes on this track, and fellow band members Sean Keane and Martin Fay play fiddle. In addition, Judy Tzuke sings background vocals.

'I think this the first time the Chieftains have been matched to a sequencer', Moore told journalist Jon Lewin. 'We did it all on the Fairlight, then we had them play over that.'[257]

'Over the Hills and Far Away' is an uplifting foot-stomper, a result of the combination of Irish folk stylings and rock guitar. Journalist Steve Newton gave the track high praise, saying it 'sports one of Moore's patented hell-bent-for-leather solo blasts and the same charismatic vocalizing as Lynott.'[258]

With its catchy chorus, 'Over The Hills And Far Away' was an obvious choice as first single from the album. A dramatic promotional video was shot, utilising a combination of music performance and story narrative. The video depicts a dramatic tale of a man falsely accused of an armed robbery who refuses to provide an alibi as that would involve exposing his romantic relationship with his friend's wife. While this story is narrated, Moore's band, along with Paddy Maloney, perform the song. Ironically, given that the percussion on the track came from a drum machine, the video features seven drummers performing a martial beat.

'Wild Frontier' is the album's second track and Moore chose it as the second single release. Moore described it as a 'pretty political song', which 'describes the fate of anybody who grew up in Belfast and then returns after many years. It's shocking how much the city has changed.'[259]

Rather than 'political', a more accurate description would be 'topical', as Moore was at pains to stress his neutrality about Northern Ireland politics. 'I'm not taking sides', he explained. 'I'm just trying to be impartial. I don't have the answer to the problems... 'Wild Frontier' is just a nostalgic thing for me, really. It's looking back at how Belfast was when I grew up there and observing how it's changed now.'[260]

Moore revealed that the track was a dedication to Lynott, and that he had played it to his old friend the previous year, hoping the two would collaborate on the song. 'It was an Irish type song, but with a rock feel on it.' Moore also thought the track, with its harmony guitars played on his Gibson Les Paul Junior, bore some similarities to Thin Lizzy.[261]

At one point, 'Wild Frontier' samples the violin section from the main title of the cowboy film, *The Big Country* (1958), the effect of which is to evoke the American frontier experience — or at least the Hollywood version of it. That frontier was a place where civilisation met disorder, and law was imposed through violence euphemistically known as 'frontier justice'. This 'Wild West' metaphor, which Moore presented visually, aurally and lyrically in the promotional video, indicates Moore's somewhat mixed feelings about returning to his native Northern Ireland.

Rather than strum full chords or power chords, Moore plays arpeggiated chords during the chorus, which has a 'softening' effect, making the track more palatable to a wider pop audience. Neil Carter explained that Moore was trying to reach a broader audience than just rock or heavy metal fans: 'Gary wants to... cross over to as large an audience as possible and that means broadening your horizons... I wouldn't even class Gary's music now as rock 'n' roll, it's rock but it's moving into the realms of people like U2 and Simple Minds. They have an edge that gives them a massive appeal and that edge is very important, it's still part of the music but it attracts a much wider audience than, say, Whitesnake.'[262]

The promotional video for 'Wild Frontier' was shot in a studio but also features stock footage of Belfast streets. In the studio, Moore wears a dark-coloured military tunic or alternatively a tan 'American frontier' jacket with tassels, while standing atop a British Army Saracen armoured personnel carrier. Armoured Land Rovers, British soldiers, burning cars, a graveyard — possible the City Cemetery in west Belfast — provide a backdrop to his performance. Perhaps to emphasise this is a narrative personal to the guitarist, other band members are absent from the video. As Moore sings a line about a lost friend, a single black rose appears on the screen, which is an obvious allusion to Lynott.

There are also some images of wall murals, which, in Northern Ireland, serve a number of functions. They record moments in history, mark out territory, make statements about current political events, and commemorate people and events, some of which are political or terrorist-related, while some are more 'normal', depicting musicians or sports stars such as George Best.

In retrospect, it's a poignant moment as, after his death Moore was commemorated in two wall murals in Belfast's Cathedral Quarter and another on the Upper Newtownards Road, closer to his childhood home. The former celebrates a selection of cultural, media, music and sporting stars, and along with Moore it features Rory Gallagher and Phil Lynott; the latter mural is dedicated to luminaries and legends from east Belfast, and it features, among others, Moore, Eric Bell and

Van Morrison.

The next track, 'Take A Little Time', has similar lyrical themes to Moore's 1985 song, 'Out Of My System', in other words, it's typical pop-rock fare about relationship difficulties. Moore called it a 'standard rock song', intended to occupy middle ground between 'Out in The Fields' and Billy Idol.[263]

To emphasise the Idol connection, Moore played a Hamer Steve Stevens model guitar on this track, and his solo, featuring syncopated licks, sounds like a tribute to the signature sound of Stevens in that time period when he composed and played with Idol on a string of hits.

The final track on side one is 'The Loner', a slow instrumental originally recorded by Cozy Powell. It was written by keyboardist Max Middleton but Moore wrote a new middle section, hence his co-writer credit for this version.[264] The song showcases Moore's softer side, with a minimalist style of playing. Perhaps surprisingly, given that instrumentals are rarely released as singles, the track was chosen as the fourth single out of five from the album. If that seems like a lot, in this era it wasn't unusual for an album to generate at least that many singles, especially if the album was already selling well. For example, Michael Jackson's *Thriller* (1982) generated seven singles from an album which only featured nine songs; and Queen released seven singles from their *A Kind Of Magic* (1986) album, which only contained nine tracks in total.

The promotional video for 'The Loner' begins with Moore playing guitar alone in an empty theatre. After that, his image is superimposed over some generic street scenes that have a sepia tone effect. The video ends with Moore carrying his guitar case off-stage. While viewers are left to decide what this all means, when viewed in the context of Moore's previous promotional videos, it fits neatly into that softer category of single releases that Moore hoped might reach a crossover audience of rock and pop fans. It was also another reminder of Moore's guitar virtuosity: journalist Steve Newton called the song the album's 'real showcase', a 'dazzling display of Moore's technical savvy and emotional style.'[265]

Side two begins with a cover of The Easybeats' 'Friday On My Mind', which was an international hit single in 1967 for the Australian group. Throughout the 1980s, Moore had made it something of a habit to record a cover version of a popular song for his albums. In this case, Moore mainly stays faithful to the original arrangement, but updates it by toning down some of the psychedelic stylings of the Easybeats' version. The original song intro begins with the guitarist picking 16th notes on two strings of the E power chord. The first verse features this same recurring pattern, then transitions to D major via an implied A chord as dominant of D. In contrast, Moore's version begins with some heavy power slides before following the picking pattern of the original song intro. However, Moore simplifies the second bar of the verse by omitting the melodic open A string picking, and instead repeats the basic picking pattern of the intro on the D power chord shape. Moore did this not because he couldn't emulate the original, which features some tricky but not expert picking, but instead to give the song a heavier feel.

The song was the third single release from the album, and it made a favourable impression on a number of reviewers. Larry Kilman called it 'the highlight of this album', and 'a maniacally hepped-up, satisfying version [which] maintains its innocent 1960s appeal.'[266]

Hard Report, a US radio industry news sheet, promoted the 12-inch vinyl release of the track, writing, 'Virgin has come up with a remix that is a segue monster and contains a guitar bridge that could stop your heart... a couple of listens should convince you that this classic Easybeats track has lotsa [sic] life left in it.'[267] It wasn't unanimous praise though: in an otherwise positive album review in *Kerrang!*, Derek Oliver called the song 'truly horrendous'.[268]

'Strangers In The Darkness', written by Moore and Carter, was a product of Moore's admiration for singer-songwriter-musician, Sting (Gordon Sumner). Moore, who was transitioning into that type of musician, said, 'I got Pete Smith who did the Sting LP [*The Dream Of The Blue Turtles*, 1985] to work on it with me, and we went for that sparse sound.'[269]

In fact, though, at first, the track sounds more like U2 than Sting, but it transforms later into more mainstream AOR, although The Edge couldn't emulate Moore's closing guitar lines. The song's subject matter is about young people arriving in London in hope of a better life, only to get hooked on heroin and then forced into prostitution. Moore told Mark Putterford: 'It's something I felt very strongly about after Phil died, and I think if you can do something to stop that happening to other people, even if it's just writing a song, then you will.'[270]

'Thunder Rising' is another Moore/Carter track, which features Paddy Moloney on pipes. It sounds like something from the Thin

Lizzy catalogue, and the main riff that begins around thirty seconds into the track seems to be inspired by the 1976 Lizzy song 'Massacre'. Moore said, 'a lot of this stuff was written intentionally to carry on the Lizzy tradition', and he specifically cited 'Massacre' as an influence.

Furthermore, the lyrics reference legendary Ulster warrior, Cú Chulainn, as they do in Lizzy's 'Róisín Dubh (Black Rose): A Rock Legend'. This isn't a celebration of a war, however, and instead the sentiments are more in line with those expressed in 'Wild Frontier', that war equates not to heroism and victory but instead to sorrow and loss. Comparisons with popular Scottish trio Big Country are inevitable, but, of course, Thin Lizzy's embrace of Celtic themes long predates that band.

Continuing the Irish link, *Wild Frontier* ends with 'Johnny Boy', a gentle track, with a traditional Irish folk feel. Moore plays acoustic guitar and provides passionate vocals. Paddy Moloney accompanies him on Uillean pipes, while Sean Keane and Martin Fay play fiddle. It was originally recorded with Don Airey playing piano, but in the end Moore preferred the cello sound of string synthesizer. 'When I lived in Dublin', Moore revealed, 'we used to go to these folk clubs, see these guys singing all these old ballads, finger in one ear, and this song's a throwback to that.'[271]

In the 1980s there was something of a revival in interest in Irish folk music among general pop listeners. For example, in 1982 the Irish folk group Clannad broke out of the 'World Music' category to achieve mainstream pop success with their song 'Theme From Harry's Game'.

Former Planxty member, Paul Brady, achieved a level of mainstream visibility when he wrote a song entitled 'Steel Claw' for Tina Turner's hugely successful 1984 album, *Private Dancer*.

Artists such as Enya, The Pogues, and Van Morrison incorporated aspects of Irish folk into their music. And, of course, The Chieftains had made Irish folk music a global brand. So this wasn't necessarily a risk or particularly ground-breaking from Moore, more that he chose this moment to utilise some musical ingredients from his past. Moore saw it as a response to those critics who thought his musical output was aimed too much towards the American market. He told *Kerrang!* that the Irish theme of the album would answer 'all those "American" criticisms and give the music some roots. This is me saying "I'm not American. I'm Irish!"'[272]

Wild Frontier was an international hit, charting high in the UK,

Finland, Norway, Sweden and Spain. While still not reaching the *Billboard* top 100 albums, it did well enough in the States to allow Moore to tour the album there. Reviewers were generally positive. For instance, *Kerrang!* called it, 'probably his most complete effort so far, with a consistency of personnel and a distinct theme (that being Irish) which binds this project together and ensures that it appears strongly united rather than patched together.'[273]

Journalist Paul Elliott wrote: 'At its most reflective, *Wild Frontier* is full of melancholic charm. At its rowdiest, it's as uplifting as rock has ever been.'[274]

North American reviewers were also supportive. For example, *Music & Media* named *Wild Frontier* one of their albums of the week.[275]

Canadian music industry publication *RPM* called it a 'solid effort' from Moore, 'who has put together an album bound to surprise many listeners.'[276]

Billboard considered it Moore's 'strongest to date', with 'tough vocals and driving guitar'.[277] And an Associated Press review praised *Wild Frontier* for 'tradition and freshness mixed in a muscular rock 'n' roll package... *Wild Frontier* is an uncivilized album. It screams. It shrieks. It's rugged.'[278]

Wild Frontier was a transitional album for Moore. Now that he had produced a second hit album and proved he had rediscovered whatever enigmatic alchemy it takes to write hit singles, the future seemed to offer yet more success. From March through to early September 1987, Moore toured extensively to promote the album, playing gigs in the UK, Europe, Japan, and the United States, this time with ex-Black Sabbath drummer Eric Singer on board. Once more, reviews were very positive.

For example, journalist David Sinclair was impressed with the band's late May performances at the Hammersmith Odeon, praising Moore for 'constructing a show that has put him in the major leagues as a solo artist... There was a variety of impressive lighting changes, judiciously applied pyrotechnic devices, and thoughtfully arranged material'.[279]

The Hammersmith show on April 2 was recorded and broadcast by the BBC as part of its BBC Radio 1 'In Concert' series. Bootlegs of this show, and of the Stockholm, Sweden gig on April 24, indicate a set list comprised of the following songs: 'Over The Hills And Far Away', 'Thunder Rising', 'Shapes Of Things', 'Wild Frontier',

'Military Man', 'Empty Rooms', 'Out In The Fields', 'All Messed Up', 'Rockin' Every Night', and 'The Loner'.

Based on a bootleg of a Japanese show that year, it's likely that 'Wishing Well' was also performed during encores. Finally, a bootleg from the gig at Club New York in Milwaukee from August 14, shows that 'Murder In The Skies' had been added to the set list for the American leg of the tour. The American tour was successful: just prior to its launch, a Virgin advert in *Hard Report* proclaimed, 'See why 40,000 people a night are going to see Gary around the world'. Three weeks later, Virgin marketing guru Jeffrey Naumann told *Hard Report*, 'Gary Moore continues selling out the house on his very successful tour and is getting rave reviews everywhere'.[280]

Moore also made several television appearances to promote the album and tours. For example, he performed 'Friday On My Mind' and 'Take A Little Time', the album's final single, on *Peter's Pop Show* in Germany. He also performed 'Over The Hills And Far Away' on a Japanese television show during the Japanese leg of the tour. Perhaps the most remarkable of these media appearances was when Moore and The Chieftains gave a live televised performance of 'Over The Hills And Far Away' in Ireland on RTE's *The Late Late Show* with Gay Byrne. As well as providing a foot-stomping, raucous rendition of the song, this performance is notable for the moment Moore joins in with The Chieftains just before his solo, causing Paddy Maloney to let out an unplanned whoop of delight.

Yet for all these plaudits, hit records, successful tours, and acknowledgements from his musical peers, Moore was not a happy man. A few years later he would tell interviewers, almost in the form of a confessional in which he would unburden himself of his past sins, that in the 1980s he felt like a fraud in the way that he dressed and in the music that he played.

Performing was his strongpoint: Moore loved an audience, and in contrast generally disliked being in the studio. Yet, in 1988 he didn't play a single live gig. But before he finally found his musical home in the 1990s when he immersed himself once more in the blues, there was one more album to come at the end of the 1980s, the much anticipated *After the War* (1989).

After The War (1989)
Moore started composing songs for his next album with writing

partner, Neil Carter, in Dublin in January 1988. The pair spent two months working together on new material, much of which, Moore revealed, sounded similar to tracks from *Wild Frontier*. In fact, Moore had originally intended the new album to continue the same theme as the previous release, with a distinct Celtic tone. While in Dublin, Moore and Brian Downey even re-recorded Thin Lizzy's 'Emerald' for a possible single release, with Moore playing lead and bass guitar on the track.[281]

However, Moore soon changed tack. He told Dave Shack of *Metal Forces*, 'it would be playing it too safe... I didn't want to do a Wild Frontier II'.[282] While Moore enjoyed his time in Dublin, taking time while he was there to meet up with and jam with members of Skid Row, in March Moore and Carter travelled to PUK studio in Denmark for a change of scenery, and this seemed to be the creative catalyst which enabled them to compose four new songs.

After a short break, Moore returned to the UK for the first time in over a year to record the rest of the album at Outside Studios at Henley-on-Thames. The album then had a final mix at Sarm Studios. Moore disclosed that writing and recording took around three and a half months in total, but that process was spread over a period of around nine months.[283]

Moore also revealed that while the *Wild Frontier* tour was lucrative, he chose to exile himself from the UK from April 1987 to April 1988 to avoid the worst effects of British tax laws.[284] It was likely this tax exile status that caused British tabloid newspaper *The Sun* to begin referring to him soon after the new album was released as, 'millionaire guitarist' Gary Moore.[285]

Due to the popularity of compact audio discs in the late 1980s, with sales of audio CDs in the United States surpassing those of vinyl records for the first time in 1988, it is around this time that it becomes difficult to distinguish whether an artist's definitive album release was on CD or vinyl. CDs allowed artists some flexibility as to how much music they could offer: 74 (later 80) minutes on CD compared to approximately 44 minutes on a single vinyl album (22 minutes on each side). However, vinyl and audio cassette tapes remained popular, and the release of multiple formats of the same title offered artists the chance to experiment with track listings, or perhaps even to offer edited versions of the same track on vinyl and the full version on CD.

However, the most common marketing tactic was to offer bonus material on the CD format that was not available via other mediums. Cassette tapes had previously served a similar function because they could contain 60 or 90 minutes of music; however, CDs were marketed as having improved sound quality over vinyl, whereas the same claim could not meaningfully be made about the cassette tape format. [286]

Because CDs were normally more expensive to buy than vinyl, this option proved very tempting to artists and fans alike: artists generated more revenue and fans got more of their favourite music. On occasion the differences between the vinyl and CD version of an album had a meaningful effect on how it was perceived, and that turned out to be the case with *After The War*.

The original CD release of the album contains three more tracks than were on the vinyl release, all of which were instrumental, and Moore clearly gave some thought as to their placement. For example, the CD opens with 'Dunluce (Part 1)', which was named after the abandoned castle on the north coast of County Antrim in Northern Ireland. As well as demonstrating his musicianship, the song serves to establish Moore's Irish roots.

In addition, *After The War* ends with 'Dunluce (Part 2)', which suggests Moore had a concept in mind, intending the album to trace his musical journey beginning and ending in Northern Ireland. The track 'Livin' On Dreams' is also autobiographical in exploring Moore's childhood in Belfast, while 'Blood Of Emeralds' traces Moore's teenage journey from Belfast to Dublin and beyond. The album makes further musical references to Moore's teenage idol Jimi Hendrix and his old band Colosseum II, all of which suggests that at some point in the conceptualisation process, Moore may have considered making *After The War* a full-blown concept album.

In contrast, the vinyl album begins with the track 'After The War' and ends with 'Blood Of Emeralds', which creates a different narrative impression. On the CD version, Moore's cover of Roy Buchanan's instrumental track 'The Messiah Will Come Again' is the pivotal point, bisecting the closing track on the vinyl ('Led Clones') and the opening track of side two ('Running From The Storm').

So instead of the natural break of the vinyl while switching from side one to two, 'The Messiah Will Come Again' offers a dramatic, fiery guitar overture that completely alters the album's dynamics. On balance, the CD version seems, therefore, to be the definitive version. It isn't quite a fully realised concept album, but it does have a more reflective, autobiographical theme running through it than the vinyl version, together with a cohesiveness that is absent from the vinyl release.

Compared to *Wild Frontier*, *After The War* has a harder edge. Moore had recorded a ballad entitled 'Peace In Our Time' which never made it onto the album and, in fact, still remains unreleased. A few months before the album release, Moore told *RAW*'s Dante Bonutto that he would like to include a bluesy ballad because 'that's part of what I do', but it couldn't just be a 'poor man's Empty Rooms'.[287]

Evidently, Moore thought 'Peace In Our Time' wasn't of sufficient quality to merit inclusion; besides, he wanted more of a role for his guitar playing on *After The War* so perhaps that was a factor in consigning 'Peace In Our Time' to obscurity.[288]

Because Moore was 'really enjoying being a guitarist' in the recording sessions for the album, one consequence was a diminished role for keyboards when compared to the previous album.[289]

Furthermore, on this occasion Moore chose to use real drums instead of a machine, and for most of the album that drummer was the unmistakable, hard-hitting Cozy Powell, with Simon Phillips appearing on just two tracks, 'Blood Of Emeralds' and 'Speak For Yourself', while session drummer Charlie Morgan performed on the title track.

In a promotional interview for the album, Moore explained his thinking process: 'having a real drummer definitely influences the whole sound. Basically I think you get that edge, that "snap", which you don't get from machines.'[290] Moore also revealed that Powell was only meant to appear on two tracks but ended up playing on six. 'He was so quick', Moore explained, 'and learned them as we went. It was all done in a couple of takes.'[291]

This new approach, which was really nothing more than a return to Moore's early 1980s style, but with modern technology, would be Moore's definitive hard rock statement of the decade, and also his last.

Somewhat ironically, *After The War* was released just before Moore abandoned the rock genre to focus entirely on playing the blues. Although that decision is often spoken of as if it were an abrupt change in direction that came totally out of the ether, Moore had previously indicated that he was somewhat disillusioned with the state of rock-metal music in the late 1980s.

He told *RAW*'s Mark Putterford, 'I just got sick of hearing all these guitarists who sound so generic and clone-ish… they're a bit like robots off a production line. So I… thought it was about time someone made a record with *this* sort of guitar playing on it. I mean, my style of playing comes from the blues, but these American whizz kids aren't going much further back than Yngwie [Malmsteen], and consequently they're missing out on the whole emotional dimension of the guitar.' (Somewhat ironically, around the time of this interview a poll of *Metal Hammer* readers placed Moore second only to Malmsteen in the magazine's 'Guitar Hero' category.)[292]

Crucially, to offer a counterargument to those critics who would soon accuse Moore of following trends, Moore told various interviewers of his reignited love for the blues. For example, he explained to Putterford, 'I wouldn't mind putting together a blues band just so I could play a few clubs and be the Peter Green of the 80s!'[293] A month later he told Paul Henderson of *Kerrang!*, 'I'd love to make a blues album. I really feel like I'm getting back more into it and getting more and more interested in that kind of guitar playing again.'[294]

After The War opens with 'Dunluce (Part 1)', a short instrumental track lasting just 77 seconds. This evocative, Celtic-themed opener offers a tantalising glimpse of the album which never was, the Celtic-rock fusion *Wild Frontier* follow-up which Moore decided against. 'Dunluce (Part 1)' is a slow-tempo track with Moore playing evocative Celtic licks set against the drone of a synthesiser and punctuated by sound effects of waves crashing against the shore.

Sisters of Mercy frontman Andrew Eldritch provides backing vocals on the album's title track, as well as on 'Speak For Yourself' and 'Blood Of Emeralds'. Moore said that he wanted someone with a deep voice to sing those parts, and his willingness to seek help with vocals demonstrates that he was happier to serve the song rather than egotistically insist that his own voice be heard on every line of every track. The lyrics are autobiographical, dealing with Moore's feelings and memories of his teenage years when the Vietnam War was a major talking point even in parochial Belfast. He was, of course, not directly affected in the way that American youth was: many of them faced the real prospect of being drafted into the US military and being sent to Indochina. Nevertheless, the war's impact was felt across the world and its nature and consequences clearly affected Moore.

Of course, for many British or Irish youths in that era, all things American were of consequence, especially its music, television, cinema and politics. Moore told Dave Shack, 'I always try to write one anti-war song, like 'Victims Of The Future', 'Nuclear Attack' or 'Wild Frontier' and this time Vietnam was just appropriate' because of the album's autobiographical theme. Moore accepted that 'Belfast was a long way from America' but insisted that the war created a 'pervading atmosphere' that affected him in those years.[295]

The title track was released as the album's first single and was offered in multiple formats including 7-inch vinyl with gatefold sleeve, 7-inch picture disc vinyl, 12-inch vinyl single, and 3-inch CD single. While the reverse of both the 7-inch and 12-inch vinyl featured the album track 'This Thing Called Love', the 12-inch vinyl also featured a live version of 'Over The Hills And Far Away', while the 3-inch CD, which was packaged in a round tin with tour patch, featured the two album tracks, the re-recorded version of 'Emerald', and a live version of 'Thunder Rising'.

It was released a few weeks ahead of the album to positive reviews. For example, *Music & Media* called it: 'Up-tempo rock with a very radio friendly production.'[296]

Despite good reviews, the various marketing tricks of the trade, and having the benefit of a promotional video, 'After The War' failed to match the chart success of 'Over The Hills And Far Away', the lead single from the previous album, or even *Wild Frontier*'s title track single. In fact, 'After The War' reached only mid-30s in the UK singles chart and top 20 in Ireland. While it charted highly in Scandinavia, it failed to make any impact in the United States. Moore blamed the single's relatively poor performance in the UK on lack of radio play, which he claimed was due to a backlash against rock at that time, especially on BBC Radio One.[297]

'Speak For Yourself', a mid-tempo rocker, was written by Moore and Carter. Moore said it was directed against groups in the United States such as the League of Parents who had been protesting about the supposed evils of rock and metal music.[298] Nevertheless, its lyrics are generic enough to defy easy interpretation. On one hand, it could be about freedom of speech; or the lyrics could be interpreted in an entirely personal way about, for example, relationship difficulties.

Not only does Ozzy Osbourne provide backing vocals on the track, Moore's main guitar lines sound very similar to Jake E. Lee's playing on Osbourne's 1986 album *The Ultimate Sin*, albeit the solo is very much in the style Moore had developed by the end of the 1980s with use of pitch harmonics to add colour to guitar fills, and with Moore using a hammer-on technique so that every pick stroke generated two notes instead of one.

Moore revealed that 'Livin' On Dreams' was about his time growing up in Belfast, 'when I was about 11 and listening to a lot of blues'. The lyrics reference a band named the Alleycats that Moore was familiar with from Saturday night gigs in Belfast's Maritime Club. In addition, Moore played some blues riffs on the track that he remembered from those days, as well as a riff lifted from Hendrix's 'Highway Chile'.

At one point, Moore even imitated Hendrix's vocals by slowing the tape to alter his voice. Moore also revealed that he used his 1959 Les Paul on the track as he wanted to achieve a Peter Green-Fleetwood Mac sound.[299] This track also features Moore playing bottle neck guitar, which was something of a rarity for him.

'Livin' On Dreams' was the album's fourth and final single release. Moore explained, 'it's got the feel of that [1970s] Thin Lizzy era, and that's something I'm very fond of, and there's nothing like that around anymore.'[300]

The track was remixed for single release, with Moore recording a new solo and adding new harmonica licks which replaced the original heavier guitar lines. *Music & Media* called the single 'An energetic roots rock & roll song with hooks aplenty'.

RAW magazine was less complimentary, asserting that the track was one of the least impressive from the album and that the additional harmonica made this sound like a Billy Joel release.[301] Regardless of these diverging opinions, however, the song failed to chart.

'Led Clones' is a Moore-Carter composition, featuring Ozzy Osbourne on lead vocals. Moore explained that it was a sarcastic song rather than a 'piss-take': 'that's why I got Ozzy to sing it, because he could sneer through it.'[302]

Given Moore's falling out with Jet over the release of *Dirty Fingers* and the *Live At The* Marquee album, as well as the nebulous circumstances which led to Moore, Jet, and Sharon Arden parting company, it is perhaps a little surprising that Moore and Osbourne remained friendly enough to collaborate in this way. In fact, Moore revealed in a 1984 interview that Osbourne was so angry that the guitarist had turned down the opportunity to join his band that Osbourne began 'slagging off' Moore in the Press. Moore explained, however, that Osbourne quickly apologised and the two were now 'on good terms.'[303]

'Led Clones' title is self-explanatory, and in interviews Moore specifically named American rock band Kingdom Come as an example of musicians openly copying Led Zeppelin yet denying they were doing so. Moore explained the song's origins: 'The riff came about when I was just sitting at home one day, and I thought, "Oh, that sounds a bit like Led Zeppelin, so I can't do it seriously or it's gonna be people saying, "Led clone!" Then it all came together very quickly, probably in a couple of hours.' Despite the provocative title and theme, Moore insisted that his main intent was humorous, and he hoped people would recognise that.[304]

The song mirrors the drum signature and main guitar riff of Zeppelin's 'Kashmir' and features musical and lyrical references to Zeppelin's body of work, particularly 'Stairway To Heaven' and 'Whole Lotta Love'. At one point, Osbourne imitates Robert Plant's emotion-filled wails. The solo features Moore playing bottle neck, which is multi-tracked and given a backwards echo effect to emulate the raga rock sound that Page achieved on 'Kashmir'.

Ironically, of all the popular UK guitar heroes of the early 1970s, Moore considered Page the least gifted, and he thought the likes of Jeff Beck, Eric Clapton and Peter Green 'wiped the floor with him.'[305] Despite receiving a fair amount of publicity due to its topic, when 'Led Clones' was released as the album's third single, with 'Speak For Yourself' on the B-side and with a picture cover featuring a design similar to Zeppelin's famous rune-like 'symbols' logo, it failed to chart.

'The Messiah Will Come Again' is a lengthy instrumental, originally written and performed by American blues guitarist Roy Buchanan, which Moore recorded live in one take. Before Buchanan's death in August 1988, Moore had considered covering the song, but that never came to pass. When Buchanan died while Moore was working on *After The War*, Moore decided the time was right to record it as a memorial tribute.[306]

Taken at face value, 'Running From The Storm' is a simple narrative of a ship caught in stormy weather. Yet, one senses deeper, perhaps autobiographical meaning below the surface. The sea is a ripe topic for lyricists in search of an apt metaphor. With 'Running From The Storm', stormy seas suggest difficulty and uncertainty, perhaps even a journey and rite-of-passage experience.

The line about sailing towards the sun could suggest hope, although often that depends whether the sun is rising or setting, and that information is not evident here. Or it could refer to danger, in the way that Icarus flew too close to the sun. The track features Don Airey on keyboards and during the solo section Airey and Moore duel as they had done a decade previously in Colosseum II.

Although this is an album on which Moore acknowledges some of his influences, he denied that 'This Thing Called Love' was a homage to Van Halen's 'Hot For Teacher', despite the opening drum sound and main riff being very similar to that track. Moore did allow, though, for some unconscious influence.[307]

Given the very distinctive double bass drum pattern in 'Hot For Teacher' that Cozy Powell virtually replicated on 'This Thing Called Love', as well as 'Hot For Teacher's memorable promotional video that was played regularly on MTV, it is highly likely that Moore and Powell were familiar with the song and that there was, therefore, some conscious or unintentional influence.

Moore admitted that 'Ready For Love' was a 'joke', a satire on the dating culture of the 1980s medallion man, complete with cheesy pick-up lines. Its driving synthesiser and bass beat is similar to any number of popular ZZ Top songs from that era, but especially their 1986 hit, 'Stages'. It is evident with this song, as well as with 'Led Clones', that Moore had added more than a touch of humour to his repertoire.

In fact, in interviews Moore sometimes revealed a different side to his character: he was quick to crack a joke and break into a smile. Up to this point, this aspect of his character had rarely been demonstrated on his studio releases. Perhaps this was a sign of growing confidence now that he had several hit albums and singles in the bag, and that he had achieved his goal of developing into a singer, composer, and guitarist.

An edited version of 'Ready For Love' was the second single released from album, as usual, in multiple media formats. The 7-inch vinyl version featured 'Wild Frontier' recorded live in Stockholm in April 1987, and the 12-inch also included 'The Loner' from that concert. The version of 'Ready For Love' featured on the 12-inch vinyl was remixed for this release, which came in a gatefold sleeve. The 3-inch CD single substituted 'The Loner' with 'Military Man', also recorded live in Stockholm.

The single was supported by a tongue-in-cheek promotional performance-style video, which intended to satirise similar exploitative-style rock videos featuring scantily-clad women cavorting provocatively. Moore wore his trademark leather jacket and, for the purposes of the video, played a white Gibson Flying V guitar. *Music & Media* called the song: 'Simple, effective and unpretentious pop rock with some splendid vocal touches and an off-the- wall guitar solo.'[308]

A *Metal Hammer* reviewer also singled out the guitar solo as something special: 'Never mind the lyrics', Valerie Potter advised, 'listen to that guitar break. Should be a big hit.'[309]

A *RAW* magazine review was less complimentary, designating the song 'corny, cliched and, as such, consummately commercial... pop fodder'.[310] Despite having all the ingredients of a hit single, however, it was only moderately successful in international markets, and failed to break the top 50 in the UK.

'Blood Of Emeralds' was written in early 1988 when the song's co-writers, Moore and Carter, were ensconced in a Dublin rehearsal room and when their initial thoughts were to continue the Celtic theme of the previous album. At over eight minutes in length, it is the longest track on the album.

Moore revealed in several contemporary interviews that the song was both a tribute to Lynott and also a solo version of Lizzy's 'Róisín Dubh (Black Rose): A Rock Legend', which, of course, he co-wrote with Lynott. The main body of the song begins with a guitar line that bears some similarity to the folk tune 'Bonny Light Horseman', which had been recorded by Irish folk band Planxty, among others. Another instrumental line incorporates a melody from the traditional folk song 'Rocky Road To Dublin', which was brought to a popular audience in the 1960s through releases by The Clancy Brothers and Tommy Makem, and by The Dubliners. Some hard rock, Celtic-sounding riffs provide the song's framework.

Unlike some of the other autobiographical tracks on the album, which merely allude to Moore's childhood and teenage years, the track's lyrics refer directly to events and places in Moore's life such as his birthplace and the river Lagan which runs through Belfast. A river is, though, also a commonly used metaphor for life's journey from birth to death.

In chronological order, Moore refers to crossing the border in

1969 on the way to Dublin where he would join Skid Row and meet the 'darkest son of Ireland' (Lynott). The water theme continues as the lyrics refer to thunder and rain, then crossing stormy seas, which, at face value, is likely a reference to crossing the Irish Sea to England to tour with Skid Row and later with Thin Lizzy.

However, it also serves as a metaphor for life's trials and misfortunes. The track's 'middle eight' — it actually lasts longer than eight bars, but it serves the same purpose as a middle eight in creating a change in tone and acting as bridge between different sections of the song — is probably the apex of Moore's musical talents, with beautiful poetic lyrics, gentle vocals, classy arrangement, and melodic playing. Moore's poignant and delicate lyrics reveal his deep friendship with Lynott and his sorrow at his friend's demise.

The album's closing track, 'Dunluce (Part 2)', is an extended version of the opening track, and it bears some similarity to the Mark Knopfler tune 'Going Home (Theme From Local Hero)'. As the album's final track, and coming as it does immediately after Moore's tribute to Lynott and their Northern Irish/Irish roots, its evocation of atmospheric Celtic landscapes and legends is a fitting and memorable end to *After The War*.

Critical reviews of the album in the UK and USA were mainly favourable. For example, *Raw* magazine claimed that the previous album had transformed Moore's image from a 'halfway-decent singer-songwriter with formidable guitar playing skills into Thin Lizzy and Van Morrison all rolled up in a drum machine.' When *Raw* reviewed the 'After The War' single, it noted accurately that Moore had 'found himself a niche, stuck with it and embellished on it — accessible Celt-rock once again, but this with solid real drums and some impressive, heavy guitar.'[311]

While Paul Henderson of *Kerrang!* admitted that upon first listen he was 'less than bowled over' by the album, and that it might not be a 'monster release', he nevertheless found several tracks that were 'surprisingly catchy once they get even a small hook into you.'[312]

Metal Hammer reviewer Valerie Potter was perhaps most enthusiastic. Praising the album's 'strong melodies', heavy drum sound, 'vibrant' keyboards, and 'thunderous' guitar sound, Potter called the album 'one of the highlights of Gary Moore's career.'[313]

Reviews in the United States were also positive. For instance, *Billboard* magazine called *After The War* Moore's strongest effort to date, and singled out 'Ready For Love' and 'Livin' On Dreams' as potential Hot 100 chart material.

Billboard called 'Led Clones' 'hilarious' and '[n]ot to be missed'.[314] *Cash Box* thought *After The War* was 'fun, a bit old-fashioned, but very cozy' and an album wherein Moore 'struts his stuff but doesn't go overboard.' The result, *Cash Box* predicted, was that the album's appeal 'will go beyond axe aficionados.'[315]

CMJ New Music Report chose *After The War* as one of its hard rock 'killer picks', calling it a 'dynamic return to form'. Labelling Moore 'a phenomenal guitarist', *CMJ* noted the album's 'heavier' aspects compared to *Wild Frontier* and that it was 'much better' because of it.

CMJ identified the audience Moore hoped to attract, 'AOR, but metal [fans] will find plenty to their liking… and the three instrumentals will make guitar mofos' [sic] jaws drop.' *CMJ* also singled out 'Led Clones' as the song 'many of us have long been waiting for… the lyrics knock the stuffing out of Kingdom Clone and their pathetic ilk.'[316]

Gavin Report also singled out 'Led Clones' for special attention in its album review. Claiming the song would 'stir up some controversy on the hard rock front', *Gavin Report* said 'Led Clones' addressed the 'ravaging Led Zeppelin's copyright has taken at the hands of younger, less talented metal merchants. Like Jesus in the temple, this song attempts to address a purge of the "house of the holy" from snake oil peddlers and thieves.'[317]

In early March 1989, Moore began touring to support the album. Initially, Cozy Powell was involved: in interviews from that era, Powell made it known that he expected to go on the road with Moore. However, Powell subsequently was offered the opportunity to tour with Black Sabbath, and he chose that option instead.

At this point, Moore's drummers seemed to be as numerous and as temporary as those of fictional rock band Spinal Tap! At short notice then, ex-Firm drummer Chris Slade replaced Powell. From March to May, the band played 37 gigs in Ireland, the UK, Japan, Europe, and Scandinavia. The professionally filmed Belfast gig on March 9, as well as bootleg recordings from Copenhagen and Tokyo, provide good indicators of a typical set list, which began with a recorded intro of 'Dunluce', leading into a dynamic performance of 'After The War'. Surprisingly, though, it appears only two further tracks from the album were played live on this tour, 'This Thing Called Love' and 'Blood of Emeralds'. *Kerrang!'s* Lyn Guy gave the May gig at the Hammersmith

Odeon a glowing review: 'Throughout, the show was characterised by the sensitive, skilful, scintillating string work that has made [Moore] famous — a true return to form… Say what you will, the man stands alone in a sea of heroic, posing mediocrity (Yngwie clones take note!) and rings blood, sweat and tears from his axe when the chemistry is right. On this occasion it was.'[318]

Despite accomplished gigs, positive album reviews, and that Moore was following a template that had proved successful with *Wild Frontier*, neither the album nor its singles improved on the chart performance of the previous album. *After The War* reached the top 30 in the UK, the top five in Switzerland, Germany, Finland, Sweden and Norway, but failed to reach the top 100 album chart in the United States. In fact, the album was released into a diminishing market for rock music, and the rock album charts were dominated by a handful of high-profile artists such as Iron Maiden (*Seventh Son Of A Seventh Son*), Metallica (*And Justice For All*), Guns N' Roses (*Appetite For Destruction, GN'R Lies*), Bon Jovi (*New Jersey*) and Def Leppard (*Hysteria*).

Moore was never an artist content to stand still, so the performance of *After The War* must have been a disappointment. As he had indicated with previous actions, Moore did not shy away from making tough decisions for the sake of musical integrity, nor from changing direction to ensure his career remained on an upward path. And if he had the blues after the underwhelming performance of *After The War*, it would be the blues that would soon give him artistic and financial reward.

1990s:
The Story
Of The Blues

In a 1989 interview, when Moore was asked about the state of contemporary music, he singled out American blues guitarists Jeff Healey for praise, in particular Healey's expressive guitar playing in an era of guitarists, Moore felt, lacked that particular quality.

'Thank God the blues is back!', Moore exclaimed. 'People are going to hear the other side of guitar playing now. Maybe it will make another generation of blues guitarists or maybe you'll have a great blues guitarist coming out of England, like you had in the late sixties. Now that would be fantastic... like a young Eric Clapton.'[319]

Moore had little reason to suspect that HE would be the great new blues guitarist he predicted might emerge, and that in the next two decades he would almost single-handedly maintain the flame of popular blues music in Britain and Ireland.

At the end of the 1980s Moore's passion for rock music went into a steep decline. 'Led Clones' was his critique not just of Zeppelin copyists, but also of the lack of originality in rock music. He had little time for modern-day metal guitarists, whom he thought favoured technique over passion due to them learning their trade at guitar schools. 'I can't say there's a single one of these new guitarists that excites me', Moore explained. 'I have a recurring nightmare of being stuck in the Rainbow [in Los Angeles] in between Tony MacAlpine and Vinnie Moore, talking about guitars.'[320]

It wasn't only rock and metal that bothered him, however, it was the whole music scene. He berated the victory of image over talent, claiming that many modern artists couldn't play their instruments but were able to fool fans with cool videos and attractive imagery. He thought popular music was at 'an all-time low', reduced now to mere 'bubblegum'.

He was particularly scathing about house music, which he claimed was 'just an excuse for people who can't play to make a record'.[321] Declaring the BBC's flagship chart program *Top Of The Pops* 'completely unwatchable', Moore told Mark Putterford: 'The thing that I hate most of all though is that everything these days is so manufactured… Commercialism is running the music, whether it's rock or pop, and it's a disgrace.'

Moore then signalled his distaste for the likes of Kylie Minogue, Brother Beyond, and Bomb the Bass before calling the Acid House genre 'shit', reducing it to 'people with no talent poncing around like idiots'.[322]

Moore was also unhappy with his own musical contributions in the 1980s. He told Mick Wall: 'I'd just got back from tour and it had gone all right, you know? Good crowds, usual thing. But towards the end I used to look at myself in the dressing room mirror, all dolled up like some guy in Def Leppard and think to myself: "Who do you think you are?"… Suddenly I didn't know who made those [1980s] albums. I didn't recognise myself in any of them any more.'[323]

He would later tell Martin Popoff that if he were to choose the best tracks from each of the albums he released in the 1980s there would only be enough quality there for a single compilation album.[324]

Moore was disillusioned and he yearned for a return to the era in which his musical tastes were shaped, an era he believed favoured musical substance over style, and when talent and passion merged to create great music. Nowhere was this more evident than in his earliest musical influences, black American blues artists, and their white British acolytes.

He revealed: 'I found towards the end of my last rock tour, for *After The War*, that the things I'd be playing in the dressing room afterwards were all blues tunes. I remember one day the bass player [Bob Daisley] even came in and said: "Oh, that's good — you should make a blues album."'[325] Then it dawned on him that's what happened *every* time he picked up his guitar: blues patterns came first and most naturally to him.

That's when the prospect of recording a blues album became a serious option. 'I thought the last thing the world wanted in 1990 was a blues album from Gary Moore', Moore reflected.[326]

Nevertheless, he followed his instincts and began to set the wheels in motion for what would become *Still Got The Blues*. Eric Bell recalls a phone conversation with Moore in the Autumn of 1989 during which Moore asked if Bell recalled any of the blues songs they played back in the 1960s when they shared stages in Belfast. Bell reeled off ten to twelve songs and thought no more of it until around six months later when he saw a billboard in London advertising *Still Got The Blues*. 'He's actually gone and done it', Bell thought, somewhat amazed at the turn of events.[327]

The CD version of *Still Got The Blues* consists of eleven tracks, only five of which were written by Moore. The remainder are cover versions of older blues tracks, with the exception of 'That Kind Of Woman', which was penned by George Harrison. Moore's core band consisted of Don Airey on keyboards, Andy Pyle on bass, and Graham Walker on drums, and there were additional guest performances by a cast of other musicians, most notably Albert Collins, Albert King, Brian Downey, George Harrison, Bob Daisley, and Nicky Hopkins.

Moore had, of course, worked before with Daisley and Downey, but the inclusion of Harrison, Collins and King was a coup. Harrison was one of the most important musicians of the era, being a founding member of The Beatles and later forging a successful and influential solo career. He and Moore were close neighbours in Henley and had been friends since Moore moved to the area. Harrison played rhythm and slide guitars on the album and provided backing vocals on 'That Kind Of Woman'.

Just after the release of *Still Got The Blues*, Moore recorded some colourful slide and lead guitar parts on the Traveling Wilburys' track 'She's My Baby', which was released on the Wilburys' new album later that year, and was also released as a single. The band consisted of the esteemed luminaries Harrison, Bob Dylan, Roy Orbison, Tom Petty and Jeff Lynne, so when they invited Moore to record with them it was a significant moment as well as an indicator of the respect they had for his musicianship.

Depending on whether one considers the vinyl or CD release, around half the tracks on the album feature brass and woodwind instruments, mainly trumpet and saxophone. This alone marks *Still Got The Blues* as a significant change in direction for Moore.

Furthermore, it is apparent from the album's opening track, 'Moving On', that Moore's vocals are ideally suited to this style of music. Amy Bradshaw of *Metal Hammer* thought Moore's voice was the 'biggest revelation of the album' and that when Moore sang the blues it sounded authentic: 'you believe him... he doesn't sound like some white Irish guy. At all.'[328]

Moore said, proudly, 'B. B. King likes my voice, which I took as a real complement. But the point is that in the blues you're answering your voice with guitar licks all the time'.[329]

The second notable occurrence on 'Moving On' is that Moore plays slide guitar throughout, which is something he had, thus far, done only very occasionally. The track not only has the kind of high energy, buoyant quality that is ideal for an album opener, it was also a statement about Moore's musical state of mind. A few years later, he revealed the attitude he had hoped to bring to the album: 'I wasn't trying to emulate Robert Cray — that slickly produced, clean American guitar sound; I wanted something more rough and ready. And I think I succeeded.'[330]

'Oh Pretty Woman' came to public attention when Albert King covered it on his 1966 album, *Born Under A Bad Sign*. King makes a guest appearance on Moore's rendition, playing some fills that are understated when compared to Moore's more dynamic approach. Moore later revealed that the album version was only the second take of the song, which the band recorded live in the studio.

Moore was very much a believer in capturing lightning in a bottle, and that too many takes dulled spontaneity. Further down the track list, Moore penned and recorded 'King Of The Blues' as a tribute to Albert King, who is named-checked in the song to distinguish him from the other members of the 'Three Kings', Freddie and B. B.

'Oh Pretty Woman' was the album's first single release, with 'King Of The Blues' on the B-side. The 12-inch single also featured 'The Stumble', an instrumental track co-written, and recorded by Freddie King, and covered previously by John Mayall and Peter Green.

Moore revealed that the recording process for 'The Stumble' and 'King Of The Blues' was more difficult than he anticipated: 'I wanted to do ['The Stumble'] all in one take', he explained, 'which is why it took so long. It's one of those that doesn't have a particular hook in it for you to come back to, so you have to improvise all the way through. It's a shuffle so you've just got to keep it moving. Not easy at all.'[331]

In contrast, Moore's difficulty in recording 'King Of The Blues' came mainly from his attempt to copy King's style of playing. He explained: 'I had written the song in Albert King's style so I tried to adapt my playing approach to his, with the way he does string bends.'

Like most guitarists, Moore bends a string mainly by pushing it up but King's style was to pull the string down, which while giving King his signature tone, also made it harder to copy. 'That's why it's such a bastard to play', Moore explained. 'Plus it's a seven minute song; the guitar never stops; you're answering all the vocal lines; there's two solos and the outro which has a long fade out. It's hard work!'

'Oh Pretty Woman' was also the first ever 5-inch CD single released by Moore, retaining the same track line-up as the 12-inch vinyl. Quoting a representative of one large east coast record store chain, US magazine *Hitmakers* correctly predicted that with this new album and promotional single release, Moore was on the verge of a breakthrough in the United States.

With the support of local AOR radio 'it's happening', wrote *Hitmakers*. *Music & Media* claimed the song had been 'brought back to life' by Moore and Albert King. 'Excellent stuff', was the magazine's final verdict. One note of criticism came from David Sinclair of the *Times*, who thought Moore's playing needlessly overshadowed King's. Sinclair wrote, 'the imbalance of power and technical muscle between King's light, faltering rubber-band sound and Moore's treble banshee shriek is laughable.'[332]

A moody promotional video, shot mainly in black and white, was performance based, interspersed with everyday images of women on the street, or in art. Unusually for him, Moore smiles and laughs while performing with King, and one suspects he was genuinely enjoying himself. For someone who is on record as hating promotional videos, this is a revealing indicator of his upbeat mood at the time.

Moore's rendition of Jimmy Rogers' 'Walking By Myself' transforms the original sedate shuffle rhythm into high energy boogie woogie, complete with some neat harmonica fills from Frank Mead. Moore demonstrates a variety of guitar techniques to enliven this standard blues track, including pinch harmonics, hammer-ons, a descending slide down the neck, and use of the volume control to create a slide/doppler effect. For example, at one point he plays a chord with the volume set low, then quickly adjusts the volume to create what is known as a volume swell.

'Walking By Myself' was released as the third single from the album, in multiple media formats, but without a promotional video. The B-side of the 7-inch single featured a live version of 'Still Got

The Blues (For You)', while the 12-inch vinyl version featured live versions of both tracks. The CD single offered the same tracks, but also included a studio version of Otis Rush's 'All Your Love'.

The fourth track on the album was the penultimate track on the vinyl version's first side, and also the album's second single release. 'Still Got The Blues (For You)' is a blues ballad, recorded live in the studio. Moore considered the first take to be the only one required. It begins with a guitar melody that reoccurs throughout to become the song's main 'hook'. The melody consists of three phrases played in a descending scale. Moore uses tasteful and very accurate bends with controlled vibrato to give the melody character. He plays arpeggiated chords during the verses, then strummed chords during the chorus, before returning to the descending scale melody. His solo is an extended and embellished version of the recurring melody. The effect of all this is to create a soulful, melodic ballad with two catchy ingredients — the chorus and the descending scale melody — the holy grain of song writing if the aim is to attain extensive radio play.

The single was released in multiple formats: the 7-inch vinyl had an edited, shorter version of the title track, and its B-side was a non-album track entitled 'Left Me With The Blues', which was written by Moore; the 12-inch vinyl had the full length version of the title track, 'Left Me With The Blues', and another non-album track, a cover version of Elmore James' 'The Sky Is Crying'; the CD single featured the aforementioned non-album tracks, plus another song written by Moore entitled 'Mean Cruel Woman'; and the cassette single had the same line-up of tracks as the 7-inch vinyl. The single was supported by a promotional video, which is mainly monochromatic, and which features Moore performing the song, interspersed with some scenes of actors depicting the song's lyrical themes.

In the United States, the radio industry trade publication *Network 40* predicted that the single might be a turning point for Moore in the country. At one stage, just after Moore left Thin Lizzy and during the G-Force era, it appeared Moore had set his hopes on 'breaking' America, but throughout the 1980s it proved to be one of his weaker markets.

Network 40 wrote: 'Gary has earned the reputation as one of our greatest contemporary guitarists. His talent as a player and songwriter is quickly becoming known in the States, and the rock 'n' roll format is embracing his latest effort, "Still Got The Blues." New adds in

Los Angeles, Memphis and Phoenix help push the song into the Top 40 at Rock radio, and sales are starting to emerge in response to the exposure.'

This optimism turned into reality when 'Still Got The Blues (For You)' became Moore's only single release to break into the *Billboard* Hot 100 singles chart, peaking at 97.[333] It also boosted album sales, as Moore would later tell Martin Popoff: 'In the States it was a big breakthrough for me. I got my first gold album in the States because a lot of people liked that song and it is being played on the radio.'[334]

As its title suggests, 'Texas Strut' is a tribute to Texas blues musicians, including Albert Collins, the 'Houston Twister' mentioned in the lyrics, and also known as the Ice Man, which Moore references in the lyrics when he writes of that 'cold cold feeling' — which is also the name of a track from Collins' 1978 album, *Ice Pickin'* — that sends 'shivers down your back'.

Billy Gibbons is name-checked directly, and Moore also plays the opening riff of ZZ Top's 'La Grange' while imitating Gibbons' distinctive vocal phrase from that song, 'A-haw, haw, haw, haw'. Moore also makes reference in the lyrics to the ZZ Top track 'Waiting For The Bus'. The 'Stevie' mentioned in the lyrics is identified when Moore refers to the name of Stevie Ray Vaughan's band, Double Trouble, one of his albums, *Texas Flood*, and two songs Vaughan famously covered, Stevie Wonder's 'Superstition' and Elmore James' 'The Sky Is Crying'.

For most of the album Moore used a 1959 Les Paul Standard he had purchased in 1988, and for two tracks — *Midnight Blues* and *Stop Messin' Around* — he used Peter Green's famous old Gibson. However, to get that particular Texas blues sound for 'Texas Strut', Moore used the 1961 salmon-pink Fender Stratocaster that he had purchased from Greg Lake.[335]

In November 1990, 'Too Tired' was the album's final single release. Moore revealed that it took only two takes to record the song, with all guitars and vocals recorded in the original take, and horns added on the second. The result, Moore reflected, is that the 'groove' on that track 'really motors!' Moore explained his approach: 'Blues is all about the vibe between the players in the room. It's all about people playing together, not samples and sequencers.'[336]

The 7-inch vinyl was backed with 'Texas Strut'; the 3-track, 12-inch vinyl also featured a live version of 'Too Tired', recorded at the

Hammersmith Odeon earlier in the year; and there were two 4-track CD singles, a special edition version included two live tracks from the Hammersmith gig, 'Oh Pretty Woman' and the Albert Collins track, 'Cold Cold Feeling'; the other version featured live renditions of 'All Your Love' and 'Too Tired' from Hammersmith, and a studio version of 'The Stumble'.

The official video for the 'Too Tired' single featured Albert Collins and Moore on the porch of a rural house. They begin trading guitar phrases in Chicago head-cuttin' style as they wander from the porch through the streets, before finishing back at the porch again. This seems to be a tribute to Collins' trademark habit of wandering through the audience at his performances, sometimes even leaving the venue while still playing guitar with an extended electrical lead that kept him connected to his amplifier. While Moore is clearly giving a performance in the video, acting and miming, it still appears that he was having a lot of fun during filming.

The vinyl release of the album ends with two lengthy slow blues tracks. 'As The Years Go Passing By' was first made popular when Albert King recorded it on his album *Born Under A Bad Sign* (1966). On this rendition, which is over seven minutes in length, Nicky Hopkins plays piano and Brian Downey sits in on drums. Moore remains mainly faithful to King's version, causing the *Guardian*'s Robin Denselow to praise him for showing 'unexpected sensitivity' in his treatment of the song.[337]

'Midnight Blues' is another sensitive, smooth blues tune, featuring tasteful electric piano by Nick Weaver. It is evident by this point that Moore's vocals are suited both to gruff blues work-outs, and also these more tender songs.

The CD release features three further songs, 'That Kind Of Woman', written by George Harrison, Otis Rush's 'All Your Love', and 'Stop Messin' Around', performed originally by Fleetwood Mac. Moore's rendition of 'That Kind Of Woman' appeared a few months before a version sung by Eric Clapton featured on a charity album called *Nobody's Child: Romanian Angel Appeal* (June 1990).

Nicky Hopkins guests on piano and Harrison plays some melodic slide guitar accompaniment to Moore's lead guitar stylings. 'All Your Love' is a blues standard that has been covered by the likes of John Mayall, Eric Clapton, Robert Cray and Stevie Ray Vaughan.

Moore told Paul Sexton of the *Times* that, like 'The Stumble', it was a song he had been playing when he was 14 or 15 years old.[338] Moore's version is similar to the Mayall version, although he has his own distinctive guitar tone, using more gain than Clapton, Vaughan or Cray did. Moore maintained, however, that he had attempted a cross between the Clapton-Mayall version and Rush's original, but the end result still 'sounds like me'.[339]

As a fan of Peter Green, 'Stop Messin' Around' had been a live favourite of Moore's for many years. The song was first released in 1968 as the B-side of Fleetwood Mac's 'Need Your Love So Bad'; a different version of the song was then used as the opening track on Fleetwood Mac's second UK and US albums. The song bears some similarities to Robert Johnson's 'Stop Breakin' Down Blues', and it became the template for another song written by Green entitled 'Black Magic Woman'. Moore's rendition remains faithful to Green's treatment of the song.

A sample of reviews illustrates that *Still Got The Blues* was received very positively in both the UK and USA. In the United States, for example, *Billboard* wrote: 'Grab the fire extinguisher. This album burns like a house on fire from start to finish. The former Thin Lizzy guitarist just bulldozes through standards such as Too Tired and his own compositions to provide one of the finest mainstream blues /rock albums in years.'

The next month, in a follow-up review, *Billboard* wrote: 'Moore is one of the most respected contemporary musicians. His music ranges from hard rock to classic, from pop to blues. With his new album *Still Got The Blues* Gary takes us back to the roots of all popular music — the blues.'[340] The tone of this second review is particularly interesting: it is as if his choosing to record an album of blues music had somehow conferred upon Moore a degree of respectability.

Cash Box also viewed the album positively, stating: 'Hard rockin' singer/guitarist Gary Moore takes us back to hard rock/metal's roots with an album consisting primarily of blues-rock… *Still Got The Blues* is a ballsy, passionate work underscoring the debt headbangers owe to those 'sixties rockers, as well as to their influences such as Muddy Waters, Willie Dixon, Howlin' Wolf and Albert King.'[341]

CMJ New Music Report also made the point that Moore was mainly known 'in metal circles', before praising his change in direction: 'he says he's been waiting twenty years to make a blues album, and from the sounds of this half-cover/half-original LP, it's what he should have been doing all along!' *CMJ* concluded that the album was 'the best solo LP from one of the genre's greatest instrumentalists.'[342]

More positivity came from *Music & Media* magazine, which called Moore 'one of rock's finer musicians' who was now paying his dues to his blues antecedents. King and Collins 'help Moore to find the perfect balance between their traditional style and his powerful playing. New songs and cover versions are treated with respect on an album that sees singing and playing at his best.'[343]

Among these indicative reviews, the only note of disappointment came from *RPM* magazine, which questioned Moore's authority as a genuine blues artist by citing unspecified 'purists of the genre' who 'may not be overly impressed by the sound', while damning the album with faint praise: 'Moore does do enough to get the images of southern blues across', wrote *RPM*, before predicted that the album 'really can't miss for the MOR blues aficionado'.

RPM's inference is that *real* blues fans, those unnamed blues purists would not accept Moore as an authentic blues artist. While *RPM* viewed Moore's guitar playing as the 'brightest and most riveting sound on the album', the magazine's final judgement was that 'even a guest appearance and song by George Harrison cannot rescue this from being an uninspiring, though competent, work.'[344]

Reviewers in the UK also received the album with positivity, tending also to turn to the idea of 'paying dues', while pointing to Moore's hard rock credentials and subsequent change of direction. For instance, a *Guardian* reviewer wrote that Moore was 'known as a head-banging heavy rock guitarist', but on this album he 'pays tribute to his blues roots'. Album tracks were 'cheerful, rough and ready, but agreeably enthusiastic and varied', while 'Oh Pretty Woman', 'Too Tired', and 'As The Years Go Passing By' were singled out for special praise.[345]

Metal Forces, a monthly heavy rock magazine, responded to Moore's genre change by denying that it even happened. For example, reviewer Jerry Ewing called *Still Got The Blues* a 'heavy rock' album, albeit one that was 'very Bluesy'. Ewing, nevertheless, was full of praise, writing: 'Moore takes us on a journey full of feeling and fire, encompassing the very soul and passion of the Blues, and it's a treat to hear.'[346]

Perhaps unexpectedly, another heavy rock/metal magazine also commended the album. *Metal Hammer* reviewer Andy Bradshaw praised its 'astonishing attention to detail', the ingredients of which were 'classic blues bass groove; superb horn arrangements; vocals sitting comfortably in the mix with the emphasis on the song and not the arrangement; feel... Where the songs demand subtlety there is subtlety, where there is an underplayed solo demanded, it is underplayed.'

Given that Moore had set out to make an album very different from the precise, clean and somewhat sanitised blues of the likes of Robert Cray, Bradshaw's comment that *Still Got The Blues* was an album to 'rival some of Robert Cray's best', seems a little off target. Nevertheless, Bradshaw asserted that Moore 'made the change from heavy metal to blues with... aplomb' and 'redefined his entire image.' In one 'stunning manoeuvre', Bradshaw claimed, Moore had transformed himself from Gary Moore, Guitar Hero, to 'Gary Moore — Bluesman.'[347]

Meanwhile, *Independent* reviewer Andy Gill either did not know, or chose to ignore, Moore's explanation as to why he recorded a blues album and instead gave his own interpretation: 'The recent resurgence of interest in the blues, courtesy of Clapton and Cray, has prompted this former Thin Lizzy guitarist to offer his own blues album as testament to the music that first inspired him to pick up a Les Paul.' Yet, Gill's review was positive, and he singled out 'Stop Messin' Around', 'As The Years Go Passing By', 'King Of The Blues', and 'Oh Pretty Woman' as songs of particular merit.

Gill also addressed the question of authority, praising Moore for his 'authentic Texan touch' on 'Too Tired'. Gill's final word on the album was perhaps a little grudging, but still supportive. He wrote: 'All in all, a much better album than we have any right to expect.'[348]

Still Got The Blues was Moore's most successful album thus far, becoming his first solo effort to breach the top 100 in *Billboard*'s album charts. It reached number one in Sweden, the Netherlands, Finland, and Sweden, and the top three in Switzerland and Norway. While it only reached 13 in the UK album charts, this was still a significant achievement for a blues album. By March 1992 it had sold nearly 270,000 copies in the UK alone.[349]

An August 1990 *Billboard* advert for the album claimed two million worldwide sales thus far, and that it had attained platinum-level sales in Australia, Denmark, Japan, Sweden, and Holland; and gold sales in the UK, Germany, Belgium, Finland, Norway, and Switzerland.[350]

A further measure of its success was that the tour organised to support the album was initially a modest affair, with just a few UK and European dates, but after the success of the album, and with Moore's raised profile, a more extensive European tour was hastily organised including a number of large festival dates.

Moore explained that the original plan was to do a 'three-week tour of little clubs [but] it went on for four-and-a-half months. In Europe we were going back to some venues two or three times.'[351]

In the immediate aftermath of *Still Got The Blues*, Moore styled himself solely as a blues musician, disavowing much of his earlier heavy rock output and, to a lesser extent, his output with Colosseum II. He even declared that he preferred the Thin Lizzy guitar line-up of Gorham and Robertson compared to his own contributions. While *Kerrang!* magazine thought that Moore was simply taking a 'time out from his Metallurgy' [sic], and even close friend Bob Daisley thought Moore's debut blues album was 'a side project', blues music would be the subject of seven out of his next eleven studio albums.[352]

With that came commercial success and critical acclaim, but also a degree of criticism, not just from those such as *Independent* reviewer, Andy Gill, who questioned Moore's motives, but also from some blues 'purists' who disliked Moore's high-energy approach and even deemed his blues derivative and inauthentic.

The origin of the latter criticism is worth consideration as it emerged from the long, painful history of black Americans, and the exploitation of black blues musicians by white imitators and white-owned record companies. One particular allegation is that white blues musicians were guilty of the appropriation of black music and culture. What role, if any, did Moore play in this, and where should his style of blues playing be situated within the genre's eventful history?

The origin of blues music isn't entirely clear, but it seems to have developed in the southern United States in the late nineteenth century, taking some time after that to reach a wider audience. In his autobiography *Father of the Blues* (1941), W. C. Handy recalled waiting for a train in Clarksdale, Mississippi one evening in 1903 when he was awoken by an unusual sound. He observed a 'lean, loose-jointed Negro', dressed like an itinerant, playing guitar with a knife pressed against the strings 'in a manner popularized by Hawaiian guitarists' who used steel bars to create a slide guitar effect. The man sang along, repeating one line three times: 'Goin' where the Southern cross the dog', which Handy discovered was the man's destination of Moorhead where east-west trains met those travelling from north to south.

Handy called this music the 'weirdest… I had ever heard', and he noted its components: 'a simple declaration expressed usually in three lines and set to a kind of earth-born music that was familiar throughout the South' at that time, the music of 'Negroes [who] sang about everything… fast women, mean bosses, stubborn mules'.

In this way, and from these materials,' Handy wrote, 'they set the mood for what we now call Blues.'[353] Handy's observations are some of the most-quoted in blues history, partly because Handy almost singlehandedly created a lasting image of the blues player as a male down-and-out who punctuated his lonely travels with slide guitar music and baleful lyrics.

Moore chose Handy's image of a blues player at a railroad stop as inspiration for the cover image of his 2001 *Back To The Blues* album, which suggests he was aware of the story and was making an attempt to establish roots and continuity in the genre. It is a powerful, evocative image, undermined somewhat by the knowledge that the rail depot Moore and photographer Gered Mankowitz chose for the photoshoot is in Croydon, not the Mississippi Delta.

In the middle decades of the twentieth century, rural Mississippi Delta blues became influential in the development of a new genre of popular music that quickly became known as rock 'n' roll. In brief, that early brand of rock 'n' roll could be characterised as energetic dance music with saxophone, piano, and electric guitar as the lead instruments. Lead vocals were delivered with passion and humour, and the lyrics typically dealt with teenage concerns such as cars and girls.

By the late 1960s, however, rock 'n' roll experienced first a decline caused, at least in part, by a parental and societal backlash against the music's liberal values, then a reemergence under the catch-all name of rock music. In that burgeoning era of new music, rural blues performers from the Handy era such as Robert Johnson and Son House provided a template for darker-themed music that was concerned with grittier subject matter and explored the personal torments of the artists themselves.

Johnson was almost unknown in his lifetime but became commercially successful after his music was rediscovered in the 1960s. His music also became synonymous with the 'Devil at the Crossroads' legend that is often linked to troubled blues artists, then to rock stars, and then to heavy metal music.

Son House also helped bridge the gap between the players of the early part of the twentieth century and the 1960s. Like Johnson, his music was rediscovered in the 1960s, and after a long gap in his musical career he began recording and touring once more.

Despite the importance of Johnson and House, Moore tended to find his influences in urban rather than rural blues. While Moore covered House's song 'Sundown' on his album *Close As You Get* (2007), it was one of only a handful of rural, acoustic-guitar blues songs that Moore found interesting enough to record. Moore almost entirely ignored Robert Johnson's body of work except when it came to him via other musicians that he found influential, such as Peter Green.

While a simple definition of blues might be a three-chord song with a 12-bar beat, featuring a pentatonic blues scale with blue notes, and with a three-line repetitive vocal refrain — as many blues artists have testified there is more to the blues than the technical aspects of scales and structure.

In fact, it is difficult and perhaps impossible to separate blues music from its racial origins in the United States. While whites and blacks shared many historical experiences, they did not do so as equals. In fact, the black experience in America of slavery, emancipation, Reconstruction, Jim Crow and racism offered blacks a set of experiences and a perspective that whites did not share.

For this reason, when, in the 1960s a blues and folk revival led to white musicians embracing the blues, a heated discussion began as to whether white artists could perform the blues authentically or if they were simply appropriating black culture — exploiting it for financial gain, without giving back anything to black artists or the wider black community.

White blues players almost immediately faced a backlash, ironically often from white critics who did not believe these musicians could or should play the blues. They believed that due to the music's origins in slavery and then Jim Crow, white musicians could not produce authentic blues; they did not have the same cultural well to draw upon, nor could they fully understand the significance of the music they played.

In 1964, for example, popular American skiffle musician Lonnie Donegan used his appearance on UK television programme *Juke Box*

Jury to accuse The Rolling Stones of exploiting and profiteering from black blues artists.[354]

Some black cultural commentators also took issue with the Stones. For instance, in 1967, poet Leroi Jones wrote: 'What is the difference between Beatles, Stones etc, and Minstrelsy? Minstrels never convinced anybody they were black, either.'[355]

Stones guitarist Keith Richards responded to this criticism by saying the Stones never pretended to be black and instead the group's primary aim was to make modern audiences aware that this music existed.[356]

Richards also saw potential for Stones' music to connect people together. He wrote: 'We realized that the guys we were playing, like Muddy Waters, had also grown up with Robert Johnson and translated it into a band format. In other words, it was just a progression... What I found about the blues and music, tracing things back, was that nothing came from itself. As great as it is, this is not one stroke of genius. This cat was listening to somebody and it's his variation on the theme. And so you suddenly realize that everybody's connected here.'[357]

Today the question 'can a white musician play the blues' seems anachronistic and even redundant. On one very obvious level, over the last fifty years or so the music of Mike Bloomfield, Eric Clapton, Peter Green, Rory Gallagher, Billy Gibbons, Stevie Ray Vaughn and Gary Moore seems to be clear evidence that they can.

Yet, if the question is rephrased slightly, for example to 'should a white person play the blues' or perhaps, 'can a white person play blues authentically' then the answer is less immediate.

Amiri Baraka (formerly Leroi Jones) accused white blues artists of conspiring in a 'Great Music Robbery', which commodified black music and was characterised by white copyists playing diluted blues primarily to white audiences. Such was the concern about these developments that blues historian Paul Oliver pondered if blues music would survive the 1960s. He asserted that the growing trend of white musicians playing the blues resulted only in 'sterile and derivative' music that could not hope to emulate or surpass black blues artists.[358]

There is evidence that white blues guitarists like Moore and his hero, Peter Green, were aware of these concerns. Green claimed, for example, if you 'don't come from America and your skin isn't brown and you haven't had people treat you like an animal' you can't really express the full emotion of the blues.[359]

When Mick Wall asked Moore if the guitarist considered himself 'one of the greatest blues players of his time', Moore responded: 'BB King, that's a great blues guitarist. Not some white guy from Belfast.'[360] Yet, while obviously aware of the racial sensitivity associated with blues music, Moore also defended his right to explore the genre. When asked directly if an 'Irishman' can genuinely play the blues, Moore responded: 'At the end of the day, you can either play it or you can't. Peter Green was a Jewish kid from the East End, but BB King said his guitar playing made him sweat. Of course, black people have a gift for it as they started it. I don't try to sound like a black man but I have always tried to put my own style into it. It is a very honest form of music, you can't hide behind it. It is music that tells the truth.'[361]

Unfortunately, Moore's response, while honest and forthright, doesn't really advance the discussion one way or the other. In fact, as the argument has developed since the 1960s, it has become clear that genetics — skin colour — has no bearing on musical ability.

However, ethnicity rather than skin colour remains relevant because that's where the topic of authenticity comes into play. As the origins of the blues are almost entirely interrelated with the American black experience, its production, presentation, and reception meant something different to a black audience than to their white counterparts.

Nevertheless, this position relies on an assumption of shared ethnic memory, yet it seems self-evident that most contemporary black blues players have as little relationship to the historic experience of slavery, sharecropping, or the Mississippi Delta, as any contemporary white blues musician.

What then does 'authenticity' mean in this historical context? The origins and innovative development of the blues primarily occurred within the black community in the United States, developing multiple layers and levels of meaning that only black audiences would understand — a kind of hidden code that obscured meaning for white audiences. While this was more relevant in times past, this realisation gives the blues a historic aspect that is absent from most other music genres.

Therefore, the argument goes, if white blues musicians study and understand and respect the historical social circumstance of those origins, and are able to decipher the linguistic codes that black blues artists used deliberately to obscure meaning to white audiences, it is possible for them to understand not what it is like to be black, because that's impossible and irrelevant, but to understand the blues as an expressive idiom.

Furthermore, given the music industry's historic mistreatment of black musicians, there does seem to be a moral obligation for white artists to take on this challenge to gain acceptance among blues circles. In other words, if whites give back as well as take, they would not be appropriating someone else's culture as much as paying tribute to it.

Crucially, this leaves the question of authenticity to the subjective opinion of the listener, which is surely the only reasonable, consistent position to take: after all, to deny white musicians access to the blues goes against the flow of musical innovation and obstructs the development of hybrid genres (like blues rock).

In addition, judging authenticity on a case-by-case basis ties together both blues historians and those in the blues audience — probably the majority — who are uninterested in historical origins and academic debates and instead simply appreciate the sound of the music and the power of its delivery, not so much in terms of volume or speed, but the underlying power that comes from emotion and which evokes an emotional response.

It is possible that the majority of those who appreciate Gary Moore's blues music fall into the latter category; however, it is not possible to fully appreciate the power behind that music unless one understands the historical origins of the blues in the black community, and also the development of the blues into outshoots such as rock and later heavy metal.

For instance, in the 1960s the blues offered whites an alternative to the cultural conformity of the early Cold War era. Blues was an evocation of alienation and oppression that appealed to many younger white people: to them, black artists were 'guitar-slinging outlaws and macho antiheroes.'

In addition, the blues talked about sex, openly or sometimes by a secret code that only blacks (because of their shared cultural well of experience with the blues) and some hip, white teenagers might understand. It was, according to historian Jim O'Neal, 'erotic, sweaty, hypnotic; it dealt on the level with the battle of the sexes.'[362] O'Neal could easily be talking here about the circumstances that gave birth to rock 'n' roll and its off-shoot genre, blues-rock.

Given the twists and turns of his musical journey, positioning Moore primarily in the tradition of the mythic wandering blues musician helps to make sense of his constant quest for musical perfection, for the best way to express himself, and his never-ending desire to gain the respect from his peers. Some knowledge of blues history is also required to understand the charges of bandwagon jumping and inauthenticity that dogged Moore after the success of *Still Got The Blues*.

When, in the 1950s the blues gave birth to rock 'n' roll, it was a particular type of electric guitar-driven blues that helped conceive this new hybrid genre. The development of electric guitars and amplification helped the urban blues movement in particular to evolve and diverge from its rural roots. When music became electrified, and especially when it was played in smaller venues rather than the arenas favoured by later generations of popular musicians, often just the bass and electric guitars needed amplification.

As a result, the electric guitar became more of a lead instrument, and blues guitar players had freer reign to play the kind of lead fills and breaks that later became intrinsic to rock music. As journalist David Sinclair has noted, blues music was 'the primal ooze from which modern popular music has grown, and even the very sound of six metal strings amplified is 'derived in large part from the blues players' art.'[363]

Some of the first blues musicians to adopt electric guitar are among the legends of the genre, and were very influential for later guitarists like Clapton, Green, and Moore. The city of Chicago became synonymous with electric blues, and perhaps its most influential bluesman was Muddy Waters (1913-1983).

Waters moved to Chicago during the 'Great Migration' of blacks from South to North between the two world wars. He quickly swapped his acoustic guitar for an electric and began playing Delta Blues that was amplified and electrified. This development quickly found an audience and made him a star. His hit song 'Man[n]ish Boy' (1955) is a typical example of electrified Delta blues. Waters signed with Chess Records, a company responsible for much of the blues music recorded in the 1950s.

Many musicians from rural blues background signed with Chess, which provided backing musicians and amplification to create an urban blues sound. Among these is another blues legend, Howlin' Wolf (1910-1976). Originally from the Mississippi Delta, Howlin' Wolf moved to Chicago to join the likes of Sonny Boy Williamson II, Muddy Waters and Chuck Berry at Chess.

Skid Row in 1968 when Phil Lynott was lead singer.
(Gerry Gallagher)

Another shot of the four-man Skid Row line-up. Both Gary in his coat and hat, and the tall, lanky Lynott look a world away from the dynamic rock stars they were to become.
(Gerry Gallagher)

Skid Row had become a power trio by the time they had a record contract.
From left: Gary, Noel Bridgeman and Brush Shiels.

Skid Row in
1971. From
left: Noel
Bridgeman,
Gary and
Brush Shiels.

Gary first joined Thin Lizzy at short notice following the sudden departure of Eric Bell.

Gary Moore, relaxing at home,
27th March, 1979.
(Trinity Mirror/Mirrorpix/Alamy Stock Photo)

Gary at Hammersmith Odeon with
Thin Lizzy, April 23, 1979.
(Alan Perry Concert Photography)

A moment of relaxation with Thin Lizzy, Copenhagen, May 1979
(Rolf Adlercreutz / Alamy Stock Photo)

Soundcheck at a Lizzy concert during the Scandinavian tour, May 1979
(Rolf Adlercreutz / Alamy Stock Photo)

Performing under his own name at the 1982 Reading Festival, with band members Ian Paice and Neil Murray.
(Odile Noël / Alamy Stock Photo)

With blues legend Albert King in 1990.
(John Wooler / Pictorial Press Ltd / Alamy Stock Photo)

Bishopstock Festival, Devon, 2001.
(*Heritage Image Partnership Ltd / Alamy Stock Photo*)

Official photo shoot for the Montreux Jazz Festival, July 6, 2010.
(Loona / Abaca Press / Alamy Stock Photo)

He had a powerful voice and was a kinetic, energetic stage performer. He recorded songs such as 'Smokestack Lightning', 'The Red Rooster', 'Back Door Man' and 'Killing Floor', featuring Hubert Sumlin on lead guitar, songs that are synonymous with the electric Chicago blues scene of this time period, and were recorded by many later artists in the rhythm and blues and rock genres. For example, the Rolling Stones recorded a version of '[Little] Red Rooster' and Jimi Hendrix recorded 'Killing Floor'.

However, it was probably The Yardbirds, featuring Eric Clapton, who most embraced the Chicago Blues legacy. The band was initially known for live renditions of Chicago blues songs by artists such as Howlin' Wolf, Muddy Waters, Bo Diddley, Sonny Boy Williamson II and Elmore James. An example of this is the album *Five Live Yardbirds* (1964), which is an indicative record of their live performances in this time period. All of the songs on the album were written by American blues and rhythm and blues artists, and among others it featured tracks originally recorded by Howlin' Wolf, Chuck Berry, and Bo Diddley.

Moore's connection to Waters in particular, and Chicago blues in general, is mainly via Clapton and John Mayall's Blues Breakers. For example, Moore recorded one of Mayall's tracks 'Have You Heard?' for the album *Close As You Get*, as well as 'All Your Love', which was written originally by Otis Rush but was made known to British audiences when covered by Mayall and Clapton on their *Blues Breakers With Eric Clapton* album in 1966 (often referred to as the Beano album, as Clapton is pictured on the cover reading the well-known UK children's comic). In a 2006 interview, Moore revealed that the song 'turned me onto the blues, when I heard it performed by Eric Clapton.'[364]

Moore also recorded the band's instrumental 'Steppin' Out', which eventually appeared on the posthumously released album *How Blue Can You Get* (2021). It was first recorded by blues pianist Memphis Slim before Eric Clapton recorded it with John Mayall. For the most part, Moore follows Clapton's template, especially in the first verse.

Moore recorded one song written by Muddy Waters', namely 'Walkin' Thru The Park', which appeared on Moore's 2008 album *Bad For You Baby*. The song 'Someday Baby' on that album is also credited to McKinley Morganfield (Waters) but was actually written in 1936 by Sleepy John Estes.

However, Waters did record an interpretation of this song in 1955 which he entitled, 'Trouble, No More'. A further connection to Waters is through Moore's recording of 'Walking By Myself' for *Still Got The Blues*. This track was written in 1956 and performed solo by Jimmy Rogers, although he was most well known for being Muddy Waters' guitarist.

B. B. King is probably the best-known blues guitarist of the last half century and was a major influence on numerous other blues guitarists. For instance, Eric Clapton recalled that King's *Live At The Regal* (1965) was 'where it all really started' for him as a young player.[365]

King was also an influence on Moore, who covered King's 1950s hit single 'You Upset Me Baby' on his *Back To The Blues* album. Moore's rendition of that track features a full brass section and he substitutes some hot guitar licks for the saxophone break that appeared in King's original recorded version. It was initially King who approached Moore to enquire about the possibility of doing some live shows together in Britain, and playing together on the album was a way for the two men to introduce themselves to each other.[366]

Moore spoke admiringly of King's professionalism and knowledge, as well as his love of the blues. Like Moore, King preferred to work at pace but he was also happy to do multiple takes if that's what was needed to get the best recording.

In addition to 'You Upset Me Baby' Moore recorded King's song 'How Blue Can You Get', which appeared in 2021 on the posthumously-released album of the same name. On Moore's 1992 album *After Hours*, King provided guitar and vocals on Moore's track, 'Since I Met You Baby', before recording his own version for King's 1993 album *Blues Summit*. King also made a guest appearance on Moore's *After Hours* tour, duetting with Moore on two songs at The Town and Country Club in November, 1992, a performance that was recorded and can be seen in the 1993 video release, *Live Blues*.

In what may be the highlight of Moore's career, the guitarist toured with King in March and April 2006 on King's farewell UK tour. In a contemporary interview, Moore revealed: 'BB's UK promoter asked me and it seemed like a great honour, so I didn't give it a second thought and jumped at the opportunity to play with BB again.'[367]

The tour was an opportunity also for Moore to promote his new album, *Old New Ballads Blues*. While Don Airey, Jonathan Noyce, and Darrin Mooney played on the album, Moore went out on tour with a different set of musicians including Pete Rees on bass, Vic Martin on keyboards, and Brian Downey on drums. The tour's popularity took Moore and King to five large arena venues in England, namely Sheffield Hallam FM Arena, MEN Arena, Manchester, NEC Arena, Birmingham, BIC, Bournemouth, with the tour culminating on April 4 at London's Wembley Arena.

The format was for Moore to open for King, then King would play his set, before the two artists performed together to end the show. Although this collaboration brought Moore professional and personal satisfaction, it was also something of a risk in that it gave critics an invitation to compare him to King.

For example, John Fordham of the *Guardian* wrote, 'Virtuoso though he is, however, Moore was an inevitable reminder of what BB King has — in emotion, timing, dynamics and drama — that most other blues devotees don't.'[368]

Nevertheless, such comparisons don't really detract from Moore as they were intended primarily as a show of respect for King. After all, most artists sharing the stage with King, especially on his farewell tour, would pale in comparison to the legendary bluesman, a larger-than-life musician who performed with almost every blues artist of note for over four decades.

In any event, Moore appears to have risen to the occasion: in a review of the Birmingham gig, the *Evening Mail* wrote: 'Moore provided the first half's entertainment, not so much warming up the crowd as setting them alight.'

In a similar vein, the *Birmingham Post* called Moore 'the archetypal British blues man' and asserted that the guitarist 'played with passion, control and supreme dexterity... which allowed him to extend the range of his tenderness and subtlety, contrasted with... full in-your-face power... Moore plays his blues as if his life depended on every note, but he never loses sight of the emotion involved.'[369]

The music of Otis Rush, another major figure on the Chicago blues scene, was also made known to Moore primarily through Mayall and Clapton. Rush had a hit with the Willie Dixon-penned song 'I Can't Quit You Baby' in 1956. Mayall's Blues Breakers recorded a version of the song on their 1967 album, *Crusade* (with Mick Taylor on guitar). Rush's 1958 hit single 'All Your Love' (1958) was covered by John Mayall and Eric Clapton on the Blues Breakers 'Beano' album.

In 1960, Rush also recorded 'You Know My Love' by Willie

Dixon. Moore recorded all three of these songs: 'All Your Love' featured on the CD release of *Still Got The Blues* and also on the 2006 semi-compilation album, *Old New Ballads Blues*; 'You Know My Love' also featured on *Old New Ballads Blues*; and Moore recorded 'I Can't Quit You Baby' for his *Power Of The Blues* album (2004). Moore played 'All Your Love' live on several occasions, most notably perhaps at the Montreux Jazz Festival in 1990. That performance was recorded and released as part of a Montreux box set of Moore's performances at the festival.

Willie Dixon's name cannot be separated from the birth of Chicago blues. He was a prodigious songwriter, whose compositions were covered by the Likes of Howlin' Wolf, Muddy Waters, Chuck Berry, B. B. King, and Bo Diddley, and later by blues and rock artists like Albert King, Eric Clapton, John Mayall, Fleetwood Mac, Cream and, most infamously, Led Zeppelin, against whom Dixon took legal action for copyright infringement. In the 1950s Dixon worked with Chuck Berry and so is connected to the birth of rock music.

Howlin' Wolf first recorded Dixon's song 'Evil' for Chess Records in 1954, whilst Moore covered it for *Power Of The Blues*. Moore's version has a harder edge than Howlin' Wolf's. In contrast to the original, which relies on double bass, piano and Wolf's cavernous vocals to carry the beat, with only minimal guitar fills, Moore's rendition relies heavily on his trusted Les Paul, including replacing a harmonica break with a guitar solo. Nevertheless, the arrangement is similar to the original, relying on a 12-bar rhythm, and three chord structure. One reviewer claimed Moore's 'gutsy rendition' of the song was, on its own, 'enough reason to give [*Power Of The Blues*] a serious spin.'[370]

Moore's cover of T-Bone Walker's 1947 hit song 'Stormy Monday' appeared on *Back To The Blues*. It has been claimed that both Albert King and BB King were inspired to play electric guitar after hearing this song, which was played live by both men on numerous occasions. A live version by John Mayall, featuring Eric Clapton, was released on Mayall's 1969 compilation album, *Looking Back*. Albert King and Stevie Ray Vaughan played a cover of 'Stormy Monday' on a 1977 television broadcast.

Moore's version was recorded live in the studio, and he liked the rough mix so much that he included it on the finished album. Unlike T-Bone Walker's version, piano and brass instruments are absent. It is also much longer than the original, which clocked in at less than two and a half minutes compared to Moore's nearly seven minutes-long version. It is somewhat similar to Mayall and Clapton's version, which is over four minutes in length, although that version features an organ and Moore's doesn't. Aside from that, Moore does his best to emulate Clapton's sound and licks, yet somehow manages to infuse the track with more energy than Clapton.

A final link to Walker comes through the song 'Evenin'', written by Royce Swain, and first recorded by Jimmy Rushing. The most famous rendition is probably that of The Dave Brubeck Quartet, on which Rushing was a guest artist. On these occasions it had more of a jazz beat than blues.

Jazz and blues vocalist Jimmy Witherspoon recorded the song in 1963, with T-Bone Walker playing guitar, and it was released the following year on Witherspoon's album *Evening Blues*. In later years Walker also recorded a solo version of the song and he played it live on numerous occasions. Moore recorded a version for his 2007 album, *Close As You Get*. While Moore's version is closer to the Witherspoon/ Walker version than earlier jazz-influenced renditions, Moore nevertheless arranges it as a slower, more mellow interpretation.

Ironically, many of these iconic blues artists were more well-known in their heyday as singers rather than guitar players, and it was only in the 1960s when their music became popular with white audiences that had embraced guitar rock that these artists' guitar playing became as important as their vocal prowess. This was also the era when rhythm and blues artists more known for their guitar skills attained a new level of success and visibility. Two of these artists, Albert Collins (1932-1993) and Albert King (1923-1992), would later feature significantly in Moore's life.[371]

In the 1990s. Moore collaborated with Texas-based blues guitarists Albert Collins. By his own admission, Moore had never listened to any of Collins' music until Virgin A&R manager John Wooler suggested that Moore hear Collins' 'Too Tired'. Moore thought it was 'incredible' and readily agreed with Wooler's suggestion that Collins be invited to make a guest appearance on *Still Got The Blues*.[372]

Collins had some success early in his career, mostly playing in Houston clubs. Collins and his band, the Rhythm Rockers, had a hit record in 1958 with the single 'The Freeze'. As was the case with several of Collins' early songs, it is an instrumental, with Collins playing sparse lead breaks, supported by brass and wind instruments.

However, it wasn't until the late 1960s, when Collins signed a record-deal with California based company Imperium, that he really found success as both a recording and touring act.[373] In those years he was a regular on the West Coast touring scene, playing at venues like Los Angeles's Whisky a Go Go and San Francisco's Fillmore West.

In 1978, he had a hit album release with the Grammy-nominated *Ice Pickin'*, and through the 1980s he remained a popular blues artist, and was once again nominated for a Grammy award for *Cold Snap* (1986) before finally winning the award for his collaborative blues album, *Showdown!* (1985).

Collins also made an appearance at the US Live Aid charity concert that year. Such was his prominence in the late 1980s that he appeared as a guest on *Late Night With David Letterman*, and he was invited to play with B. B. King, Eric Clapton, and Stevie Ray Vaughan at the New Orleans Jazz and Heritage Festival.

Collins often went by the name the 'Ice Man', a title reflected in the naming of a number of his single and album releases. It comes from his sparse, intense picking style, which was facilitated by his use of a capo high on the neck and his use of alternative tunings. This gave him a distinctive playing style that was selective and passionate.

His playing directly inspired a newer generation of blues guitarists like Robert Cray and Stevie Ray Vaughan. It was quite a coup for Moore then when Collins agreed to make a guest appearance on the track 'Too Tired' from *Still Got The Blues*. 'Too Tired' was written by Texan blues artist Johnny 'Guitar' Watson and featured on Collins' 1978 album *Ice Pickin'*. (Moore also covered Watson's song 'Looking Back' on his *Back To The Blues* album.)

Collins also made a guest appearance on Moore's next album, *After Hours,* playing guitar on the (Little) Milton Campbell song 'The Blues Is Alright'. Collins also played guitar on Moore's instrumental piece, 'Once In A Blue Mood', and it was clearly a fruitful and enjoyable collaboration as Collins would later join Moore on stage in Montreux in 1990, and on Moore's 1992 tour [as evidenced by 'Too Tired' on Moore's *Blues Alive* album, 1993].

Albert King wasn't the most commercially successful blues guitarist in his heyday, but his influence on other guitarists was substantial and long-lasting. He was a colourful character, who was left-handed but played an off-the-shelf guitar strung for a right-hander, which he played inverted and without resetting the strings. He preferred not to use a plectrum, instead using his fingertips to pick the strings, and he experimented with alternative tunings. His single string soloing and bending were an influence on the likes of Clapton and Stevie Ray Vaughan.[374]

Indeed, Clapton covered the title track from King's album *Born Under A Bad Sign* (1966) for Cream's third album, *Wheels Of Fire* (1968). That album also featured 'Oh Pretty Woman' and 'As The Years Go Passing By', both of which Moore recorded for *Still Got The Blues*.

That Moore asked King to make a guest performance on 'Oh, Pretty Woman', as well as composing the track 'King Of The Blues' specifically for King, demonstrates Moore's respect for the older blues artist, even if King proved difficult to work with.

For instance, during the *Still Got The Blues* recording sessions, King declined to tune his guitar to concert pitch, and instead tuned it by ear, expecting everyone else then to adjust to his tuning. In addition, King chided Moore because he had made a single error when transcribing the original lyrics (Moore sang 'She is the rising sun', whereas King corrected it to 'Sure is the rising sun'). In fact, as Moore recalled it, King hated everything about this new version except Moore's singing and guitar parts. King advised the somewhat over-awed Moore, 'Man, you gotta get yo'self a good band!'[375] However, despite King's prickly nature, Moore made whatever adjustments were needed because the venerable old blues player had his respect.

Sixteen years after *Still Got The Blues*, Moore once more paid a tribute to King when he recorded Jerry Beach's 'I'll Play The Blues For You', which was a rhythm and blues chart hit for King when he recorded it in 1972. Moore's version of the song on *Old New Ballads Blues* is more blues than rhythm and blues: Moore eschews the horns and tambourines of King's rendition and uses moody organ chords in the rhythm section. He plays the song at a slower tempo with restrained guitar, focusing more on his vocal delivery than on guitar pyrotechnics.

There are further links between King and Moore. For example, in 1969 King recorded Elmore James' 'The Sky Is Crying' for the album *Years Gone By*. Unlike James, who played slide guitar on that track, King used his usual picking approach.

King also recorded a version of the song for his 1984 album *I'm*

In A Phone Booth, Baby. Moore recorded 'The Sky Is Crying' as a non-album track during the *Still Got The Blues* album sessions, and it appeared on the CD single release of the album's title track. Moore also used a picking approach as opposed to slide.

In addition, in 1962 King recorded the pre-World War Two Hudson Whitaker/Tampa Red song 'Don't You Lie To Me', which King renamed 'I Get Evil'. As it is something of a blues standard, it was covered by other notable artists including Fats Domino in 1951, Chuck Berry in 1961, and BB King in 1977. The original Tampa Red version and the Fats Domino version are dominated by boogie-woogie piano. On the Tampa Red version, minimal guitar fills punctuate the song.

In contrast, while also featuring a piano accompaniment, on Berry's version the main rhythm is carried by Berry's 12-bar guitar. In place of Tampa Red's instrumental break, which was played on kazoo, Berry plays a lead guitar break. In B. B. King's version of the song the main rhythm is carried by brass instruments and bass guitar, punctuated with electric organ fills and King's tasteful, minimalist guitar. Like Berry, King substituted a guitar break for Tampa Red's kazoo solo.

Albert King's version of the song features an Afro-Latin percussive rhythm, a funky horn section, some minimal guitar fills by King, and a piano solo break. When Moore recorded a version of the song for his *After Hours* album, he paid tribute to both the writer and Albert King versions by renaming it 'Don't You Lie To Me (I Get Evil)'. In style, Moore's version is closer to Berry's arrangement than any of the others, although it still has those trademark Moore guitar phrases that distinguish him from Berry's more basic playing. Whereas Berry's version is structured around his 12-bar guitar rhythm, Moore allows his band to provide the structure while he concentrates on vocals and searing guitar fills.

These then are the roots and routes of Moore's fascination with the blues, gaining inspiration not so much through the original American artists but instead mainly via those British musicians such as Clapton, Mayall and Green that Moore heard during his teenage years. In those early days, Moore admitted, 'white blues players were as far as I was prepared to go back at the time.'[376]

In fact, Moore's versions of these songs usually sound more like the cover versions by those British musicians than they do the original versions. Moore even conceded that he really enjoyed working with B. B. King because, 'a lot of his style was handed down to me through Peter [Green].'[377]

Moore's recollection of his teenage years is that he was 'totally swamped with blues' and the likes of Albert King. Nevertheless, as Moore remembers it, guitar playing was generally in the background of blues music and the guitar 'didn't have a really powerful voice' until Clapton made the Blues Breakers album.

This indicates that Moore's discovery of the blues in his early teenage years laid a groundwork for his playing, but it wasn't until he heard the power generated by Clapton that he began to develop the dynamic and loud electric blues style that he would become known for.[378]

Perhaps Moore also gained inspiration through the music of Stevie Ray Vaughan, whose name crops up throughout the aforementioned links between songs and artists.[379] Or perhaps he learned from the Allman Brothers Band, who recorded covers of many standard blues tracks. As Keith Richards said, 'everybody's connected here', but it was Clapton's particular style and sound that was especially impactful on Moore, that mixture of troubled lyrics and hot guitar lead work played on a Gibson Les Paul through Marshall valve amplifiers.

Moore said: 'From the age of sort of 12, 13, I was just so into blues. I first heard the British blues stuff and then Eric Clapton, John Mayall, and then Peter Green came along. It was just a great time to be growing up with all these great guitar players just coming out of the woodwork one after another.'[380]

When Moore first saw Cream play live when he was just 14 years old he thought they were 'the best band in the world.'[381] That perhaps explains why Moore was drawn to that style of blues rather than, for example, the rural Delta blues of Robert Johnson that mesmerised Clapton.

In fact, Moore's blues career mainly stays clear of acoustic, rural blues with one notable exception, when he covered Son House's 'Sundown' (1965) on *Close As You Get*, with Moore taking a rare excursion into acoustic slide guitar. 'Sundown' 'had to be treated with respect', Moore revealed. 'I had several attempts at it before I finally nailed it. I was in the studio late one night sitting on a couch at the back of the control room with a few microphones. In the end, I recorded it in one take.'[382] Moore's version stays very close to the original, although, despite a valiant effort, Moore cannot emulate House's rich vocals.

It's possible Moore discovered Sonny Boy Williamson II through his devotion to Clapton. In 1963 The Yardbirds, then featuring Clapton, backed Williamson on several occasions in December 1963 and January 1964. A gig in December at the Crawdaddy Club in Richmond, Surrey, was recorded and released on album in 1966 as *Sonny Boy Williamson & The Yardbirds*. Moore recorded Williamson's 'Eyesight To The Blind' (1951) and also the more well-known 'Checkin' Up On My Baby' (1960), both of which appeared on *Close As You Get*. 'Eyesight to the Blind' is probably most familiar to modern audiences because it was covered by the Allman Brothers Band, while an Eric Clapton version of the song appeared in the film *Tommy* (1975), featuring The Who.

Moore's version of 'Eyesight To The Blind' is closer to Clapton's electrified version that it is Williamson's original. 'Checkin' Up On My Baby' is something of a blues standard, having been covered by Junior Wells and Mick Jagger, among others. Like the original, Moore's arrangement of the song features harmonica, bass, rhythm and lead guitar parts, and piano. The harmonica is not present to the same extent as in the original, and Moore's rhythm guitar is more prominent. The main difference, however, is that Moore extends the song by adding a three and half minute guitar break which brings the song to a close.

Back To The Blues also features Moore's rendition of the Jimmy Reed song 'I Ain't Got You', which was covered by The Yardbirds in 1964 and appeared on their first American album, *For Your Love*, in 1965. Clapton played lead guitar on the track. The Yardbirds' version features harmonica and clocks in at just two minutes, whereas Moore's version retains the harmonica, but is closer to three minutes in length thanks to the addition of a second guitar break. Moore's version is also more blues-influenced than the Yardbirds pop rendition.

As well as Clapton, Peter Green was also a huge influence. Moore first met Green when he was only 16 years old and playing guitar for Skid Row. The band was supporting Fleetwood Mac for a Dublin gig. The two hit it off immediately and remained friends. At Green's insistence, Moore bought Green's 1959 Gibson Les Paul from him in 1972. Moore called Green 'one of the guitarists from that era who really had something to say.'[383]

Green replaced Eric Clapton in John Mayall's Blues Breakers, quickly establishing his credentials as an innovative and tasteful guitarist. It is possible the 10-second-long sustained notes in the instrumental 'The Supernatural', from the album *A Hard Road* (1966), was an influence on Moore's trademark sustained note in 'Parisienne Walkways'.

Green soon left Mayall's Blues Breakers to form his own band, entitled Fleetwood Mac. In his three years with the band, he penned a series of hit songs, including the UK number one 'Albatross'. Green began using LSD, however, which led to his departure from the band. Over the next few years, he suffered mental health issues and dropped out of public view. Decades later, Green's manager Stuart Taylor revealed that Green only 'resurfaced' after Moore recorded *Blues For Greeny* (1995) and 'requested his appearance at a show in London.'[384]

Moore explained his reasons for recording the album: 'It is a thank you from me to him for everything he did for me and my music, and to emphasise that his style of playing is still missing today.'[385]

Moore had previously recorded the Clifford Davis/Peter Green song 'Stop Messin' Around', which appeared on the CD release of *Still Got The Blues*. Moore resisted the opportunity to modernise the track, which was likely a sign of respect for Green.[386]

However, during the *Blues For Greeny* sessions, he recorded a version played with acoustic guitar that ended up as a non-album bonus track on the single 'Need Your Love So Bad'. On this version, Moore demonstrates impressive vocal control of falsetto and vibrato.

Moore also recorded Tony 'Duster' Bennett's 'Jumpin' At Shadows' for his *After Hours* album. This track had previously been covered by Green's Fleetwood Mac. Bennett had played harmonica for John Mayall and was friendly with Green. Moore knew Bennett from his days in Skid Row, when according to an interview Moore gave in 1994 to promote his *Ballads & Blues 1982-1984* album, Bennet and Skid Row 'did a couple of shows together.'[387]

The song's reflective lyrics bear some resemblance to Robert Johnson's 'Crossroads Blues', even mentioning the devil, but the song seems to be about a man sinking into depression as he comes to realise he hasn't made the most of his talents.

Critical reviews of *Blues For Greeny* were mainly positive, helping the album reach the top ten in *Billboard*'s blues charts. Dave Johnson of *Hard Report* wrote: 'if you doubt that Gary Moore can do complete justice to Greeny's music, just close your eyes and listen to such Green classics as 'Long Grey Mare' or 'The Same Way'. What you will hear on this new CD is simple unbridled passion and appreciation from one artist to another. And when you're dealing with two greats such as Gary Moore and Peter Green, the interpretation is phenomenal!'[388]

Jim Farber of the New York *Daily News* called *Blues For Greeny* 'a worthy tribute', with Moore paying homage to Green's music and playing style.[389]

Lyall Johnson, of the *Sunday Herald Sun* was also very positive. '[U]sing Green's distinctive guitar', Johnson wrote, 'Moore manages to reflect the slick style and grace of Green's music. All the tracks on this album are written by Green but performed with the flavour (and voice) that is quintessentially Moore — a blues legend in his own right. This is a fine addition to the collection for those who remember Green with John Mayall's Blues Breakers and early Fleetwood Mac, or fans who just love Gary Moore and the blues.'[390]

A *Vox* album review praised Moore's 'taste and respect', noting, 'Moore is more restrained than usual, making effective use of his talent for lyrical playing.'[391]

Together with these indicative positive reviews there were, however, a handful of negative outliers. For example, Australia's *Advertiser* claimed the album 'merely goes through the motions', while Canada's *Ottawa Citizen* claimed, 'this collection from Moore is more of his acquired-taste sound, with the exception of The Supernatural [which] features amazing 10-15-second sustains and lyrical lead runs.'[392]

Reflecting on these influences, it seems apparent that Moore's style is more in the tradition of urban, electrified Chicago blues, but even more is grounded in the particular dynamic of British blues guitarists who adopted the blues in the 1960s. Their hybrid blues-rock style privileged guitar prowess over vocal ability, and fans worshiped them as 'guitar heroes', as evidenced by the 'Clapton is God' graffiti that appeared around London after the release of the 'Beano' album.

Awareness of Moore's musical origins, influences, and style makes it easier to defend him against persistent criticisms that have dogged white blues players such as that of imitation, appropriation and exploitation.

For example, it is evident that if Moore was imitating anyone it was Clapton, Mayall, and Green, not the original black blues players. Moore explained that Clapton's guitar playing on the 'Beano' album was as powerful for him 'as Robert Johnson was for Eric.'[393]

The difference between Clapton and Moore, wrote music journalist Charles Shaar Murray, is that 'Clapton started out wanting to be Freddie King, but Moore started out wanting to be Clapton.'[394]

The origins of the blues are in the American black experience, as are the origins of rock, with the likes of Ike Turner, Chuck Berry, Bo Diddley, Little Richard, and Fats Domino among its foundational artists. However, the blues-rock hybrid style — defined normally as songs played with faster tempos and played more aggressively — was a product mainly of the 1960s, played in the UK by white artists like Clapton, Mayall, The Rolling Stones, The Yardbirds, and The Animals, and in America by artists such as The Paul Butterfield Blues Band, Canned Heat, The Doors, and Janis Joplin.

The genre is an example of the kind of musical evolution that comes from artists adopting and adapting various styles of music. Without that happening there would be no musical growth or innovation at all, only repetition. Ironically, it is only when critics of white blues players such as LeRoi Jones insisted on putting the blues in a glass case, telling white musicians 'don't touch!', that the genre was in danger of becoming stale and irrelevant.

Yet, these criticisms refuse to go away, not directed so much at Moore individually but instead at white blues players in general. Indeed, the amount of wealth being created by the 1990s blues revival inspired Buddy Guy to write a song entitled, 'Don't Tell Me About The Blues', in which he criticised unnamed blues imitators exploiting blues archives for personal gain.[395]

While there is no evidence that Guy had Moore in mind, Moore, nevertheless wasn't entirely immune against such criticism, and there was superficial evidence available that could lead critics towards negative interpretations of Moore's legitimacy and motives. For example, while *Still Got The Blues* is more rhythm and blues or blues-rock than it is straight-ahead blues, in later albums Moore tried his hand at more traditional blues arrangements, which could leave him open to charges of imitation.

For example, in a review of *After Hours* (1992) journalist Mike McClellan praised Moore's playing and singing but claimed Moore's original blues compositions were too familiar and did not push boundaries: 'next time out I'd like to hear him take the tradition and push it further', the reviewer opined.[396]

Others charged that Moore's high-energy style was too far removed from the original arrangements of classic blues songs. For example, in reviewing Moore's *Blues Alive* (1993) album, journalist Shane Sutton called Moore's approach 'heavy handed' and opined: 'Moore's blues packs a heavily produced punch, which bears little resemblance to any blues which has emanated from Chicago or Memphis.'[397] Music journalist Tony Green also found Moore's heavier approach problematic, claiming that it wasn't the 'genuine blues article', and that Moore was merely a 'blustery "fusionoid" rocker'.[398]

In a review of one of Moore's blues albums, the *Ottawa Citizen* wrote: 'Moore's always had this problem in the North American blues community. Street-hardened blues practitioners from Chicago and New York always had a hard time with Moore's knack for chewing up the scenery. The teeniest bit less angst would probably have worked wonders careerwise.'[399]

In a similar vein, journalist David Sinclair claimed that Moore was trying to 'claim a set of blues credentials retrospectively' but was 'just too damn noisy and speedy to do anything but murder the authentic feel of the real thing.'[400]

Finally, Sinclair claimed that *Still Got The Blues* was, 'marred primarily by the overpowering lack of restraint which has always characterized Moore's playing. His massively cranked sound, combined with the hyperactive zeal of his fret technique, simply leaves no room for the nuances that are essential to the creation of a good blues mood.'[401]

Sinclair also doubted Moore's motives for returning to his blues roots, and, worse, even accused the Belfast man of a kind of tokenism in inviting black blues artists to collaborate with him.

Another journalist, Mike Hasted of the *Independent*, complained about Moore's blues style, and also introduced race into the argument. Hasted reviewed a B. B. King performance during King's 2006 farewell tour with Moore: while dismissing Moore as merely 'another well-meaning white acolyte' who mimics blues playing, he compared Moore's 'thuggish power' style unfavourably with King's 'innate delicacy'.[402]

Of course, much of this is merely opinion presented by reviewers as fact: for example, another journalist, listening to the same music, reached a completely different conclusion, that on *Still Got The Blues* Moore showed 'not only he can play and sing the blues, but understands it.'[403]

In a review of *Close As You Get*, another reviewer claimed that Moore remained true to the roots of the blues, but also injected it with vitality. 'If you think the blues are no longer relevant', he wrote, 'spin this and prepare to change your mind.'[404]

For some critics, however, any choice Moore made was the wrong one due to his unforgiveable whiteness. If Moore veered too far from original arrangements he was 'heavy handed' (Sutton); yet if he went for a more traditional sound he was unambitious and failed to push boundaries (McClellan). These comments, together with Hasted's inference that racial origin is the distinguishing characteristic between Moore and King's approaches, suggests not only a tendency to find fault with white blues musicians no matter the circumstances or context, but also that commentators struggle to deal with the historical racism from which the blues originated.

One reviewer claimed: 'There is something unsettling about British people playing blues, even the electric variety. Like Americans playing football, it doesn't ring true.'[405] While this uncertainty and perhaps even suspicion is somewhat understandable given the nature of white and black history, it nevertheless hardly seems fair or appropriate to burden musicians with a nation's guilt over its racist past.

How much Moore paid his dues is an important part of this conversation. The discussion leads to questions of authenticity, and how access to the blues community of musicians could rest on how much effort a particular musician makes to understand the music's historical and social context.

Did Moore approach the blues on a superficial level or did he do his homework? Moore conceded he wasn't a blues historian in the way that Clapton studied the genre's history. Instead, Moore revealed: 'I'll always just enjoy listening to it and playing it. I don't claim to be an expert on the blues or anything whereas Eric — you could talk to him about any aspect of the blues and I'm sure he would know the whole history of it.'[406]

Yet, Moore clearly respected the music's depth and impact, a point noted by some older blues artists. For instance, in 1991 Albert King told *Guitar World* magazine that Moore and Stevie Ray Vaughan were two of the best young blues players and that both had 'what it takes to really do it'.[407]

In addition, Albert Collins said of Moore: 'He's a rock player, but he proved he can play the blues.'[408] Collins thought highly enough of Moore to offer him a guest spot on his 1993 album, *Collins Mix*. One reviewer claimed that Moore was the only guest on that album, which included BB King, Branford Marsalis, and Kim Wilson, who was able to keep up with King's 'fluent and attacking' style.[409]

According to some critics though, neither King nor Collins knew as much about blues authenticity as the critics did themselves.

Against the charge of chasing trends, Moore responded that when he released *Still Got The Blues* in 1990 the blues was essentially a niche market that was neither commercial nor cool. However, he claimed that after his album was successful, 'a lot of people [were] jumping on to that bandwagon, a lot of so called heavy rock guitarists saying that Robert Johnson was a big influence The thing was in Europe I was the fucking bandwagon… Eric Clapton wasn't doing anything at that time, Buddy Guy hadn't come out with that album [1991's *Damn Right, I've Got The Blues*]. I just wanted to play and hope that I wasn't going to get slagged off.'[410]

While generally true, Moore's point about the low profile of blues music before 1990 is not entirely accurate: in January 1989, for example, at George H. W. Bush's Presidential inauguration, festivities included a four-hour-long rhythm and blues show at the Washington Convention Center, featuring blues musicians such as Willie Dixon, Albert Collins, and Stevie Ray Vaughan.

Later that year, B. B. King's collaboration with U2, 'When Love Comes To Town', was a hit single in the UK, Ireland and the US. In September, John Lee Hooker released *The Healer* (1989), which won critical acclaim and reached number 62 on the Billboard album charts — a surprising achievement for a blues album. A track from the album entitled 'I'm In The Mood' won the Grammy Award for best traditional blues performance.

But in the year preceding *Still Got The Blues*, blues singer and guitarist Bonnie Raitt had the greatest success with her blues album, *Nick Of Time* (March 1989), which reached the top of the *Billboard* album chart and won a Grammy for album of the year.

Yet, the main thrust of Moore's claim is accurate: in the decade before Raitt and Hooker's albums achieved popular success only Stevie Ray Vaughan's *Texas Flood* (1983) and Robert Cray's *Strong Persuader* (1986) had achieved similar levels of sales.[411]

Furthermore, previous attempts by artists known primarily for their work in the rock genre to try their hand at the blues had little success. For example, when Brian May and Eddie Van Halen collaborated on May's concept album *Star Fleet Project* (1983) it resulted in poor sales and critical scorn.

May sent a copy to his hero Eric Clapton, who later told *Musician* magazine that he found the album's rock-orientated tracks 'really very interesting' but was 'very disappointed' by the guitar duo's performance on the May-penned song 'Blues Breaker', which Clapton deemed 'horrible'.

Clapton said that he was 'almost insulted' that May had dedicated the song to him, and he derided May and Van Halen's blues-playing skills: 'they can't play!', he insisted. 'They took turns to play solos, and just went head-at-it, with everything they knew. And there was no dynamics, no build-up, no sensitivity. I was very disappointed... I realized that, although I'd been accepting the fact that all these players knew exactly what it was about on the surface of things, underneath, they didn't.'[412]

This suggests that rather than being a self-interested sure thing, as some critics charged, Moore's change in direction was a critical and commercial gamble: releasing a blues album was far from being a guarantee of commercial success, nor was there much hope that music critics or the blues community would embrace Moore or his music. As it turned out, he became something of a trailblazer in making a success of his transition from hard rock to blues when others such as May and Van Halen had failed in that endeavour.

Sometimes criticism of Moore took on a nasty, unprofessional tone: for instance, in 1992 journalist Robert Sandall claimed that Moore 'enthusiastically hitched himself to the blues bandwagon'. Sandall dismissed Moore as a 'second-rate heavy metal guitarist' before delivering the unkindest cut of all: 'The blues would be better off without him.'[413] A few years later, Neil Slaven cited Moore as one of the 'spent rock stars hitching themselves to [the] blues [band] wagon'.[414]

Both viewpoints are, however, misleading: there wasn't a blues bandwagon in 1990 when Moore released *Still Got The Blues*, but when those criticisms were raised, Sandall and Slaven were in the middle of one, and that was at least partially due to Moore's success.

Besides, as Tony Clayton-Lea reminded readers of the *Irish Times* in his review of Moore's gig at the Olympia Theatre, Dublin, in 2001,

Moore had been a 'fan of the genre' since the 1960s, which led to Skid Row supporting Peter Green's Fleetwood Mac. As such, Clayton-Lea insisted, 'Moore couldn't be accused of jumping on bandwagons.'[415]

A few weeks after Sandall's bitter criticism, he at least offered an apology and correction: 'Moore's patronage of black American players such as Larry McCray and Albert Collins has doubled the fees they can command in concert; his current collaboration with BB King has put the grand old man of the blues within a shout of the British top 40 for the first time ever.'[416]

Given the torrent of abuse from blues purists that Moore anticipated, his return to the blues must be considered a bold gamble, not a calculated business decision.

It remains open to opinion the extent to which the success of Moore's *Still Got The Blues* acted as a catalyst for the blues revival that occurred in the 1990s. This decade saw the successful reissue of Robert Johnson's *Complete Recordings* (1990), Eric Clapton's blues-orientated MTV *Unplugged* session, which became the best-selling live album in history, Clapton's return to pure blues with *From The Cradle* (1994), a number of successful blues albums by Moore, and the emergence of a number of white blues-rock guitarists as successful solo artists, such as Walter Trout and Joe Bonamassa.

Furthermore, John Lee Hooker's two follow-up albums to *The Healer*, *Mr Lucky* (1991) and *Boom Boom* (1992) both reached the top 20 in the UK album charts, the latter helped by Levi Jeans using Hooker's song 'Boom Boom' in a well-known television ad campaign.[417]

Whether *Still Got The Blues* helped cause this revival, or if it was merely one of the first to catch the wave of resurgent interest in the genre that perhaps began with Raitt and Hooker, remains unclear. *Music & Media*'s Robert Tilli suggested that a blues revival happened every ten years, or so, but he didn't explain why.[418]

Perhaps this was all simply a product of new technology and market forces. This was the era which saw the emergence of CDs and CD box sets, and as a result many artists' back catalogues were reissued. Often, as was the case with *Still Got The Blues*, for instance, extra tracks would be offered on the CD release, encouraging fans to buy both vinyl and CD releases to ensure they didn't miss out. In addition, the back catalogues of many older blues artists could now be made available in more convenient packaging and in a format which gave these old tracks a modern makeover.

Some, however, were taking note of Moore's success. One of those was Virgin A&R manager John Wooller, who was involved in the marketing of *Still Got The Blues*. Blues enthusiast Wooler had set up the Point Blank Records in 1988 with a focus on blues music. After Moore's success, Wooler signed John Lee Hooker to the label, and it was on the Point Blank label that Hooker found further success with *Mr. Lucky* and *Boom Boom*.[419]

Venerable blues artists such as Johnny Winter, Albert Collins, Solomon Burke, John Hammond and Van Morrison were also lured to the label. To be sure, some of these artists like Hooker and Van Morrison were already popular, so there may be no direct connection between Moore's success and these events. However, it seems evident that Moore's profile-raising collaboration with Collins had, at least, made the older bluesman a marketable figure once again.

Suddenly the blues was cool again, at least in terms of sales and, it must be noted, marketed to and purchased predominantly by white audiences. This was a long-standing trend: the blues began to attract white audiences in the 1950s, while in the 1960s black audiences were drawn to rhythm and blues and soul. By the early 1970s, most African Americans had moved to soul and funk music; and through the 1980s and 1990s hip-hop and rap were more contemporary expressions of the black experience.

By the 1990s popular blues music was, with some exceptions, being played mainly by white musicians to white audiences. Another demonstration of the whiteness of the blues in this era is that while the two most popular movies about the blues in the 1980s, *The Blues Brothers* (1980) and *Crossroads* (1986), featured black actors and musicians, the main characters in both movies were white.

If white artists could avoid allegations of appropriation of black music and culture by giving something back in return for what they took, and if Herzhaft's *Encyclopedia of the Blues* is accurate, Moore self-evidently paid his dues. For example, Herzhaft asserted that 'rock star' Moore 'tried to spread [Albert King's] fame', but the older bluesman died before he could fully take advantage of their collaboration.[420]

If that was Moore's intention then a case could be made that Moore was reciprocal towards a black blues artist and not simply appropriating that music, a charge some critics maintain is the sin of all white blues artists. For his part, Moore thought his main achievement with *Still Got The Blues* was in exposing the genre to a more youthful audience. He told Mark Putterford: 'It really is nice to be responsible for bringing something as important as the Blues to a younger audience's attention. On the last tour I had people of all sorts of ages at the shows — kids with their fathers, teenage Metal fans...'[421]

It might be argued also that in recording *Blues For Greeny*, Moore was giving something back to Peter Green in particular, but also blues music in general. Moore stated, for example: 'The idea behind that album is… like a thank you… because it was a big thank you from me to him for all the great music and all the great things he did for me and all the great things I learned from him as a musician over the years and I just thought his music had been ignored [and] I felt I was in a position to maybe draw attention to it as I was doing pretty good myself at that time and I just thought it might be nice if somebody pointed people in his direction again and maybe they might see what a great musician he was.'[422]

While Green was already making his way out of semi-retirement before Moore recorded his 'thank you' album, there is no doubt that Moore raised Green's profile for a modern audience. As one reviewer put it, Green was now 'enjoying the spotlight again thanks to Gary Moore's tribute'.[423]

Moreover, as B. B. King acknowledged after touring with The Rolling Stones in 1969, his association with such popular, white musicians exposed him to new and bigger audiences, while boosting record sales. In a similar way, Moore's association with black American blues guitarists Larry McCray and Albert Collins ensured those artists had a raised profile in the UK and it gave them more bargaining power with promoters when they came to tour.

In addition, when Moore covered older blues songs it often led to the original rights owners earning substantial royalties: for instance, when Moore recorded Jimmy Rogers' 'Walkin' By Myself' it earned Rogers more than his original recording. Indeed, one newspaper report claimed that Moore's cover ensured that Rogers could live off the royalties and never have to work again.[424]

In any event, often in these discussions of origins, influences, and authenticity, a rather simple point is missed, even when musicians openly expressed it. Sometimes simply the sound of an electric guitar is enough to inspire a young man (or woman) on the road to a musical career. That was the case with Gary Moore. As a teenager he had become interested in music and performing but he recalled a particular moment that was such an epiphany it set the template for his musical career. 'The first time I heard Clapton play guitar, it changed my life', he recalled. Something very profound happened when I heard that record [1966's *John Mayall's Blues Breakers With Eric Clapton*]. Within two seconds of the opening track, I was blown away. The guitar sound itself was so different. You could hear the blues in it, but prior to that all the guitar you heard in rock, well pop, music had been very staid, very polite... Clapton transcended it completely... I could just relate to it somehow, it was all about the emotion of the electric guitar.'[425]

It's impossible to understand Moore's musical trajectory without realising how profound the sound of a particular electric guitar can be, how certain chords ring out or notes sustain, the sounds of different amplifiers, the use of effects, how a change in pick up selection affects sound, not to mention various playing techniques from basic strumming and arpeggiation to bending strings, tapping, muting, using volume and tone controls, choosing pickup configurations, using a pick in various ways including where to pick strings, to more complicated sweep picking.

Without being able to play even the simplest of these techniques, a layman fan can still hear the effects and feel the emotion or raw power, and for some these sounds trigger a desire to pick up a guitar and learn how to use these techniques. And so it is with the blues: while it can be played on a variety of instruments, in a band situation or as solo performances on piano, trumpet, or saxophone, for some, like Gary Moore, the sound of an electric guitar playing the blues was inspirational and transformative.

Moore recalled the impact of hearing Peter Green play in a Belfast club: 'I had never heard anyone play a Les Paul live before. I remember the walls kind of resonating and the floors shaking... It was an incredible moment for me... [Green] just walked onstage and fucking blew everyone away with his tone and everything. And when I heard all that, it was just so pure and so full of emotion and passionate, I really didn't want to play anything else.'[426]

Having noted already most of the guitarists who inspired Moore, there is one more important and enduring figure in blues history that ties together Moore's two main influences, Clapton and Green, and that is the spectral, legendary figure of bluesman Robert Johnson.

In his own lifetime, Johnson was an extremely minor figure, yet decades after his death Johnson came to be considered as one of the most talented blues artists of all time, a major influence on the likes of Bob Dylan, Keith Richards, Jimmy Page, Peter Green and Eric Clapton. Partly, this unfolded because Johnson's recordings resurfaced in the 1960s. For instance, Columbia records released *King Of The Delta Blues Singers* (1961), which exposed much of Johnson's music to a record-buying audience for the first time. Almost immediately, the cream of that era's rock, pop and folk community began to namedrop Johnson as a major influence in their work.

Perhaps the musician most influenced by Johnson in the 1960s was Eric Clapton, who recalled: 'I don't think I'd even heard of Robert Johnson when I first found [*King Of The Delta Blues Singers*]. I was around fifteen or sixteen, and it came as something of a shock to me that there could be anything that powerful... It was as if I had been prepared to receive Robert Johnson, almost like a religious experience.'[427]

In his autobiography, Clapton testified: 'It was hardcore... I realized that, on some level, I had found the master, and that following this man's example would be my life's work.'[428]

Peter Green was also a fan of Johnson's work, both in his early days with John Mayall and Fleetwood Mac, and in his later years. For example, Johnson's song 'Hellhound On My Trail' appeared on Peter Green's debut album with Fleetwood Mac; decades later, Green released *The Robert Johnson Songbook* (1998), an album featuring only Green's renditions of Johnson songs.

What drew Clapton and Green to Johnson was the power of his music, his ethereal guitar playing, and tortured lyrics. However, Johnson's legend also featured an element of the supernatural. In 1966, Son House told *Downbeat* magazine that Johnson 'sold his soul to the devil in exchange for learning to play like that'.[429]

Of course, none of the musicians who admired Johnson actually believed it as fact that he made a Satanic pact, although the tragedies and trials that afflicted the lives of Johnson, Clapton, Green, and perhaps even Moore, might suggest otherwise.

Yet, Moore never recorded any of Johnson's songs, not even the ones he discovered through Clapton and Green. 'I'd heard the name Robert Johnson,' Moore told one journalist, 'but the acoustic blues didn't mean anything to me at all.' However, Johnson's mythic history, and especially the apocryphal story of his deal with the Devil — what

Vox called the 'most potent blues myth of all'[430] — is relevant to Moore's life and his position within the blues framework. The story, in fact, works as a metaphor to describe the personal demons that many musicians faced, such as the pressures of fame and expectation, addiction, relationship break-ups, musical successes and failures.

Keith Richards expressed this idea most eloquently, and in a way that remains relevant to the trajectory of Gary Moore's musical career. Richards equated the Johnson legend to The Rolling Stones' journey from the obscurity of playing the blues in small London clubs to becoming world famous rock stars.

Richards said: 'It's not that easy being famous; you don't want to be. But at the same time you've got to be to do what you're doing. And you realize you've already made the deal at the crossroads… You're now set on the path, along with all those people you wanted to follow anyway, like Muddy Waters, Robert Johnson. You've already made the fucking deal. And now you have to follow it, just like all your brothers and sisters and ancestors. You are now on the road.'[431]

The rock star life Richards referred to was a travelling and touring culture following in the footsteps of those itinerant blues artists who chose a life 'associated with all manner of fast living and ungodly pursuits — a veritable underworld of promiscuous sex, drinking, here-today-gone-tomorrow hell-raising, gambling and generally living the life of a drifter.'[432]

The alternative for these early black blues musicians was poverty and the daily grind and stultifying boredom that seemed to be all that was available for them in Jim Crow America. As Werner notes, Keith Richards was just one of many white musicians to 'bear witness to how black music helped them escape the suffocating communities they grew up in.'[433]

Richards' interpretation of the 'deal' is a useful way to frame the similar rite-of-passage journey taken by Moore. Being a musician required him to leave home and adopt a life on the road. To become a popular and financially successful musician meant making deals and compromises for the sake of success. Being a rock star in the drug-fuelled 1970s sometimes meant losing friends, either as victims of their habit, or by leaving them to ensure one's own good health.

Moore was an admirer of rock band ACDC, and as their lead singer Bon Scott once wrote, the everyday experience of a rock 'n' roll band involves getting robbed, beat up, ripped off, and underpaid, all of which Moore experienced at some point in his career.[434]

Moore's musical journey began and ended with the blues. The series of successful and critically acclaimed blues albums he released in the last two decades of his life brought him the respect of fans, critics, and fellow musicians. In them, he explored different aspects of the genre: for example, his 2002 *Scars* album was more in the style of Jimi Hendrix blues than the more accessible 'pop-blues' of *Still Got The Blues* or the more traditional, more sparse style of *Blues For Greeny*.[435]

In addition, on his *After Hours* album, Moore utilised the talents of The Memphis Horns — Andrew Love and Wayne Jackson — to get that unmistakable Stax-soul sound, most notably on the Albert King-influenced ballad 'Story Of The Blues', and on his emotional ballad 'Separate Ways'.

After decades of searching for the mode of expression that best suited his talents, he was finally ready to raise his colours proudly: 'I'm a blues musician now,' he said. 'I consider myself a blues musician.'

Gary Moore Live!

'Moore remains a guitarist to be seen playing live. It's in the sweat of a stage show that he shines, Strat poised and Marshalls steaming...' [436]
Tony Bacon

It's no secret that Gary Moore preferred playing to a live audience to recording in the studio. He told one interviewer, 'I just want to get out there... I just like the atmosphere of playing live a helluva lot more than recording.' [437]

Moore's attitude towards live performances is illustrated by an anecdote from Eric Bell, the ex-Thin Lizzy guitarist, and Moore's friend. 'I saw him play one night at Liberty Hall in Dublin and he was amazing', Bell recalled. 'But when I went to see him in the dressing room afterwards he was sitting in the corner with a big bottle of Marcus Rose wine knocking it back. I sat down beside him and said, "Fucking great gig, Gary." He looked at me. "What? Fucking load of shite! I've never played so bad in my fucking life!"' [438]

This was the elevated standard Moore set himself, and that he expected from those around him, including promoters, stage crew, and the musicians he worked with. He told *Guitar World*, 'I'm not impressed with doing things in half measures… I feel you have to give it 200 per cent all the time — play every gig as if that's it.' [439]

Because of this intensity and these high standards, Moore developed a reputation for being 'prickly' and difficult to work with. But for every complaint like this, there is also an example of Moore being generous in praising others and giving credit where it was due.

In addition, Moore also had a sense of humour that undermines his dour image: for instance, he told *Metal Forces* magazine that when he discovered a particular fan would come to his shows with a stopwatch to time how long he held his famous extended note in 'Parisienne Walkways', Moore would try to 'make his night' by holding the note longer than he had done the previous night. [440]

Moore's attitude to his stage shows changed over time. The main issue he had to consider was who would sing his songs. Initially, he relied on others to do that until he gained enough confidence to undertake all live lead vocal duties by himself.

In a 1987 interview, Moore reflected on that decision: 'There came a point when I said, if I want people to recognise me as a musical entity, I have to sing my own songs, It was really hard to get the confidence on stage to be at the front — I had to get drunk every night, I was so nervous. I was so used to being able to hide behind a singer and jump around onstage. Also there was the physical hassle of getting to the pedals, switching things around, and getting back to the stand. I was out of puff all the time but I've learned to pace it now.'[441]

Moore also had to adjust to the times. In the 1980s, when he was playing heavy rock, his stage show reflected the standards and expectations of that era. He dressed like a hard rocker, and his concerts were a visual spectacle of lights and pyrotechnics. He later told Vox magazine: 'There were times when you had to be a set designer before you were a guitarist.'[442]

When, in 1990, he started playing the blues, he changed his stage garb and toned down the spectacle. When *Still Got The Blues* proved successful and Moore found himself highly in demand and therefore required to play more shows in larger venues, how might audiences react to his more muted stage show? Would they accept the erstwhile hard rocker now that he dressed in a suit instead of his trademark leathers and denim? Given that music would now be at the forefront and spectacle in the background, would he still be able to connect with audiences as successfully as he had in the past?

In 1989, Neil Carter told journalist Mark Putterford: 'We're not Iron Maiden… so I don't think our image is that important', but while it was true that Moore had never burdened himself with the supernatural imagery that the likes of Iron Maiden had embraced, audiences nevertheless expected rock gigs to offer an aural and visual spectacle.[443]

The lengths some bands went to ranged from having a life-size prop of Stonehenge on stage (Led Zeppelin & Black Sabbath) or wearing an exploding codpiece (Blackie Lawless/W.A.S.P.), parading semi-naked women around (The Rolling Stones), biting the heads off bats and chickens (Ozzy Osbourne), having a lighting rig shaped like a World War Two bomber (Motörhead), landing a UFO onto the stage (Electric Light Orchestra), swinging through the air above the audience (David

Lee Roth), using a revolving stage (Def Leppard), shooting flames into the air (Kiss), interacting with an animatronic monster (Iron Maiden), driving onto the stage on a motorbike (Rob Halford/Judas Priest), and pretending to be beheaded by a prop guillotine, then continuing the show while holding his own severed head (Alice Cooper).

Moore never went to any of those lengths and, in fact, tried to minimise his reliance on image, gimmicks and spectacle. 'If someone comes up to me at the end of the show and says, "The lights were great!" I know I'm in trouble', he explained. Moreover, Moore spoke about the cost of such productions and was acutely aware he did not yet have the drawing power of artists such as Pink Floyd, who could afford to create bigger productions for each new tour.

Furthermore, he was cynical about bands who 'hide behind their stage gimmicks. Rock is the perfect game for bluffers', he insisted, 'and over the years plenty of people who can't sing or play have made a lot of money out of it.' Nevertheless, Moore admitted to hiring professional stage designers who would suggest ideas and provide drawings and models for Moore to consider.[444]

Moreover, Moore was happy to use the standard concert effects of lights and pyrotechnics that were an audience expectation. 'We do have visual effects', he explained, 'and I don't like the thought of going out on stage without some kind of visual accompaniment that complements what you do as a musician, but it doesn't take over'.[445]

For example, on the *Victims Of The Future* tour in 1984, at the beginning of the title track twin sheets of flame arose from either side of the PA stack, and at certain points the performance was accompanied by clouds of dry ice, thunder flashes, and lighting that synchronised with Moore's guitar solo. In addition, during the song 'End Of The World' Moore was raised twelve feet above the stage by a lighted riser.

These were typical not just of Moore's stage show during this period but were standard fayre for almost every rock band of the era. Occasionally Moore would use effects that tied in with the imagery of the album art or promotional videos.

For example, during the *After The War* tour in 1989, two huge flags were projected onto a screen behind the stage to emulate the title track's promotional video. For this tour Moore wanted the stage set to look 'a little bit tougher' than the 'modern', angular design of the *Wild Frontier* stage set up.

Moore recalled that one magazine had described that tour's stage as 'either a very clever use of minimalism or a parody of Andy Pandy's playpen' (Andy Pandy was a BBC children's television series about a marionette who lived in a picnic basket).[446] This was evidently not the look Moore was after, and although Moore told this story in a humorous way, it does demonstrate that he paid attention to feedback about stage design and acted upon it when necessary.

The closest Moore came to having an iconic stage outfit was in the mid-1980s during the *Run For Cover* and *Wild Frontier* tours, when his stage wear included a historic military tunic and military great coat adorned with chevrons on each arm. Moore insisted: 'It is important that the band entertain people onstage… and if the band look right then that helps — you don't want them all wearing Marks & Spencer T-shirts, but then again you don't want them wearing Batman costumes, having pigs flying from the ceiling [a reference to Pink Floyd] and monsters walking across the stage! [a reference to Iron Maiden's 'Eddie' mascot]. I am conscious that people pay good money to come and see us, but I'm more concerned with giving value for money with the music not the looks.'[447]

Moore attributed his relative lack of success in the United States to the fact that he didn't have an image like some of the aforementioned rockers. 'We're regarded as a heavy rock act', he explained, 'but because I don't have make-up and blond hair we don't fit into their idea of how a heavy rock band should look… I come up with an album cover that doesn't have fourteen girls being chained to a wall and eating raw meat or something, and it doesn't fit in.' Instead, Moore insisted that the success he had achieved in Europe and Japan, two key markets for his music, was the result of his band's musical ability, a fact, he said, meant more to him 'than selling 10 million records through some kind of hyped-up image.'[448]

Further to that sense of honesty and integrity, Moore was insistent that live album, CD, and video releases remained true to the original performance, and that, as much as possible, what a fan saw or heard was what was played on the night. For example, *We Want Moore!* (1984) features only one track with additional studio recording and that was because Moore's guitar went out-of-tune. 'I didn't change anything else like a lot of people do who record so-called "live" albums', he explained.[449]

Moore revealed that when his *Blues Alive* album was released in 1993, some thought it sounded so polished that it couldn't possibly be a true record of his live performances at the time. However, Moore explained that his band was so well-rehearsed for that tour that he only had to do a few minor fixes on that album.

And when Sanctuary Records released a DVD of Moore's performance in Sheffield on the 2003 Monsters of Rock tour, the closing credits said: 'This DVD contains no overdubs.'[450] This attitude was very much in keeping with Moore's no-nonsense personality, as well as his desire for respect from both fans and peers.

Rockin' Every Night – Live In Japan (1983)

Moore's first live release as a solo artist was *Rockin' Every Night – Live In Japan* (1983). It came soon after Moore signed with the Virgin label and initially was only available in Japan. Although it could be found in some record stores in the UK as an expensive import, it wasn't given a full European release until 1986.

Rockin' Every Night is a record of Moore's *Corridors Of Power* tour, and it features four tracks from that album. Moore performs lead vocals on two tracks, his cover of Free's 'Wishing Well' and on 'Back On The Streets'. He also shares lead vocals with John Sloman on 'I Can't Wait Until Tomorrow'. The set includes two instrumentals, 'White Knuckles' and 'Sunset', the latter being a song Moore wrote and first recorded on Cozy Powell's 1981 album, *Tilt*, and which he performed on this occasion as a tribute to the recently deceased guitarist, Randy Rhoads.

A *Sounds* review of the UK import LP gave the album four stars and was mainly positive. Reviewer Dave Roberts considered Moore 'Britain's finest rock guitarist' and a 'sleeping giant' on the verge of popular success. Roberts viewed Moore as a 'responsible but volatile technician… only now fulfilling his true potential.'

In retrospect, Roberts' comments about lead vocalist John Sloman point to his pending departure from the band, with Moore thereafter taking on most live and studio lead vocal responsibilities. Roberts wrote: 'Sloman manages to sing reasonably well but little more, while Gary does a surprisingly good job on his own lead vocals.' Roberts concluded his review with a plea to fans to buy the album: 'Whether you can afford this import LP is another matter, but support the man whatever. Gimme more, gimme Moore.'[451]

Writing in *Kerrang!*, Neil Jeffries also noted Sloman's predicament. Jeffries called Sloman 'a fine singer' but on this tour he was 'seemingly only there to take over the duties from Gary on the faster songs so the latter could jump around more!' Jeffries singled out 'Wishing Well' and 'I Can't Wait Until Tomorrow' for particular praise. Jeffries wasn't convinced by Moore's studio cover version of the old Free song but when performed live, Jeffries thought the song transformed into something special. In addition, Jeffries thought the live rendition of 'I Can't Wait Until Tomorrow' took on epic proportions, surging 'majestically… to a mighty climax.' Jeffries concluded that *Rockin' Every Night – Live In Japan* was an 'excellent album' and predicted success for the band if they could retain the touring group line-up.[452]

When the album was finally released in the UK in 1986, *Kerrang!* reviewed it once more, this time with Mark Putterford offering his thoughts. Putterford gave an equally positive assessment, singling out Moore's playing and singing. Putterford viewed Moore's vocal performance as evidence that Sloman wasn't required. 'Sloman', Putterford asserted, 'comes across as awkward and out of place.' However, it was Moore's guitar playing that Putterford found most impressive, not just his 'devastating digital displays' and '100mph soloing', but also his playing on 'Sunset', with Moore 'gliding gracefully on the breeze of Don Airey's keyboards to create a marvellous atmosphere of melancholy.'[453]

Gary Moore Live/Live At The Marquee (1983)

After the break-up of G-Force, Moore formed a new band for some live gigs in the Autumn of 1980. This line-up featured Kenny Driscoll on vocals, Andy Pyle on bass, Tommy Aldridge on drums, and Don Airey on keyboards. Gigs in November at the Marquee Club in London were audio recorded, but a full live album was not made available until 1983 when Jet released *Gary Moore Live*. Future iterations would be released under the title, *Live At The Marquee*.

The setlist included unrecorded material that Moore had been working on, such as 'Nuclear Attack', 'Dallas Warhead', and 'Run To Your Mama', some material from the *G-Force* album, and the crowd-pleasers 'Back On The Streets' and 'Parisienne Walkways'.

Driscoll sings lead vocals on the opening track, 'Back On The Streets', with Moore adding backing vocals. 'Run To Your Mama', a fast-paced rocker with a memorable hook chorus, is, for the most part, better suited to Driscoll's bluesy Lou Gram-style vocals than it was to Charlie Huhn's vocals on *Dirty Fingers*. However, on the studio vocals, Huhn performs what can best be described as a heavy metal scream in the final chorus, a feat Driscoll was either unable or unwilling to attempt on stage.

'Dancin'', originally from the *G-Force* album, has all the hallmarks of the forthcoming wave of 1980s hair metal, but with few of its highlights. Unfortunately, this live performance isn't much of an improvement on the *G-Force* version. Driscoll and Moore share lead vocals on another *G-Force* track, the dramatic 'She's Got You'. Until about the halfway stage it remains faithful to the album track, with Moore once more playing a Charvel guitar.

However, the solo is very different to the recorded track, and the live performance is extended to allow interplay between Moore and Don Airey. Furthermore, the live guitar sound is an improvement on the overly processed studio version. There is some powerful drumming by Tommy Aldridge on the live version, and Aldridge's performance is a reminder that throughout his career Moore worked with some A-list drummers, including Downey, Hiseman, Powell, Aldridge and Ian Paice.

The opening track on side two of the vinyl release is 'Parisienne Walkways', which features an extended guitar introduction before Moore launches into the song's familiar guitar melody. This version is entirely instrumental, as Moore originally intended it to be until Lynott jotted down some lyrics and persuaded Moore to proceed in that direction. Moore uses the volume pots to add colour to the notes and to create an effect that simulates whispered vocals. Moore plays his trademark extended single note but doesn't hold it as long as he would in later live renditions.

The melodic 'You', from the *G-Force* album, follows, staying close to the album version. It is a coin toss between Dee and Driscoll as to who sings it better, while Moore's guitar is punchier than on the album version, and the harmonies between Moore and Airey bring to mind their days together playing in Colosseum II.

Moore introduced 'Nuclear Attack' as 'another new song' because it had yet to be recorded for what would become the *Dirty Fingers* album. It's a powerful live performance with some notable guitar effects deployed by Moore to create dissonance and an uneasy ambience.

The album ends with the instrumental 'Dallas Warhead', which is mainly a vehicle for an extended drum and guitar thrash featuring Moore and Aldridge.

We Want Moore! (1984)

Moore toured extensively throughout 1984 to promote the *Victims Of The Future* album. At the end of January, Moore, Gruber, Carter and Paice undertook a British tour which lasted until late in February. The concert at Golddiggers in Chippenham at the end of January was recorded for the BBC's Sight and Sound in Concert programme. Then the band flew out to Japan for a short tour, playing five prestigious gigs in six days, from 24-29 February. A European tour followed from March 10-30, with gigs in all the Scandinavian countries, then on to West Germany, Switzerland, Netherlands, Belgium and France.

In April, Paice unexpectedly parted company with the band, so Moore brought in Bobby Chouinard as a replacement for the forthcoming, extensive summer American tour in support of Canadian rockers, Rush.

At this time, Rush was at the height of its popularity. The band made its reputation in the 1970s playing progressive hard rock, but had adapted its sound in the new decade by focussing less on Alex Lifeson's guitar virtuosity and incorporating more keyboards into the band's sound. In the process, Rush gained a new pop audience. Consequently, Gary Moore's brand of hard rock wasn't best fitted to Rush's audience. Besides, Moore had a low profile in the States, and unknown support bands always ran the risk of playing to half empty arenas, or facing a hostile or indifferent audience.

Nevertheless, it appears Moore fared well with American audiences. For example, British music journalist Malcolm Dome wrote that Moore arrived onstage at the Los Angeles Forum to a muted reception but after a 45-minute set the band had 'won recognition' from the audience. Dome mused: 'In a city where the hairspray can is more important than the amp, Gary's mob must be an unpretentious novelty.' Dome praised Moore's guitar playing and singing and predicted that the single 'Empty Rooms' might give Moore the breakthrough hit that he needed to gain traction in the United States.[454]

In August and early September, with Paul Thompson replacing Chouinard, the band played several festivals, including Monsters of Rock at Castle Donington, a two-day festival in Paris on August 29-30 entitled 'Breaking Sound', another Monsters of Rock festival this time in Germany on September 1, and an arena gig at the Stadthalle in Vienna.

The line-up for the Paris festival billed Moore ahead of the likes of Accept, Motley Crüe and Metallica, but below Whitesnake, Dio and Ozzy Osbourne, whereas the German festival line-up placed Moore again ahead of Motley Crüe and Accept, but below Dio, Van Halen and AC/DC. This was a fair reflection of Moore's popularity and drawing power in mid-1984, and Moore acknowledged that at Donington, England he wasn't surprised or offended to be billed below Ozzy Osbourne, Van Halen and AC/DC, all of whom were having massive chart and sales successes at the time.[455]

It appears, however that Moore — dressed on this occasion in a red jumpsuit, and with backing vocals provided by actor/singer Jimmy Nail — at least held his own with some of those above him on the Donington bill. For example, in *Kerrang!*'s festival report, reviewers expressed some dissatisfaction with the performances of AC/DC and Van Halen, whereas Moore made a good impression on journalists Mick Wall and Derek Oliver.

Playing to an audience of around 65,000, and under sunny skies and in 80-degree heat, Moore's setlist was comprised mainly of tracks from *Corridors Of Power* and *Victims Of The Future*. Wall said Moore 'paraded his talents with assurance and the natural aplomb of the true Guitar Hero', and whereas Oliver thought Ozzy Osbourne's band stole the show and asserted that Jake E. Lee 'trashed just about every other guitarist' at the festival, he added a qualifying clause: "cept maybe Mr Moore'.

Wall noted the crowd's positive reaction to Moore's setlist, and that they were particularly energised by 'Parisienne Walkways', which Moore played as an encore: 'The crowd reacted... as if Bob Dylan had just walked on with a harmonica hanging outta his gob singing 'Blowing In The Wind'. You know, massive applause!'[456]

In retrospect, the 1984 Donington bill is remembered as perhaps the strongest ever, with Moore's performance often recalled as a highlight. For example, *Metal Hammer*'s 1989 review of the decade singled out Moore as a 'guitarist's guitarist' whose Donington performance 'dragged the crowd around by their hair, slamming riff to riff in a rocking ecstasy.'[457]

At the end of the month, Moore performed at the Breaking Sound festival at Le Bourget, Paris. Moore played on the first day of the two-day festival, along with minor acts such as High Power, Sortilege, Bullet and Heavy Pettin [sic], and more well-known acts such as Metallica and Ozzy Osbourne. Osbourne topped the bill, while Moore performed after Metallica and just before Osbourne's set. (On day two the headliner was Dio, with Blue Oyster Cult given second billing.)

Once more, Derek Oliver reviewed the festival for *Kerrang!*, comparing Moore's performance unfavourably with Donington. Oliver wrote, 'His performance on this occasion was good but not exceptional. His guitar and/or equipment seemed to be playing nasty tricks throughout the show and it was probably for this reason that the set seemed bitty and non-committed… with Moore looking ruffled'. Oliver, nevertheless, singled out 'Wishing Well', 'Murder In The Skies', 'Victims Of The Future', and 'Rockin' And Rollin' for praise, as well as 'Empty Rooms', which he called 'spine chilling', with an 'exceptionally evocative' guitar break. 'Moore's middle name must surely be class', Oliver concluded.[458]

The Gary Moore band played five more gigs in December, with bass player Bob Daisley replacing Gruber. The first took place at London's Marquee Club, then Moore played two 'homecoming' gigs at Belfast's Ulster Hall, and two more in Dublin at the SFX Centre. Phil Lynott gave guest performances at the Belfast and Dublin gigs. A number of gigs that year were recorded, and a selection of songs from the UK, Japan and American tours were chosen for the live album *We Want Moore!* (1984).

This double vinyl album, released in a gatefold sleeve, consists of four tracks from the gig recorded at Harpos Concert Theatre in Detroit, one track from the Nippon Budokan concert in Tokyo, four tracks from the gig at The Apollo in Glasgow, and one track recorded at the Hammersmith Odeon. The album showcases four tracks from *Victims Of The Future*, three from *Corridors Of Power*, one from *Back On The Streets*, and one from *G-Force*. It also features one non-album track, a cover version of 'So Far Away', which acts as an instrumental introduction to 'Empty Rooms'. 'Rockin' And Rollin'' was recorded at the Hammersmith Odeon, where actor and part-time singer, Jimmy Nail provided guest background vocals.

A UK magazine advert for the album proclaimed: 'If you are one of the 90,000 people who have seen Gary playing live in England this year you can find the entire set plus encore on We Want Moore!' This was, however, a little misleading. Except for the American leg of the tour, when Moore supported Rush, his concerts consisted of around 15-16 songs.

However, in his supporting slot, Moore had only around 45 minutes to play his set, which was therefore shortened to around 8-9 songs. Therefore, at only ten tracks in length due to the imitations of vinyl, and even though it only features four tracks recorded in the United States, the setlist featured on *We Want Moore!* is more representative of those on the American leg of the tour.

Eight of the ten tracks were either written entirely or co-written by Moore, with the exceptions being his covers of 'Shapes Of Things' and Mo Foster's 'So Far Away'. The album offers an authentic record of Moore's dynamic live show at this time, accompanied by some very able musicians. Moore revealed that it contained only one overdub, and called it 'an exciting album' on which he 'played some good solos.'[459] It proved moderately successful, reaching 32 in the UK album chart, and 21 in Finland and Sweden. Once again, however, it failed to chart in the United States.

Emerald Aisles. Live In Ireland (1985)

As well as *We Want Moore!*, the other official live release from the 1984 tour was the videotape *Emerald Aisles*. This was mainly a recording of Moore's performance on December 18, 1984, at the Ulster Hall in Belfast, his first performance in the city for a decade. In the video Moore revealed that (unnamed) musicians from his previous bands had declined to play in Northern Ireland due to the perceived risks involved, and this was the first line-up that had no qualms about that.

The video also features backstage footage, interviews, and stock footage of Belfast side streets. Narrated by disc jockey and music presenter David 'Kid' Jensen, and with the music of The Chieftains opening and ending the documentary, *Emerald Aisles* provides an evocative snapshot of Moore's live show, his relationship with Lynott, and also of Belfast in the early 1980s — or at least, the cliched media version of Belfast.

Emerald Aisles includes the entirety of the 'Out In The Fields' promotional video, which features non-complimentary images of the city that were intended to illustrate the song's plea for peace. In contrast, other footage shows the rural beauty of the countryside. One scene shows Moore travelling on a bus along the north-east coast towards Dunluce Castle, while Moore provides commentary on the soporific beauty of the natural environment.

Moore then gives a short description of the derelict castle's history, and this is followed by a performance of 'Empty Rooms' set against the ruins and environs. In contrast, Moore is then shown walking past burnt out, abandoned homes in a Belfast street that, he reveals, is where some of his relatives used to reside.

While such sights were typical of certain areas of Belfast in the 1970s, usually in places that later became known as 'interface' areas where one community rubbed up against another, and where such sectarian strife had led to people voluntarily or through coercion relocating, such scenes were atypical by the 1980s.

As journalist and humourist P. J. O'Rourke noted when he visited Belfast in that decade to write a piece for *Rolling Stone* magazine, 'The Belfast pictured in *Time* magazine, the rubble, and barbed wire, litter and graffiti Belfast is, in fact, a patch of highly photogenic impoverishment no more than a mile long and half a mile wide. It is as though *Architectural Digest* came to "do" a house and took pictures of the closet in the teenager's bedroom.'[460]

Unfortunately, *Emerald Aisles* gave into the temptation to depict Belfast through this very narrow lens. Still, Moore makes a relevant point that Belfast was a tough place in which to grow up and he attributes some of the aggression in his playing to that upbringing.

The set list for the Ulster Hall gig consisted mainly of tracks from *Victims Of The Future* and the forthcoming album *Run For Cover*, as well as concert favourites 'Back On The Streets', 'Parisienne Walkways', and 'Stop Messin' Around' — with Phil Lynott joining Moore onstage for the latter two songs.

Moore's stage garb was red leather waistcoat and trousers, one of those outfits that in later years he would disown as ridiculous. Still, the crowd was clearly enthusiastic, the music dynamic, and the stage show a spectacle to behold.

Emerald Aisles also features footage of Moore's performance at the SFX Theatre in Dublin on December 20. The set list for this gig was almost identical to the Belfast concert, missing only 'Stop Messin' Around' from the encore. However, it had one notable addition, which was the first live performance of 'Out In The Fields'.

Neither song featured on *Emerald Aisles*, however. At the Dublin gig, locally born singer Dave Clark of the rock band Fastway joined Moore onstage for a rendition of 'Rockin' And Rollin''. Paul

O'Mahony's review of this gig for *Kerrang!* offers a snapshot of Moore's live show at the time. O'Mahony began by observing how difficult it was for Irish artists to gain traction in Ireland, noting that with the exception of U2, almost all had to gain acceptance internationally before being respected at home.

O'Mahony situated Moore within a group of artists such as Van Morrison, Vivian Campbell, Mama's Boys, Taste, Rory Gallagher, Skid Row, The Boomtown Rats and Thin Lizzy as belonging in this category. O'Mahony called Moore an Irish musician who had been 'through the rock mill' but had come out 'as a solo performed of truly exhibitionist proportions!' O'Mahony branded Moore's performance 'Grossly Excessive Rock Music', which drove the audience into a fervour, and the more excited they became the more Moore fed from the energy produced. Moore was 'High on adrenaline', O'Mahony claimed, and he 'slogged and sizzled all night long.'[461]

Emerald Aisles remains a powerful video release, which captured a great live rock spectacle and showcases Moore's exceptional guitar skills.

Live At Isstadion Stockholm:
Wild Frontier Tour (1987)
From March to September 1987, Moore toured extensively to promote his *Wild Frontier* album, with various legs of the tour seeing him play in the UK, Europe, Japan, and the United States. While Moore's gig at the Hammersmith Odeon on April 2, 1987, was recorded and broadcast by the BBC, the only official commercial release from the *Wild Frontier* tour was *Live At Isstadion Stockholm*. The video captures ten of the fourteen songs on the set list from the April 25 gig. These are 'Over The Hills And Far Away', 'Thunder Rising', 'Wild Frontier', 'Military Man', 'So Far Away', 'Empty Rooms' 'All Messed Up', 'Out In The Fields', 'Rockin' Every Night', and 'The Loner'. Notable tracks from the performance that were omitted from the video release were 'Shapes Of Things', 'Murder In The Skies', 'Victims Of The Future', and 'Wishing Well'. During the performance of 'Military Man', some stock images of the Vietnam War are interspersed.

Eric Singer's drum kit was positioned high above and to the back of the stage, while Carter's keyboards were situated on a raised platform stage left. So, while Moore and Daisley were the only musicians on the main stage area, the lay out ensured that every member of the band could be seen clearly by the audience in this large stadium. Despite his reputation for hogging the limelight, the guitarist made sure that the musicians he worked with got their share of recognition. Nevertheless, Moore chose to wear the attention-seeking, eye-catching military jacket from his 'Over The Hills' video shoot. It was his name on the ticket, after all.

For those fans and critics expecting two hours of heavy metal, *Live At Isstadion Stockholm* probably came as something of a surprise. While Moore never strays far from his hard rock stock in trade, with songs such as 'All Messed Up' and 'Rockin' Every Night', the performance offers many melodic moments. The gentle ballad 'Empty Rooms' is probably the best example of this with its traditional verse and chorus structure, and soft melody, punctuated by a gentle guitar solo and outro, all of which has Moore occupying ground shared by contemporary pop-rockers such as Dire Straits.

Furthermore, while Moore had a deserved reputation for speed, 'So Far Away' offers proof that he can play in a sparser style while still imbuing the notes with emotion. Yet, Moore puts the same amount of energy into both his fast and slow playing, as if every note was his last.

The showstopper, however, is undoubtedly 'Out In The Fields', which is extended significantly here to provide space for crowd interaction. During one chorus, Moore plays slow arpeggiated chords to allow the crowd to sing along. Not only is this a poignant track, given Lynott's sad absence, but Moore's showmanship demonstrates that he had learned a few tricks from his old friend about being a frontman.

Unlike the concert performance on the night, which ended with the song 'Wishing Well', the video release ends with Moore very much in the spotlight, playing the mostly instrumental track, 'The Loner' (Moore sings the line 'He was a loner' a couple of times). To add colour and variety, Moore uses gentle tremolo and finger bends, as well as adjusting the volume control much in the style of Jeff Beck. It was likely an artistic decision made by the film director to end the video with Moore's guitar playing in the foreground as opposed to the band performance of 'Wishing Well', and while it may have annoyed hardcore fans who felt short-changed by the truncated video, for the purposes of a commercial release aimed at as wide an audience as possible, it was probably a sensible decision.

Still Got The Blues Tour

Before he set out on tour to promote *Still Got The Blues*, Moore decided that his set list would comprise only of blues tracks and not any of the rock songs from his previous albums, not even the popular hits. He admitted this was a risky strategy: 'The biggest problem I have at the moment is whether people coming to the show are going to expect to see my other material. We are only going to be playing blues. There's going to be no 'Over The Hills And Far Away' or 'Out In The Fields'… It wouldn't work out if we did those in the middle of a blues set.' When asked if he thought this was a brave decision, Moore responded: 'It's either very brave or very stupid but I guess I'll soon find out!'[462]

The wisdom of Moore's decision is evident in two official releases. The first is the 1991 video, ***An Evening Of The Blues With Gary Moore And The Midnight Blues Band (Featuring Albert King And Albert Collins)***, which documents Moore's gig at the Hammersmith Odeon in May 1990. The second is ***Gary Moore & The Midnight Blues Band – Live At Montreux 1990,*** which wasn't made commercially available until 2004. This release documents Moore's debut performance at the Montreux Jazz Festival in July 1990, one of five he made at the event.

A career highpoint for Moore was playing alongside Albert King and Albert Collins on this tour. Collins played around thirty dates but Albert King was flown in only for the filming of one of the two nights at Hammersmith Odeon. It's evident from the energy of his performances and the joy on his face, that Moore had the time of his life on this tour. For example, at one point during the Montreux gig, just after their dramatic rendition of Collins' song 'Cold, Cold Feeling', Moore asks the audience 'Do you want to hear some more?' When they reply in the affirmative, Moore smiles, looks over to Collins and says 'me too'.

An Evening Of The Blues features eight (out of nine) tracks from *Still Got The Blues* vinyl, excluding only 'As the Years Go Passing By'.[463] Non-album tracks include 'Farther Up The Road', 'Stormy Monday', and 'Caledonia'.

'Farther Up The Road' is a Texas shuffle-style song, originally recorded by Bobby Bland but which probably came to Moore's attention as it was a staple of Eric Clapton's live set in the 1970s, and it appeared on two Clapton live albums. It was also heard on the concert films and soundtracks of *The Last Waltz* (1978) and *The Secret Policeman's Other Ball* (1982).

'Stormy Monday' was originally a hit for T-Bone Walker in 1947. It was a live favourite of Albert King, and was likely performed here for that reason. Moore would later record it for his *Back To The Blues* album.

A bit like Moore and Phil Lynott, Albert King and Albert Collins were long term friends and musical rivals. King was a particularly intimidating figure, at six foot two inches in height, and not slow to offer an opinion or raise a complaint just to show everyone who was top dog.

For example, at the rehearsal for the Hammersmith gig, King told Moore that he was playing too loudly and needed to turn it down. He also advised Moore to play fewer notes and leave space between his phrases. During the live show, he insisted the song 'Stormy Monday' be played in the key of A Flat, despite learning from an earlier conversation with Moore that the younger guitarist did not particularly like playing in that key.[464]

Nevertheless, Moore did enjoy the experience, and he took King's advice for future recordings, for example, when he recorded *Blues For Greeny* in a more restrained style.

While this is mainly a concert video, interviews with the participants, shot in black and white, are interwoven between songs. Collins and King share the stage with Moore, together and separately. 'Those two go back a long way and they've got that real gun-slinger thing between them', Moore revealed.[465]

This is evident in their performances with each vying to outdo the other, trading licks and cracking jokes. However, Moore was no third wheel and was easily able to keep up with the older bluesmen. Indeed, due to his superior technical ability, wider range, and the variety of licks at his disposal, he often left both men just a little bit in the shade.

Collins and Moore duet on 'Too Tired', repeating their album performance. Moore introduces Collins as the Master of the Telecaster and indeed the contrast between Moore's Les Paul and Collins' Telecaster makes for interesting listening.

While Moore performs lead vocals, Collins plays most of the guitar fills and is clearly having fun. When Moore plays a lick, Collins offers some vocal encouragement. At one point after King joins Moore for a rendition of 'Stormy Monday', King smiles broadly at one of Moore's trickier fills before performing a little theatre when he pretends to be shocked by Moore's speedy playing, then holds out his long white coat to hide what Moore is doing on the fretboard.

King provides lead vocals and Moore lets the older bluesman have centre stage. There does seem to be a little tension in the performance though, with King frequently motioning to and talking to the band as if he is unhappy perhaps with the pace or volume. During the space for his main guitar solo, he slows the pace and deliberately picks single notes as if to illustrate the difference in styles between his more traditional playing and Moore's more rock-influenced style.

This tension wasn't lost on music journalist Andy Bradshaw, who was in the audience and would soon after review the gig for *Metal Hammer*. Bradshaw had previously written a very positive review of *Still Got The Blues* for the magazine, but he wasn't as impressed with those songs when performed live that evening. For a start, he thought the sound quality was 'abysmal' and far too loud. However, he was most disappointed with Moore who, Bradshaw felt, had lost some of the feel and subtlety he displayed on the album.

'Blues is not a race to see who can finish first', he complained: 'The phrase "too many notes" springs to mind'. Bradshaw thought Albert Collins stole the show due to his 'immense feel and understated approach' which 'showed the whizz kid [Moore] that there is more to blues than technical bombast.'[466]

King, however, was impressed with Moore's playing, saying in one of the interwoven interviews that he thought he might have to throw some water on Moore's guitar, because his playing was 'hotter than pepper pudding.'

All three play guitar on the song 'Caledonia', while Collins provides lead vocals. In a competition as to who can sustain a note the longest, there could be only one winner between Moore's Gibson Les Paul and Collins' Fender Telecaster. At times King seems to struggle, searching for the right notes in the right key as he takes a backseat to Moore and Collins. Nevertheless, with King playing a Gibson Flying V, the three men onstage must surely have been a sight for guitar lovers to behold.

Reviews of the VHS video release were positive. *Billboard* wrote, for example, that Moore 'astonishes the viewer with his incendiary playing and the sheer joy that it brings him, the band, and the audience.'

Together, *Billboard* proclaimed, the trio of Moore, Collins and King were 'a bonanza for not only guitar fans or blues fans but just fans of great playing.' *Billboard* also noted Moore's toned-down stage show compared to previous rock tours, saying, 'this video smartly relies on guitar pyrotechnics rather than fancy lighting or special effects to keep the viewer's fascination.'[467]

The UK's *Sounds* magazine made the predictable comment that this video showed Moore 'returning to blues roots' and predicted that 'Blues and Gary Moore fans alike will appreciate it, but non-fans will be comatose after ten minutes.'[468]

Live At Montreux 1990 features eight tracks from the *Still Got The Blues* vinyl album, excluding only 'As The Years Go Passing By'. The set list features seven non-album tracks, some of which were B-sides and some which would appear on Moore's next album, *After Hours*.[469]

Moore likely played 'You Don't Love Me' as a tribute to Albert King, who recorded an instrumental version of the track on his 1969 album, *Years Gone By*. However, Moore's rendition includes the lyrics that were in Willie Cobb's 1960 original. Moore also plays a cover of Roy Buchanan's 'The Messiah Will Come Again', which Moore had recorded previously for his *After The War* album.

Collins performed on four tracks at the Montreux gig. These were 'Too Tired', 'Cold, Cold Feeling', 'Farther Up The Road', and 'The Blues Is Alright'. Although both clearly enjoyed each other's playing, their contrasting styles sometimes led to discordance. Moore's superior technical ability was clearly demonstrated during 'Farther Up The Road' when the guitarists pretended to have an on-stage argument, using guitar licks in place of words.

Moore did most of the work, probably because his background playing rock and metal gave him the edge in wringing unusual sounds from his guitar, in this case making it 'talk'. Steve Vai did much the same thing on the track 'Yankee Rose', from Dave Lee Roth's *Eat 'Em And Smile* album (1986), so this was a trick rock guitarists were well aware of, whereas there had not been much call for traditional blues guitarists like Collins to attempt this. Even so, it's clear both guitarists were having a lot of fun.

The tour to promote *Still Got The Blues* was rejuvenating for Moore, and his rediscovery of the blues led to some inspired guitar playing, earning him the respect of both fans and musicians. Don Airey, who had played with Moore for over a decade, noted Moore's new-found enthusiasm and creativity, saying: 'His playing was unbelievable on that tour, just unbelievable. Sometimes I couldn't believe what

I was hearing. Jon Lord came up to me and said something very complimentary about my Hammond playing. But he said, "Don't take this wrong, but it's not surprising given what's going on out front."'[470]

The After Hours Tour

Moore's follow-up to *Still Got The Blues*, was *After Hours* (1992), another album of blues tracks done in Moore's hard rock style, but with female backing vocalists and a horn section. It was received positively, and sold well, but was not as big a hit as its predecessor despite having arguably a stronger song line up, tighter playing, and a bluesier sound.

The *Independent*'s Andy Gill wrote, for example, that the album set Moore's 'paint-stripper tone and dazzling fretboard agility in a more soulful context than on *Still Got The Blues*', whereas the *Sydney Morning Herald* called *After Hours* 'a well-produced blues-'n'-soul outing swinging between the urbanity of Robert Cray and the sting of Albert Collins.'[471] *Billboard* also heaped praise on *After Hours*, calling it a 'masterfully crafted collection... best appreciated when cranked to maximum volume.'[472]

Moore decided to take the backing singers and horn section out on the road as part of his 'Midnight Blues Band' for the *After Hours* tour, which lasted from May to November 1992. From those gigs, nine shows were recorded and a representative selection of tracks appeared on the 1993 live album **Blues Alive**.

A video entitled **Live Blues** was also released that year. Unsurprisingly, the tour's set list drew mainly from Moore's two most recent blues album, although Moore also dusted off 'Parisienne Walkways' for another run out. Once again, Albert Collins made on-stage guest performances, although he only appeared on one track on the album, 'Too Tired'. *Blues Alive*, released on compact disc, double vinyl LP, and cassette, is possibly Moore's best-sounding and strongest live album, reaching number eight in the UK album chart, and also charting highly in Austria, Switzerland, and Finland.

What is immediately striking about *Blues Alive*, especially when compared to Moore's previous live recordings, is how the horn section fills out the live sound. Moore wrote songs for *After Hours* knowing there would be a horn section available in the studio, so the new onstage sound is smooth and unforced. Perhaps surprisingly, Moore's guitar onslaught integrates slickly with both the horns and his female backing vocalists.

Nowhere is this more evident than in the opening track 'Cold Day In Hell', which opens with dynamic guitar and horns, before Moore's confident vocals kick in for five and a half minutes of dynamic blues.

The next track, 'Walking By Myself', is the sole example of when Moore's aggressive approach seems a little overwhelming on what is a very basic blues shuffle, which can't really bear the weight of such powerful playing. For example, during the first solo on that song Moore plays a fast progression that is more suited to hard rock than blues.

However, Moore makes immediate amends with the next track, the joyous 'Story Of The Blues', which is surely one of the highlights of his career. The lyrics are a deliberate pastiche of phrases from standard blues songs, beginning in the opening line with a nod to the Sonny Boy Williamson song 'My Baby She Left Me' and in the third line with a reference to B. B. King's 'Sweet Little Angel'. Moore's voice has never sounded better, and the horn section is powerful and emotive. Moore's tasteful guitar fills demonstrate the restraint he is often accused of lacking, and even when he lets loose in a lengthy guitar solo with some very fast playing, it remains melodic and tasteful.

Moore's rendition of 'Oh, Pretty Woman' stays close to the studio version, albeit the horn section is more prominent than in the album mix. This is followed by 'Separate Ways', a slow-tempo ballad about an impending relationship break-up, sung beautifully by Moore. Like 'Story Of The Blues', this is another highpoint in Moore's song book. The next track on *Blues Alive* is 'Still Got The Blues (For You)', which by this point had become Moore's signature tune, equal in that respect only to 'Parisienne Walkways'. In this version, the horn section fills in for the string section on the studio version.

The *After Hours* studio version of 'Since I Met You Baby' features Moore and blues legend B. B. King 'cutting heads' in a respectful guitar duel. Sometimes this involves one guitarist beginning to play even before the other has finished, which is the case in the studio version. American rock magazine *Hit Parader* wrote that on this song, Moore made his guitar 'cry, beg and moan like nobody else around.'[473]

Moore and King also share lead vocal responsibilities, mainly with Moore covering the verses and King the choruses before both take turns singing the chorus line in call-and-response fashion. Of course, King was not present for this live rendition, so Moore sings all the lead vocal parts and plays all the guitar fills and solos. His backing singers take King's role in the call-and-response section. It is not as powerful as the studio version, but how could it be in the absence of King's massive musical presence.

Moore and Albert Collins then form a duet for the song 'Too Tired'. Compared to previous live duets with Moore, one simple change is noticeable and that is that Collins plays more notes. Perhaps that was because the two were now more comfortable in each other's company, but Collins perhaps had come to realise that to compete with the younger guitarist he would have to bend a little towards Moore's busier style of playing.

Moore performs a powerful version of Elmore James' 'The Sky Is Crying', in which he plays some very the fast fills. However, he changes the dynamics in the middle section by playing more slowly and picking fewer notes before ending the song in a blaze of fast picking and strong sustained vibrato.

'Further On Up The Road' was a favourite live choice for Moore. At the filmed Montreux 1990 concert, Moore and Collins cut heads but in Collins' absence from this rendition a guitar-keyboard duel between Moore and Tommy Eyre fills in. Regrettably, this version doesn't have the same impact, arguably because keyboards don't work as well as guitars in such a 'battle', and unlike Moore's duels with Don Airey in Colosseum II, the blues format doesn't allow for a keyboardist to be too innovative.

'King Of The Blues' follows, which is Moore's tribute to Albert King from *Still Got The Blues*. Indeed, as King died in December 1991, Moore dedicated the entire *Blues Alive* album to the legendary blues player. Moore's blistering guitar solos on this live rendition might be due to that turn of events, and Moore name checks King during one of the choruses.

The album's penultimate track, 'Parisienne Walkways', is taken from a performance at London's Royal Albert Hall. It must have been something to behold to witness Moore's Gibson Les Paul ringing out around that venerable arena, especially hearing Moore's trademark sustained note. The album's final track is the slow blues number 'Jumpin' At Shadows', which offers an elegant and mellow end to the evening's entertainment.

Reviews of the album were mainly positive. *Vox*'s Max Bell wrote, for example, that Moore was 'high on adrenaline-soaked twelve-bar panache'. Songs like 'Cold Day In Hell', 'Too Tired', 'King Of The

Blues', and 'Since I Met You Baby' showed Moore was, 'pickled in the relevant vats of misery and sufferin'.'[474]

Cash Box's Troy J. Agusto wrote that Moore's return to his blues roots proved that 'you can indeed go home again', and he singled out 'Parisienne Walkways' and 'Too Tired' as high points of this 'pleasing live recording'.[475]

Music & Media called the album a 'tasteful live registration of one of blues music's "heavies"... Blues Alive makes for an enjoyable "powertrip" through some classic blues territory.'[476]

The most positive of these indicative reviews was by Nick Krewen of the *Hamilton Spectator* (Canada), who praised the album's 'Searing fretwork and amazing arrangements', which combine to 'make this undoubtedly the best live effort of the year so far.'[477]

Despite these mainly positive viewpoints, an occasional reviewer was unhappy. For instance, Tony Green of *St. Petersburg Times*, Florida, wrote that Moore has 'guitar chops galore [and] near-legendary status among the guitar-mag crowd [but] unfortunately, little subtlety... the more sublime aspects of blues playing seem lost on the fleet-fingered former Thin Lizzy axman.' While an exact explanation of these 'sublime aspects' remained undisclosed, Green did complain about Moore's 'overplaying', and compared him to 'Billy Gibbons in a steroid rage'.[478]

Shane Sutton of the *Advertiser* went a bit further with his criticism, claiming that Moore's blues were 'heavy-handed' and 'metallic', bearing 'little resemblance to any blues which has emanated from Chicago or Memphis.' While Sutton praised Moore's 'impeccable chops', he found Moore's aggressive blues-rock approach too much to handle: 'the hammer blows are just too heavy', he griped.[479]

Perhaps Sutton and those other critics who found Moore's blues not to their taste were used to a more traditional style such as that of B. B. King, who didn't play rhythm guitar. King's style was to sing, then play a phrase on guitar in the 'call-and-response' blues tradition. Moore, however, was accustomed to playing rhythm and lead guitar, as he had done when playing live with Thin Lizzy. Moreover, it is a basic requirement for any four-piece rock band that the lead guitarist also plays rhythm guitar, as well as fills and lead breaks. The Who's Pete Townshend is probably the best example of this. When Moore transposed this style on to his blues playing, it did make for a heavier sound than that of the King and other traditional blues players.

Additionally, while many blues tunes build to a climax with guitar used sparsely at first before progressing to a more intense finale, Moore's style was dynamic throughout. He would often begin with an intense phrase, play complicated fills throughout, and end dramatically, either with a dynamic solo or with a slower play-out. It is easy to see, in retrospect, how some critics might mistake that for lack of variety when, in fact, to the untutored ear, all blues songs might sound very similar. But it is true also that Moore played many fast fills and solos that were more at home in the rock and metal genres than in the blues. It's a matter of personal taste as to whether that was 'too heavy', as Sutton thought.

A videotape recording of the *After Hours* tour was also made available for commercial release in 1993, and that was entitled **Live Blues**. Unlike *Blues Alive*, which is comprised of tracks from four separate concerts (Royal Albert Hall, Hammersmith, Universal Amphitheatre, and Le Zénith De Paris), *Live Blues* is a recording of a single gig at The Town And Country Club, London, on November 11, 1992. Unsurprisingly, it has much the same track list as *Blues Alive*, missing only 'Parisienne Walkways' from that album.

Because B. B. King made a guest appearance at the Town and Country Club, Moore added 'The Thrill Is Gone' to the set list, and he also dusted off 'Stop Messin' Around' for this gig. The only other notable difference to the set list of *Blues Alive* is the inclusion of a three-minute guitar instrumental which served as the introduction to 'Separate Ways'. That instrumental was edited out of the *Blues Alive* CD release.

The visual aspect of the video opens a window into the intimate, smoky atmosphere of this gig. Moore is dressed in a trim, burgundy-coloured coat and black shirt, a style far removed from his earlier rock outfits. King wore an emerald green waistcoat, possibly as a compliment to Moore's Irish heritage. The video provides evidence of the physicality of Moore's performance, from his trademark grimaces to the energy and intensity of his playing. After 'King Of The Blues' Moore apologised to the audience for all the 'messing around' between songs and explained that 'it's a bit different tonight'. Most of this 'messing around' was edited out, but his comment provides a little insight into recording a live show where everything must be 100 percent correct and in tune for posterity's sake. And, of course, B. B. King's guest appearance made the show 'a bit different' in a special way.

After the pair played a searing version of 'Since I Met You Baby', with both artists sharing vocals and guitar fills, King told Moore 'You are hot tonight young man', before Moore plays the opening notes of King's classic track 'The Thrill Is Gone', surely one of the greatest blues tracks ever recorded.

In deference to King, Moore takes a backseat for the most part, playing the main melody, while King sings and plays tasteful fills, although some space is reserved after the first chorus for Moore to show his chops. There is a respectful slow guitar 'battle' wherein King plays a phrase which Moore then repeats, all of which is done theatrically and with an element of humour. When King left the stage it was to thunderous applause from both the audience and from the musicians on stage.

Moore switched from his beloved Gibson Les Paul to a Fender Telecaster for the next track, 'The Sky Is Crying'. He name-checked two of his influencers, Albert King and Stevie Ray Vaughan, as having previously covered this Elmore Leonard original. Moore and Eyre repeat their guitar-keyboard jousting during 'Further On Up The Road', but to no greater effect than on *Blues Alive*.

During 'King Of The Blues' Moore lays down some lightning fast guitar fills that would never be heard on a traditional blues track. The final two songs performed as an encore, 'Jumpin' At Shadows' and 'Stop Messin' Around', are Moore's tribute to Peter Green, so much so in fact that the slow, sparse blues of 'Jumpin' At Shadows' seems more like Moore imitating Green's style rather than simply being influenced by it.

Billboard's Catherine Applefeld gave *Live Blues* a positive review, writing: 'Bluesman Moore and his Midnight Blues Band let it rip to considerable effect at this gig filmed in a small, smoky London nightclub'. Applefield singled out 'The Sky Is Crying', 'Walking By Myself', 'Separate Ways', and the 'stomping show-opener' 'Cold Day In Hell' as high points, as well as King's 'The Thrill Is Gone'. Applefield concluded that *Live Blues* constituted 'a soulful night blues fans will savour', and predicted success for both the video and the *Blues Alive* album which had a simultaneous release in the United States.

Blues For Greeny Live

On April 27, 1995 Moore and the Midnight Blues Band played to around 2,000 fans at the Shepherds Bush Empire to launch his new album, *Blues For Greeny*, which would be released at the end of May. The gig was recorded and released on videotape that year. The footage captures Moore paying tribute to one of his benefactors in an intimate theatre setting, and as there was not a major tour to promote the album, this release remains the most comprehensive live example of Moore's fascination with Peter Green.[480] The video format consists of song performances from the gig, interspersed with interview excerpts with Moore, plus some rehearsal footage.

The concert set list contains mainly Peter Green and Fleetwood Mac tracks, with one original song written by Moore, 'Since I Met You Baby'. While to this point in his own personal blues revival, Moore had played the blues with a rock star's ear for rhythm and pacing, here Moore was heavily influenced by Green's more stripped-down style.

He told *Rolling Stone* magazine that Green had 'a special thing… his touch. The restraint and the emotional content was far above anything else at that time. Peter's style of playing is just as important as Eric (Clapton)'s or Jeff (Beck)'s, but because he wasn't around to promote himself, he was forgotten. That is why I did this album.'[481]

In keeping with Green's minimalist, stripped-down approach to the blues, stage lighting effects were kept to a minimum. Moore also toned down his stage garb: in sharp contrast to the more dapper, besuited Moore of the *Still Got The Blues* and *After Hours* period, here he wears dark trousers and waistcoat with a white shirt that remained un-tucked in throughout the performance. He also adorned himself with a silver cross necklace, giving him a bohemian 'artists-in-residence' look.

The opening song, 'World Keep On Turning', is somewhat unusual in that Moore play acoustic guitar throughout. Aside from one song, 'Showbiz Blues', where he plays a Gibson SG, for the remainder of the show Moore plays the famous Gibson Les Paul 1959 previously owned by Peter Green. There is nowhere to hide for a vocalist accompanied only by acoustic guitar, but Moore had nothing to fear here as 'World Keep On Turning' is a testament to how well Moore's vocal timbre is suited to the blues genre.

After an interview excerpt, Moore performs 'I loved Another Woman', a slow blues track during which Moore plays soulful and passionate fills. 'Merry Go Round' is another slow blues song, with Moore making good use of finger bends to imbue emotion into each note. The vibrato in Moore's voice is pleasing to the ear and suits the song. Like the sounds Moore coaxes out of his guitar, this vocal vibrato adds colour to the notes.

After a further interview excerpt, Moore plays 'If You Be My Baby', with prominent saxophone and piano accompaniment. This is the first time Moore really lets loose with some fast blues fills. He also coaxes a 'wolf whistle' effect from his Gibson to emphasise a racy lyric. The audience, which to this point had mostly been polite and subdued, for the first time responds loudly and raucously to what's happening on stage. The next song draws a similar crowd response. The mid-paced 'Long Grey Mare' is filled with sexual innuendo, and the harmonica accompaniment helps the song move along.

In the next interview excerpt Moore voiced his thoughts about Green's music. He explained that he approached it 'very respectfully' because it had been such an important part of his life. Unlike Moore's interpretations of other blues artists' songs, he felt Green's music was almost 'written in stone', and he was therefore determined to stay close to the original compositions. Moore also explained how challenging the project was. He listed a number of factors that made for a nervous evening, for example that *Blues For* Greeny wasn't due for release until a month after the concert, so the audience hadn't yet heard his versions of Green's songs.

In addition, he hadn't played live in about a year, so he was a bit anxious about that. More pressure came from the concert being filmed and recorded. Finally, Peter Green would be at the event, and given Moore's respect for Green, he had high expectations of his own performance. Might he fail to rise to the occasion?

Moore, though, had always challenged himself, and he made high demands of his own performance and from those around him. That's partly why he had a reputation for being difficult to work with. He need not have worried, however, as the concert ran smoothly, his knowledge of and passion for Green's music was very evident, and his playing tasteful and exciting. On 'Need Your Love So Bad', a slow, blues ballad written by Little Willie John and recorded by Fleetwood Mac, he was accompanied by a string section for the first and only time only time during the show. Moore showed uncharacteristic restraint with his slow picking, and this combination of delicate picking and classy strings made for a passionate and beautiful performance.

Next came 'You Don't Love Me', a mid-paced blues rocker with saxophone, harmonica, and keyboard accompaniment, all of which are prominent in the mix. A brief harmonica solo adds some variety to the performance. 'Driftin'' is another slow song, with prominent piano accompaniment, during which Moore uses his guitar's volume controls to manipulate notes and add colour. He plays fast, passionate fills and an intense solo comprised of slow and fast phrases. While the song maintains the same tempo throughout, it builds to a climax due to the light and shade of Moore's playing.

In the next interview excerpt, Moore explained how he obtained Green's Gibson guitar. Green had become disillusioned with the worst capitalist excesses of the music business, and he wanted out. He first tried to sell the guitar for £120 to musician Snowy White, but White declined Green's offer.[482]

He then approached Moore, who told Green he couldn't afford it. Green then asked Moore to sell his current guitar, a Gibson SG, and to give him the proceeds in return for the Les Paul. Moore revealed that the amount raised wasn't close to the value of the Les Paul, but Green took it anyway. 'It wasn't a money thing, he just wanted it to go to a good home', Moore recalled.

Moore offered to return it upon request, but Green never asked. Many years later when *Mojo* magazine asked Green if he wanted the guitar back. Green responded with characteristic humour: 'No, I don't like Les Pauls anymore. Too jazzy for me. Too Parisian, too French. He's welcome to it.'[483]

Moore makes good use of the guitar on 'The Same Way', a rhythm and blues shuffle that Green wrote and sang originally on John Mayall and the Blues Breakers 1967 album *A Hard Road*. Moore's original track, 'Since I Met You Baby', follows, staying close to the original recording. The song doesn't appear out of place among Green's catalogue, although Moore seems less restrained playing his own licks and the energy level seems to jump a bit. 'Love That Burns' is a slow tempo song on which Moore again makes effective use of vibrato in his vocals. Moore plays slow, intense fills, and emotion shows on his face with every note and bend. His Gibson has never sounded better, as he squeezes every bit of emotion from the instrument.

Moore then plays a slower, more restrained version of Green's 'Stop Messin' Around', a song he had previously performed live as a raucous encore.

After another interview excerpt, in which Moore explained how this project was a celebration of Green's music rather than a tribute, as well as a personal thank you to Green, Moore performs 'Showbiz Blues', a Fleetwood Mac track written by Green. Moore opens with slow slide guitar before launching into a fast-repeating riff while still using the slide for fills, a solo, and an outro. Moore's use of a slide is almost as rare as him playing acoustic guitar, but it is needed here to emulate the Fleetwood Mac version.

The concert ends with 'Dust My Broom', written by Robert Johnson but covered by Green with Fleetwood Mac. Moore also uses a slide on this song and, perhaps surprisingly, Moore's version is less aggressive than the Fleetwood Mac version. And then a surprise, as Peter Green is led onto the stage. Perhaps because Green had become physically unrecognisable from his younger days, Moore gave him a simple introduction, saying: 'This man here is Peter Green' before bidding the audience good night. Inevitably, perhaps, an encore followed, with Moore performing the haunting 'Jumpin' At Shadows', which made for a beautiful, melancholy end to the evening.

Almost apologetically, Moore told the crowd, 'Thank you very much for coming this evening. I know it was a bit unusual but... there you go.' However, Moore had nothing to be apologetic for as this was a sincere recognition of Green's contribution to British blues. Except for 'Dust My Broom', Moore's live arrangement and performance retained faithful to Green's original recordings, although Moore played them with just a little bit more aggression and intensity.

He told *Rolling Stone*, 'I didn't try to copy him, just to have the same sort of feel. I could never sound the same as Peter.' While *Blues For Greeny Live* is primarily remembered as Moore's heartfelt thank you to Green, it is also serves to display the virtuosity and range of Moore's playing.

Not only could he play in a rock-blues style, he could also emulate the economical style of Green's more traditional blues playing. In addition, he displayed his considerable skills on acoustic guitar and with a slide, while demonstrating that his voice was particularly well-suited to this genre.

BBM (1993), A Different Beat (1999),
and the Dark Days In Paradise tour (1997)

Since 1990, and until his death in 2011, blues songs were the main content of seven out of eleven of Moore's studio albums. If live albums and compilations are included, that ratio would be even more weighted in favour of blues music. However, the non-blues albums he released are important indicators of his thinking processes, demonstrating his willingness to take risks, while providing evidence as to how his song-writing had progressed.

The three albums that don't fall strictly into the blues category are *Around The Next Dream* (1993), featuring Moore, Jack Bruce and Ginger Baker, *Dark Days In Paradise* (1997), and *A Different Beat* (1999).

Around The Next Dream was originally a Moore solo project, which developed into a collaboration. It came about after Bruce asked Moore to fill in at a gig in Esslington, Germany after Bruce's guitarist, Blues Saraceno, left to join Poison.

Bruce's drummer, Gary Husband, recalls how quickly Moore grew into the role: 'I was immediately very impressed by Gary's "lightning strike" impact as a guitarist. He meant every note, and that means a lot to me... Gary came in and owned those songs, seemingly from moment one, almost as if he had been guitarist in the original band.'[484]

It went so well that Moore asked Bruce and Husband to work with him on his next solo album. But when Husband had to drop out, Bruce suggested asking Ginger Baker to join the project. Baker agreed, and when they started playing together Moore soon realised this could not now be labelled as a Gary Moore solo album. Instead, it would have to be released under a band name, and with three large egos and considerable musical heritage in the mix, they chose the neutral and original band name of BBM.[485]

The trio released one album and two singles, and undertook a concert tour in the UK and Europe to promote the album, which helped it reach the top ten in the UK album chart.

Of the ten studio tracks on *Around The Next Dream*, Moore wrote two and co-wrote six. One of the two covers on the album, 'I Wonder Why (Are You So Mean To Me?)', was written by Albert King. In an era in which fans and critics had embraced the gloomy 'Gen-X' rock of the likes of Jane's Addiction, Nirvana and Soundgarden, critical reaction was surprisingly good.

For example, *Billboard* called the album 'modern-edged classic rock'; *Vox*'s Andy Robson said it was 'shamelessly retro and gorgeously indulgent'; and while Charles Shaar Murray found the album too close to being a mere clone of the original iteration of Cream, he applauded Moore for having Clapton's tone 'absolutely nailed.'

In contrast to Murray, Bill Bengle insisted BBM was no mere clone of the original Cream line-up but was the real deal, especially when compared to Clapton's more recent output. Bengle conceded that Moore's playing on the album recalls the late sixties Clapton era, especially on tracks such as 'City Of Gold' and 'Why Does Love (Have To Go Wrong)', but Moore achieved this 'without sounding like some hack imposter'. Bengle praised Moore's guitar playing, noting that the guitarist 'let more of himself shine' on bluesy tracks such as 'I Wonder Why (Are You So Mean To Me)' and 'Can't Fool The Blues'.

Robson also singled out Moore's playing, calling it 'orgiastic', while praising the guitarist's contributions as a songwriter, especially the album's two 'gorgeous' romantic ballads. But perhaps the biggest enthusiast of Moore's playing was *Cash Box*'s Steve Baltin, who viewed *Around The Next Dream* as an affirmation of Moore's blues credentials. He wrote: 'Moore asserts himself enough that fans will recognize his input, which is strongest on the blues tracks. Long a child of the blues, though known as a rocker, Moore's work on the standard High Cost of Living should once and for all remove any doubt about Moore's blues capabilities.'[486]

No official live recordings emerged from the project. A handful of bootleg audio and visual performance are available, however, and they reveal BBM as a dynamic and very professional live act. The tour set list for May and June, 1994 stayed consistent, with BBM playing approximately fifteen songs each night, eight of which were from the new studio album, with the rest being Cream songs and other covers. The two songs from the album that are missing from these set lists are 'Where In The World', which was co-written by Moore and Bruce, and Moore's 'Wrong Side Of Town'. Of the Cream tracks played live, 'I Feel Free', 'Sunshine Of Your Love', and 'Tales Of Brave Ulysses' were the most well-known and biggest crowd favourites.

Promoting the band's live appearances was undermined a little by the BBM band name. For example, a promotional poster for the gig in San Sebastian, Spain on June 18 failed to mention BBM and instead listed Gary Moore as top of the bill, with Baker and Bruce named in smaller typeface. This was likely the idea of the local promoter as BBM had little name recognition whereas Moore had been touring for over a decade under his own name, and he had some previous commercial success in Spain.

Despite positive critical reviews, a UK top ten album, and a successful promotional tour, internal tensions meant BBM was a short-lived combination. Moore later revealed that, for once, the cantankerous Baker wasn't at the heart of the band's problems, and instead it was friction between himself and Bruce, two leaders who were used to making all the decisions: 'It wasn't Jack and Ginger', Moore admitted, 'it was Jack and me because we were both used to leading our own bands. A lot of the attention was getting put on me, and it was like the Eric Clapton situation again. That helped break Cream up, all the attention was going on Eric but who was writing all the fucking songs? Jack. So he felt really pushed out in that situation and I think there was echoes of that.'[487]

In 1999, Moore attempted a radical change in direction in deciding to release an album on his new label, Castle Music, that combined modern drum and bass rhythms with electric guitar. Moore was inspired by the exciting sounds he was hearing on the streets in London and wondered if and how he might engage with them on a musical level.

The resulting album, entitled ***A Different Beat***, was a daring effort to reinvent himself in the year leading up to the millennium, and into the fifth decade of his music career. Earlier the same year Jeff Beck had also embraced electronic and techno music on his album *Who Else!* But if there was any suggestion that Moore was inspired or encouraged by Beck's move, it's worth pointing out that *A Different Beat* had been recorded in 1998, months before Beck's album hit the shops.

While on the surface, some of Moore's experiments seemed unlikely — for example, 'Go On Home' sees Moore play slide guitar blues set against electronic noises and drum beats — the album is very melodic, with a prime example being the outro to 'Lost In Your Love'. There is even an attempt to bring Jimi Hendrix's 'Fire' into the modern era, albeit with mixed results.

Moore's vocals are warm and powerful on this album, even tender at times, for instance on the soulful 'Surrender'; or they are down and dirty, as heard on the track 'We Want Loving'. His guitar playing is innovative and intricate, but Moore uses the guitar not to carry the song but instead just to add colour, although no doubt fans of his playing would want to see it more in the foreground.

The album includes a track called 'Fatboy', which is Moore's light-hearted appreciation of the huge-selling DJ, artist, and music producer, Fatboy Slim. Moore told the Newcastle *Evening Chronicle*, 'I'm a great admirer of Norman Cook [Fatboy]. Here's a guy who has really brought the fun back into the business and has opened up dance music to a whole new audience.'[488]

Yet despite its many positive attributes including its contemporary vibe, *A Different Beat* failed to spark the public imagination and the rock and blues audience that he had cultivated over the last two decades failed to follow him through this somewhat confusing maze. For example, fans of 'Still Got The Blues (For You)' or 'Story Of The Blues' might have expected more of the same when viewing 'House Of Blues' on the track list, only to be disappointed by the song's back beats and electronic harmonies. Yet if they managed to move beyond that track to reach 'Bring My Baby Back', they would have recognised its origin in the blues and back country music of the American south, albeit set here against a modern trance beat.

In a perceptive album review, *Uncut* magazine's Mick Meikleham noted that Moore's career saw him embrace a variety of musical genres including hard rock, jazz-rock fusion, and pure blues, and he cited *A Different Beat* as a further example of the guitarist continuing to 'lay down his licks in different contexts.' Meikleham called Moore a 'musician's musician' and 'one of the few movers left in the medium.'[489]

Yet, critical praise doesn't pay the bills and, as Moore himself admitted in an interview for the *Irish Times*, in retrospect the album was a mistake: 'the last record… was an attempt to marry guitar with dance rhythms. With something like that, you're really crucified before you start. People who would be into what I do would probably hate those rhythms and the people into dance music would probably hate me!'[490]

A Different Beat failed to chart and, unsurprisingly, after this musical mid-life crisis, Moore returned once more to the blues with his next album, the appropriately titled *Back To The Blues* (2001). The only tracks from *A Different Beat* to ever get a live run out were 'Lost In Your Love', 'Surrender', and Moore's cover of Hendrix's 'Fire', all of which he played on tour in 2000. Moore also performed 'Fire' at Montreux in 1999 and 2001, and at his tribute gig to Hendrix in

October 2007.

Sandwiched in between *Around The Next Dream* and *A Different Beat* was **Dark Days In Paradise**, which, along with *A Different Beat*, is probably the best material evidence available for those critics who accused Moore of chasing trends. Yet, if considered in a more positive light, *Dark Days In Paradise* is a fine example of Moore engaging with a younger, modern-day audience.

In a contemporary interview with Paul Sexton Moore said that the album encompassed all of his influences over the years, 'and a few new ones.' 'There's a bit of everything in there', he revealed. 'I've been listening to a lot of hip-hop, drum 'n' bass, reggae, R&B, very rhythmical stuff.' Was he chasing trends? Moore said simply that the album style was 'just what I wanted to do... I just felt it was time for a change.'[491]

Sexton revealed a bit more from this interview in a piece he wrote for the *Times*. Moore told him that dance music, hip-hop, drum and bass, reggae, and rhythm and blues were all 'very rhythmical music' that is 'happening now, and if you ignore all those new rhythms, you're a dinosaur before you know it.'

Moore told Sexton that after his BBM collaboration, he wanted to move in a more melodic direction and if, instead of *Dark Days In Paradise*, he had recorded and released another blues album, 'it wouldn't have been with my heart.'

Tellingly, in an era of 'Brit-pop', when bands like Oasis, The Verve, Ocean Colour Scene, and Radiohead were both popular and critically acclaimed, Moore told Sexton, with a broad smile, 'Rock is happening again', and he revealed that the set for his forthcoming European tour would, for the first time in many years, include some material from his heavy rock period.

Preceding the album's release in May, 'One Good Reason' became the first single release in the UK, whereas 'I Have Found My Love In You' was released in Europe. Moore made several promotional television appearances, including the *Mississippi Show* in Spain in early June, and *Ohne Filter* in Germany in early July, notably in countries which were strong markets for his music.

Moore rehearsed in London for a European tour which started at Dynamo Stadium in Moscow on June 27, and included some European festival dates such as Montreux Jazz on July 9, with further British dates following later in the year. Moore seemed very happy with his change in direction. For instance, he told Sexton the musicians he was taking with him on tour (Magnus Fiennes on keyboards, Guy Pratt on bass, and Gary Husband on drums) formed 'the best band I've ever had.'[492]

The official live release from this tour took over a decade to materialise and when it did, it was merely part of a 5 CD box set entitled ***Essential Montreux*** (2009). A visual record of the 1997 Montreux gig was made commercially available in 2007, entitled ***Gary Moore - The Definitive Montreux Collection***. It was a 2 DVD release, featuring tracks from all five of Moore's Montreux performances to date. Moore played six tracks (out of eleven) from *Dark Days In Paradise*. These were 'One Good Reason', 'One Fine Day', 'Cold Wind Blows', 'I've Found My Love In You', 'Always There For You', and 'Business As Usual'. He also played two blues songs, 'Oh Pretty Woman' and 'Walking By Myself', two eighties hits, 'Out In The Fields' and 'Over The Hills And Far Away', and his 1978 hit 'Parisienne Walkways'. The set list is evidence that Moore was falling back in love with at least some of his earlier rock output.

The Montreux CD begins with 'One Good Reason', a track with a catchy chorus and ELO-style synth strings. Moore plays a Gibson ES-335 and uses a slide. The next track, 'One Fine Day', is a nostalgic throwback to 1960s Beatles raga rock. In the late 1990s that was a sound bands such as Oasis, The Stones Roses and The Seahorses took inspiration from, so it sounded both nostalgic and contemporary.

Moore uses an inflection in his voice to stretch the last syllable of the last word in a vocal line, a technique similar to the vocal delivery of Oasis's Liam Gallagher. 'Cold Wind Blows' has a drum pattern composed to sound like native American percussion, somewhat in the style of The Cult's debut album, *Dreamtime* (1984) and continuing through until their *Ceremony* album in 1991. Moore uses a slide on this track to tease some haunting patterns from his guitar.

'I've Found My Love In You' is a soulful blues ballad on which Moore plays a black Stratocaster, using its tremolo arm and a wah-wah pedal to imbue every note with emotion.

On 'Always There For You' Moore returned once more to his faithful Gibson Les Paul, despite not using it at all on the studio album. Perhaps this was his attempt to break from his past traditions. The song — a soulful funk-ballad — begins with phasing and echo effects, and Moore's solo has a Carlos Santana vibe. On the studio recording of this track, and when he recorded 'Like Angels', Moore used a screwdriver as a slide. When he performed 'Like Angels' on the *Ohne Filter* television show on July 2, Moore used the screwdriver, but he declined to play that track at Montreux, and he didn't use the slide on 'Always There For You'.

Moore then played fairly straightforward run throughs of 'Oh Pretty Woman' and 'Walking By Myself'. Moore played his biggest hit from the 1990s, 'Still Got The Blues (For You)', at Montreux, but that performance was omitted from the CD release, possibly because it is too similar in tone to 'Parisienne Walkways'.

On 'Business As Usual' Moore played rhythm guitar on a Stratocaster and he sang live with a delay on his vocals to give an echo effect. The guitar solo also has a delay effect, reminiscent of the style of Dave Gilmour. While the song unfolds slowly as Moore narrates his youthful memories, the guitar outro builds to a dynamic crescendo. Moore said of 'Business As Usual', 'I thought as an experiment I would let the memories come out, from the first thing I could remember. And whatever came out that was it. It wasn't going to be changed.'[493]

Moore uses the black Stratocaster once more on 'Out In The Fields', the first of the 1980s' rock tracks reintroduced into his set list. During the song, Moore took the opportunity to interact with his audience, inviting them to clap along in the middle section. While this goes on, he uses tremolo bends and echo effects to enhance the informal mood. The band then leaves the stage but returns for a two-song encore of 'Over The Hills And Far Away' and 'Parisienne Walkways'.

On the former, Moore plays his black Stratocaster and, clearly in nostalgic mood, asks the audience, 'Has anyone got any Irish in them?', echoing Phil Lynott's crowd banter from the pair's Thin Lizzy days. Unsurprisingly, for 'Parisienne Walkways' Moore returns to his Gibson Les Paul again. This is a playful, informal version, on which Moore sings only the first verse. The other lines are played on guitar with single note picking. Moore's trademark extended note is also different to usual. Moore takes a break during the song to accommodate some drum-bass jamming before the song picks up once again in a more familiar pattern. Moore then introduces the band before exiting the stage.

The DVD release, *The Definitive Montreux Collection*, features only six songs from the 1997 performance, five of which were from *Dark Days In Paradise*, with the other being 'Out In The Fields'.

Moore chose new stage garb, probably to highlight his musical change in direction, and also to reinvent himself as a contemporary artist. He looked sharp in a designer yellow shirt, white slacks, black shoes and dark glasses. He told one interviewer he felt 'totally rejuvenated musically' with *Dark Days In Paradise*, and his change from darker stage wear to those brighter colours emphasises this.[494]

Live At Monsters Of Rock (2003) – DVD & CD

In 2002, Virgin released *The Best Of The Blues*, a compilation of tracks released while Moore was under contract to the label. Moore, meanwhile, was taking another detour away from the blues with his **Scars** album, which was released by Sanctuary records in September that year.

Moore auditioned Richard 'Cass' Lewis, formerly the bass player of Skunk Anansie, and Darrin Mooney, ex-drummer for Primal Scream, who had worked with Moore previously on his *Back To The Blues* album: he was immediately struck by the chemistry he felt between the three of them. At the time, Moore said, 'I'm really excited about the group. It's a very different dynamic with just three [musicians] and although we have different styles it works really well on stage. Cass and Darrin are brilliant to work with and this sound is a lot heavier than what I've done in the past.'[495]

The album took only a few months to record, and it contains no keyboards, only pedals that Lewis persuaded Moore to use. Moore revealed: 'Cass has a huge pedal board and he got me to use it to make more eccentric sounds. It's all effects pedals, although they are synth-like sounds, but the good thing is that because they are pedals we can do it live as well.'[496]

The resulting album is heavy blues-rock, in the style of Cream, Jimi Hendrix, and early Led Zeppelin. It is also a stripped-down album, that sounds like a record of the group playing together live in the studio, with only a few overdubs added.

Reviews were mainly positive: for example, Alan Poole, of the *Coventry Evening Telegraph*, claimed the album had 'some of the Irish veteran's heaviest songs and sharpest performances in years.'[497]

The *Irish News* wrote: 'Many guitarists of Moore's age and stature might be content to go through the motions, but *Scars* is streets ahead of much of the rock output around at present.'

And the *Southland Times* (New Zealand) wrote: 'If doubt existed over Moore's guitar-playing talent it has been dispelled with this blistering 10-track offering… Moore plays the guitar meaner than a junkyard dog, while being supported by the brilliant rhythm section that is Cass Lewis and Darrin Mooney.'[498]

The band toured in the Autumn of 2002, playing gigs in small venues around Britain such as Newcastle City Hall, Gloucester Leisure Centre, Bristol Colston Hall, and Oxford Apollo. In a review of the Bristol gig, journalist Keith Clark wrote: 'Scars is a threesome… that Moore describes as a "power trio". And boy is that an understatement. There were times when you had to wonder if Moore had actually made a pact with the devil. Surely no one can play that fast and get such sounds from a plank of wood and six strings without some form of supernatural intervention? And in some of the earlier solos it was a good job it was loud or the sound of jaws dropping would have been deafening.'[499]

While reviews of the album and live gigs were encouraging, sales were not, so when Moore was offered a chance to tour in support of Whitesnake in May 2003 on the nine-date Monsters Of Rock Tour, he jumped at the opportunity, as did Lewis and Mooney.

After all, the proposed venues were the likes of Birmingham National Exhibition Centre, Manchester Evening News Arena, Glasgow SECC, Wembley Arena and Cardiff International Arena, all of which were larger than the small halls and leisure centres that were a feature of the Scars tour. Of course, it wouldn't be the first time Moore had toured in support of Whitesnake, although he perhaps didn't have the fondest memories of his G-Force days.

The gig at Sheffield Hallam FM Arena on May 21 was recorded for future CD and DVD release. As well as the full concert set list, the DVD features soundcheck footage and an interview with Moore. The set list is interesting in that Moore eschewed almost all of his 1990s blues catalogue, focusing instead on three tracks from *Scars*, two well-known songs he covered on 1980s solo albums, 'Shapes Of Things' and 'Wishing Well', two hit singles from his solo career, 'Out In The Fields' and 'Parisienne Walkways', one instrumental track from his *Corridors Of Power* album (listed as 'Guitar Intro' on the album and DVD but this was actually a track from *Corridors* entitled 'End Of The World'), the Thin Lizzy track 'Don't Believe A Word', and finally, 'Walking By Myself', the up-tempo blues track from *Still Got The Blues*. In the DVD interview Moore explained that he deliberated about adding 'Empty Rooms' to the set list, but considered this impractical as he didn't have a keyboardist on this tour.

Moore therefore put together a set of songs at least some of which would have been known to the audience: such familiarity normally creates a good atmosphere and encourages audience participation. In addition, he chose rock songs but omitted any songs from his solo catalogue that could be categorised as heavy metal; given this was a Monsters Of Rock tour, this seems like a prudent decision.

Finally, he was stubbornly determined to keep promoting the *Scars* album, despite it having sunk without trace in the UK and US album charts. This single-mindedness was a character trait that shaped much of Moore's musical career. Add to this his perfectionism, his desire to gain the respect of his musical peers, and his restless search for musical self-satisfaction, and these would be the four traits that sum up the man and his music.

Moore came onto the stage carrying a white Gibson Explorer. In the interview footage Moore spoke about using a black Explorer on the track 'Rectify' from the *Scars* album. However, he chose a white Explorer for the tour as it made more of a visual impact on stage, plus, as it turned out, Moore thought it sounded better than the black one. After introducing the band, Moore put the Explorer to good use on 'Shapes Of Things', which he had recorded for the *Victims Of The Future* album. After being conditioned to years of Moore's great vocals on years of blues tracks, his return to singing rock songs is something of a shock. It's immediately clear that his vocals don't sound as clean or cultured as on most of his blues output, and, in fact, are a bit 'shouty' here.

Moore follows on from one familiar, crowd-pleasing cover version to another, with 'Wishing Well' from his *Corridors of Power* album. The studio recording featured keyboards by Tommy Eyre. However, because Moore hadn't added any new musicians to his Scars line-up, this three-piece had no keyboard player. As such, the live rendition of 'Wishing Well' sounds a bit thin at times, especially during the bridge section where Moore plays arpeggiated chords to fill the gap, but this still leaves his vocals a bit exposed. Nevertheless, the Explorer sounds particularly hot on this song, and as with 'Shapes Of Things', the composition and structure of these live performances remain faithful to the studio version.

Moore introduces 'Rectify' as 'one off the Scars album'. It is reminiscent of the aggressive style of Rage Against The Machine, with heavy riffing and a song structure with a wide range of volume dynamics, light and shade. The guitar solo is Hendrix-like, and Moore even used the 'Hendrix Chord' (E7#9) [pronounced E 7 sharp 9] more as punctuation than as an integral part of the song structure. Tom Morello of Rage Against The Machine is also a Hendrix fan and he used this chord in the same way on the song 'Testify', from the Rage Against The Machine album *The Battle Of Los Angeles* (1999).[500]

By this stage of his career, Moore was a seasoned stage performer, a point noted in the interview when he spoke of the amount of effort that goes into creating the right guitar effects on stage while also performing lead vocal duties. Part of being a 'frontman' was also being a performer, and while Moore was no Mick Jagger or Freddie Mercury, he did have a few tricks up his sleeve as to how to engage an audience. For example, before performing his instrumental guitar solo, 'White Knuckles', he got the audience on his side by announcing that the gig was being filmed and that he specifically chose Sheffield as it was 'a great fucking crowd!'

Moore then launched into 'Stand Up', which he introduced as, 'Stand Up For Your Freedom'. In another possible link to Rage Against The Machine's radicalism and anger, Moore instructed the audience: 'Don't believe anything those fucking cunts tell you, right?' Throughout this song, Moore plays with distortion and wah wah pedals, which is another hint of possible Morello influence.

Morello is known for his use of guitar effects pedals, which are among the tricks he has at his disposal to wring unusual sounds from his guitar. Moore again uses the 'Hendrix Chord' and displays some of the fastest shredding he has played in many years.

Moore then switched to a Gibson Les Paul Standard for 'Just Can't Let You Go', the third and final song on the set list from *Scars*. It begins as a slow blues elegy, like The Rolling Stones' track 'Love In Vain', with arpeggiated chords during the first verse and chorus, until some aggressive power chords during the bridge transform the song into something much heavier, before Moore returns once more to the arpeggiated chord-playing of the verse and chorus. These dynamics of light and shade are reminiscent of the Radiohead song 'Creep'.

This live version of 'Just Can't Let You Go' is heavier than the studio version, something that often happens due to the absence of studio tools to level and mix the instruments and perfect the vocals.

Here, however, it appears Moore has given the song some extra dynamism, perhaps to suit audience expectations on this Monsters Of Rock tour.

After an energetic but unremarkable rendition of 'Walking By Myself', Moore introduced the classic Thin Lizzy song 'Don't Believe A Word'. There are two studio versions of this song: the first by Lizzy was a fast tempo rocker, and Moore recorded the other as a slow blues track. When Moore introduced the song to the audience he promised to play both versions, and the result was a hybrid mix of slow blues adjoined to the faster Thin Lizzy version, with vocals by Moore. Not having Lizzy's two-guitar attack meant Moore played rhythm, fills and the solo, while also finding a way to make one guitar sound like the two used by Lizzy.

Because the main melody of the next song, 'Out In The Fields', is carried by keyboards that are absent here, Moore plays the melody on guitar. Moore, of course, doesn't have Phil Lynott's voice to help deliver the vocals, as was the case on the studio version, and because the recorded version features a chorus that slightly overlaps with verses, it is a tricky vocal performance for a lone singer to perform on stage. Due to these limitations, it feels like Moore just 'gets through' this audience-pleasing song as best he can whereas choosing a different song to perform would have resulted in a better live performance. Nevertheless, Moore used the song's middle section to generate some fan interaction, with the audience clapping at Moore's instigation while he guides them along with arpeggiated chords.

'Out In The Fields' is the final song on the set list but the band returned for 'Parisienne Walkways'. Moore paused playfully before playing the song's trademark long note. Before leaving the stage for the final time, Moore introduced Lewis and Mooney once Moore, then somewhat undermined his reputation as a curmudgeon by thanking Whitesnake's stage crew for their help when issues arose due to a 'really long soundcheck'.

Moore's performance on this tour, as well as the CD and DVD releases, received generous praise. Journalist Alan Poole insisted that Moore 'pretty much stole the show' on the multi-artist tour and the new release was a 'welcome souvenir' of his performances.[501]

During the DVD interview, when Moore was asked how it felt to do rock again, he responded that it was 'really good fun', and that if it hadn't been for the Monsters Of Rock tour he probably would never again play the likes of 'Shapes Of Things' or 'Wishing Well'.

He also revealed that he had to relearn some old solos, which meant having to buy some of his old records because he no longer had his own copies. Like many artists, it seems Moore was always looking forward, not backwards. Yet, he was pleasantly surprised to rehear his original solo in 'Shapes Of Things', which he had composed in three separate sections.

Looking forward to the future, Moore believed the Scars project still had some life in it. He revealed, for example, that the band had already written some more 'chunky' riff-based songs that were dark and melodic. However, Moore's optimism was tempered by hard-headed, perhaps even ruthless determination to be successful. Moore had shown that previously when band mates, particularly vocalists, had failed to meet his expectations.

In addition, Moore was very much aware that as a professional musician he needed to be turning a profit from his endeavours, and Scars, by any commercial measure, was a financial failure. Perhaps that was due to the band's lack of name recognition. Gary Moore had name recognition but did the general public know about Scars?

In what was surely a crucial marketing error, the album cover didn't even feature a band picture. When the Monsters Of Rock tour ended, Scars faded away in much the same way G-Force, another band undermined by marketing problems and lack of name recognition, faded from existence without achieving any commercial success.

Moore then returned to safer, more financially lucrative material. His next studio album was firmly based in the blues genre and was entitled *Power Of The Blues* (2004). This was also the case with his final two solo albums, *Close As You Get* and *Bad For You Baby*. Nevertheless, Moore and Mooney stayed close, and Mooney played drums on *Power Of The Blues*, an album credited solely to Gary Moore, and whose 'brand' name features prominently on the cover.

Several Moore gigs were given posthumous releases. These include: *Live At Montreux 2010* (CD & DVD), released in September 2011; *Blues For Jimi* (CD & DVD), which is a recording of an October 2007 tribute gig that wasn't released until September 2012; *Live At Bush Hall* 2007, which was released in September 2014; and *Live From London*, which is an audio recording of Moore's gig at the Islington Academy on December 2, 2009, and which wasn't released until January 2020. In addition, some previously unheard live tracks appeared on the 2017 box set release, *Blues And Beyond*.

Numerous radio and television appearances have been bootlegged over the years. Details of most of these appearances can be found in the *Gary Moore Bible*, an online work by fans and the product of a great deal of research and love. In light of that, there is, therefore no need to discuss those performances here. It is enough just to note that, in some crucial ways, they capture more of the spirit of Moore live than some of the official releases.

For example, Moore's gig at the Kings Hall, Belfast on March 9, 1989, was recorded and broadcast by BBC Northern Ireland in July that year. Although it was never made an official release, the broadcast demonstrates the quality, energy, and intensity of Moore at the peak of his heavy rock period. In addition, it marked the return to the live set list of the old chestnut, 'Parisienne Walkways', which Moore had dropped for a few tours but saw fit to reinstate to mark the tenth anniversary of its success as a hit single. There is no official, comparable recording from 1989, so the BBC broadcast is an important record of that time period.

The last live performance made commercially available before Moore's untimely demise was *Live At Montreux 2010*. Released on CD and DVD, the 13-song set list is basically a greatest hits package with a distinct Irish theme, featuring songs such as 'Over The Hills And Far Away', 'Thunder Rising', which was inspired by the Thin Lizzy track 'Massacre' and is about legendary Irish warrior, Cúchulain, 'Military Man', written by Phil Lynott, 'Blood of Emeralds', Moore's tribute to Lynott, 'Out In The Fields' and 'Johnny Boy'. It also featured three new songs with an Irish feel that were to appear on Moore's next album, which of course never came to pass. These new songs are 'Days Of Heroes', 'Where Are You Now?', and 'Oh Wild One'.

'Days Of Heroes' is about the warrior Cúchulain, the legendary 'Hound of Ulster'; 'Where Are You Now?' begins with a Celtic-sounding guitar phrase, which becomes a refrain through the song, while the mournful lyrics seem to be about a lost companion; and 'Oh Wild One' is an up-tempo Celtic rocker whose lyrics about a wild Dubliner friend who is no longer with us of course brings to mind Phil Lynott.

The recurring Celtic-sounding phrase Moore plays on that song is, perhaps, in danger of becoming a bit twee, except Moore unexpectedly extemporises the first time he repeats it, playing an astonishingly fast phrase, and then each time he repeats it afterwards he continues to improvise with a different phrase, all of which serves to keep the song fresh and exciting.

It is fascinating to speculate where this new Celtic direction would have taken Moore, especially as the Montreux set list was rock rather than blues orientated. Certainly, the intensity of Moore's playing had not diminished over the years: for example, he played an emotional and very dynamic version of 'Parisienne Walkways', a song which by that point was so familiar to him that he might have been forgiven for merely going through the motions.

With Darrin Mooney once more returning to play drums (Moore had briefly reunited with Brian Downey for the *Close As You Get* album) and the surprising reunion with keyboardist Neil Carter, who was a key ingredient of Moore's rock era and who also provided backing vocals and rhythm guitar on this tour, it seems likely that Moore was planning to record a Celtic rock album and possibly a concept album.

A few years earlier Moore was interviewed by the *Belfast Telegraph* when he revealed: 'I got a lot of inspiration [when] I was just walking around in Belfast, a lot of little melodies came into my head. I found it very inspiring to be back there.'[502]

While Moore released two further blues albums before the Montreux performance in 2010, perhaps that Belfast trip was the inspiration for those three new songs. Regrettably, no further tracks from that planned album have come to light since the Montreux performance, and Moore's tragic death brought the curtain down on those plans.

In Memoriam

Gary Moore died of a heart attack in Estepona, Spain on February 6, 2011. There was an immediate outpouring of compassion and sympathy from fellow musicians, and obituaries appeared in press outlets in the UK, Ireland and internationally. Of course, it's only human nature that when someone passes away those in mourning remember only positive things about their life. While some of those post-mortem elegies are quoted below, I've also included comments garnered from throughout Moore's career. Perhaps these carry a little more weight as they weren't articulated during a period of mourning and remembrance.

Perhaps, though, the tribute Moore would have found most fitting was musical rather than verbal, and it came from his hero Eric Clapton. On May 10, 2011, just a few months after Moore's death, Clapton's current world tour took him to Belfast's Waterfront Hall. Clapton, of course, had any number of classic tracks to select from, including legendary hits from his stints in The Yardbirds, John Mayall's Blues Breakers, Cream, Blind Faith and Derek And The Dominoes, as well as from his solo career, yet Clapton found room to play an acoustic version of Moore's signature song, 'Still Got The Blues (For You)', which he had added to his set list in Dublin the previous night as a tribute to the fallen bluesman. (A few years later, Clapton recorded a studio version of the song for his 2013 album entitled *Old Sock*).

Clapton, Dublin, Belfast, the blues… if Gary had known this was going to happen, he might even have cracked a smile.

***

'Gary Moore is a celebration of why the electric guitar exists.'
Michael Palmisano, guitar teacher, YouTube and social media star

'Gary Moore is one of the best rock guitarists in the world.'
Harry Doherty, journalist[503]

'Belfast-born Gary Moore is undoubtedly one of the most exciting and innovative rock guitarists around today... he plays with genuine feeling, and that is a rarity.'
Grim Reaper guitarist, Nick Bowcott[504]

'Moore is unquestionably one of the greatest guitarists alive today, his impossibly fast but endlessly tasteful playing gaining him reams of respect from feisty guitarists of every genre the world over.'
CMJ New Music Report[505]

'He was a fantastic composer and guitarist who rose to greatness.'
Tony Newton, G-Force[506]

'I've played with the greatest guitar players. Gary Moore was the jewel in the crown.'
Glenn Hughes, Deep Purple[507]

'The best guitarist in the world, if only he'd settle down and not grimace quite so much, is Gary Moore.'
David Coverdale, Whitesnake[508]

'Gary was a very special guitarist, truly phenomenal in what he could do.'
Jon Hiseman, Colosseum II[509]

'I've always liked Gary. He's easily one of the best new guitar players around. He's a technical wizard, and he's got great feel, a really inventive player.'
Scott Gorham, Thin Lizzy, 1977[510]

'Gary was an amazing guitarist. I mean, truly amazing.'
Kit Woolven (engineer & producer)[511]

'One of the world's truly great guitar players.'[512]
Cash Box

'Moore has made his name as one of the finest rock guitarists around... He is a technically excellent guitarist but it's the passion and lyricism in his screaming guitar that has made him his name.'
New Sunday Times[513]

'I always loved Gary's playing — he had something extra.'
Dave Flett, Manfred Mann's Earth Band[514]

'Gary was an unbelievable guitar player — one of the best I've ever heard. He was also a lovely man.'
Ozzy Osbourne[515]

'He's a very exciting musician, full of ideas, a very daunting talent.'
Don Airey, Colosseum II[516]

'I'd never be as good a guitar player as Gary Moore. For me, he ranks No. 1 in the world as an electric guitar player.'
Greg Lake, Emerson, Lake & Palmer[517]

'I didn't think he could play. I thought he was just another kid trying to get off into the blues guitar world... but listening to that kid play the wildest things... Golly Moses, where did he come from?'
Albert King[518]

'He's a great guitarist and tremendous soloist.'
Paddy Moloney, the Chieftains[519]

'Gary Moore, it seems, is a real person in a rarefied business. He just happens to have an extraordinarily rich musical history.'
Irish Times[520]

'I really enjoy working with Gary, he's so respected by fans and in the industry.'
Bob Daisley, musician & songwriter[521]

'Jimi Hendrix was the greatest thing I had ever seen... and then I saw Gary Moore.'
John Pettersson, music producer[522]

'Gary Moore is superb, perhaps the best in the world. He's fast, but also plays with feel. That's rare.'
Glen Tipton, Judas Priest[523]

'Gary Moore is good... he's very good.'
Jimmy Page, Led Zeppelin[524]

'Gary Moore blew me away from the first time I heard him — it was like hearing Jimi Hendrix or Stevie Ray Vaughan... I don't know why he wasn't more popular in America — he played with George Harrison and B. B. King, and they saw him as a peer.'
Kirk Hammett, Metallica[525]

'I was a mad fan of his because he was probably the most technically proficient guitar player that has ever been in Thin Lizzy. As a young guitar kid, that is what I gravitated toward, and I think I probably ripped him off more than any other guitar player.'
Vivian Campbell, Def Leppard[526]

'One of the finest and most expressive blues and rock guitarists of his generation.'
Daily Telegraph[527]

'He had incredible enthusiasm for music, great energy, very dedicated musician. He was a good laugh as well; a lot of people said he was kind of grumpy but I never saw him that way... His enthusiasm for the instrument was remarkable. He had a feel for it.'
Eric Bell, Thin Lizzy[528]

'Gary Moore was the next in line in the lineage of historically important British blues guitar players; from Peter Green, Eric Clapton, Jeff Beck and Jimmy Page, the baton then passed to Gary. In my opinion he was quite simply the best blues rock player on the planet, and he made some truly moving music.'
Bruce Dickenson, Brighton Institute of Modern Music[529]

'A giant of modern-day guitar playing whose work stretched far beyond rock and heavy metal to pop, jazz and even experiments with techno. Moore will be remembered as a true modern bluesmen whose ability to make a guitar seemingly cry in pain touched many... an unpretentious, unassuming, prodigiously talented man.'
The Guardian[530]

'While rarely fashionable, Moore was acclaimed as a musician's musician, held up by blues pioneers such as BB King and Albert King as a worthy inheritor of their craft and passion.'
Sunday Times[531]

'Without question one of the great Irish bluesmen. His playing was exceptional and beautiful. We won't see his like again.'
Bob Geldof, Boomtown Rats[532]

'Playing with Gary during the Black Rose era was a great experience, he was a great player and a great guy. I will miss him.'
Scott Gorham, Black Star Riders[533]

'I have known Gary since 1967 when he was in Platform Three and he's been an amazing friend ever since. It was a pleasure to play with Gary again in 2006 after his days with Lizzy. He will always be in my thoughts and prayers, and I just can't believe he is gone.'
Brian Downey, Thin Lizzy[534]

'A man with rather colourful shirts, who possessed a childlike quality and was an inspiration to many and the kind of person you could never forget.'
Gary's daughter Lily Rendle-Moore[535]

'He didn't do it through any gimmicks. He did it through sheer ability, and anything he has recorded he can stand up on that stage and do.'
Robert Moore, Gary's father [536]

NOTES TO PREFACE

1 Harold Mac Wonderlea and Christine Rebmann, 'Gary Moore, The Wild Irishmen: The former Thin Lizzy is becoming a fat cat, indeed', Guitar World, Sept 1987, pp. 26-? Reprinted on Sept 15, 2011 as 'Gary Moore Discusses His Latest Album, Gear and Phil Lynott in 1987 Guitar World Interview at: https://www.guitarworld.com/gw-archive/gary-moore-discusses-his-latest-album-gear-and-phil-lynott-1987-guitar-world-interview

2 Mark Putterford, 'The Wild One' Kerrang!, No. 141, March 5-18, 1987.

3 Derek Oliver, 'Happy Together, an interview with Gary Moore and Phil Lynott', Kerrang! No. 94, May 16-29, 1985, pp. 20 & 25.

4 Christopher Booker, The Seven Basic Plots: Why We Tell Stories (London & New York: Continuum, 2004.

5 Sian Llewellyn, 'I jumped on the Blues bandwagon? I was the bandwagon!', Louder, March 23, 2007. Available online at: https://www.loudersound.com/features/gary-moore-i-jumped-on-the-blues-bandwagon-i-was-the-bandwagon

NOTES TO CHAPTER ONE

6 David Hepworth, Overpaid, Oversexed and Over There (London: Penguin, 2021), p. 104.

7 Mat Snow, 'Gary Moore: No Sweat', Q, April 1992, pp. 36-41.

8 Mat Snow, 'Gary Moore: No Sweat', Q, April 1992, pp. 36-41.

9 Steven Rosen, 'Gary Moore: Guitar on a Rampage', Guitar World, November 1984.

10 'Gary Moore Remembers Rory Gallagher', Hot Press 1995. Available online at: https://www.hotpress.com/music/gary-moore-remembers-rory-gallagher-14356584?fbclid=IwAR2pdanaNpPpMeZbRR_hAGYjqgj_VWozTQvfY8Of-7HMCem48HDpvxXZdRpg

11 Neville Marten, 'Catch Him If You Can!', Guitarist, March 1989, pp. 33-40; Dave Shack, 'After the Moore', Metal Forces, March 1989, pp. 32 & 41; and Valerie Potter, 'Soldier of Fortune', Metal Hammer, Vol. 2, No. 2, February 6, 1989, pp. 10-13.

12 Mark Putterford, 'The Wild One', Kerrang , No. 141, March 5-18, 1987.

13 Colin Harper, Review of Back To The Blues, Irish Times, February 23, 2001.

14 Richard Walmsley, 'Moore Music', International Musician and Recording World, November 1985, pp. 90-95.

15 Ivan Little, 'Gary Moore's teenage kicks; Chubby lad became a Thin Lizzy Legend', Sunday Life (Belfast), February 13, 2011.

16 Colin Harper, Review of Back To The Blues, Irish Times, February 23, 2001.

17 Mark Putterford, Phil Lynott: The Rocker (London: Omnibus Press, 2002), pp 31-2.

18 'Moore's Almanac', Belfast Telegraph, May 24, 2007.

19 Neville Marten, 'Catch Him If You Can!', Guitarist, March 1989 pp. 33-40.

20 It's possible Moore was driven by a conservative 'protestant work ethic' that occasionally alienated him from bandmates. For example, Eric Bell called Moore a 'very serious guitar player', who 'played all the time. I've never seen anybody play the guitar as much as Gary He would just be playing all day. That's how deeply he was into it, and so he was very sort of serious about it all in those days.' Scott Gorham recalled an incident from his Thin Lizzy days with Moore when Lynott, Gorham, Moore, Mark Nauseef, and Huey Lewis flew to Nassau in the Bahamas for a couple of weeks in in June 1979, ostensibly to do some song writing. There, everyone except Moore sat by the pool every day, whereas Moore mainly stayed in his room at the hotel to practice his guitar. A few weeks later, when Lizzy and AC/DC played some gigs together in the United States, Moore advised Lynott to follow the example of guitarist Angus Young: 'Look how hard that guy works – that's how we should be!' A few weeks later, Moore left the band mid-tour because he was unable to cope any longer with what Moore thought of as Lynott's unprofessionalism. For Bell quote, see Martin Popoff, From Dublin To Jailbreak: Thin Lizzy's 1969-76 (Bedford: Wymer, 2011), p. 90. For Moore's comment about Angus Young, and his split from Lizzy, see Mark Putterford, Phil Lynott: The Rocker (London: Omnibus Press, 2002), pp. 163-65.

21 'Moore's Almanac', Belfast Telegraph, May 24, 2007.

22 David Mead, 'Classic interview (1995): Gary Moore', Guitarist, December 23, 2019. Available online at: https://www.musicradar.com/news/classic-interview-gary-moore-talks-blues-for-greeny-jack-bruce-bb-king-albert-collins-and-never-playing-with-clapton

23 Tony Bacon, Interview with Gary Moore, Music UK, No. 13, January 1983, pp. 18-22.

24 Top 50 albums. Record Mirror, October 17, 1970, p. 8.

25 Paul Charles, '"Universities are the worst" say Skid Row', Record Mirror, August 7, 1971, p. 3.

26 Paul Charles, '"Universities are the worst" say Skid Row', Record Mirror, August 7, 1971, p. 3.

27 Review of 34 Hours, Billboard, August 28, 1971, p. 50.

28 Paul Charles, '"Universities are the worst" say Skid Row', Record Mirror, August 7, 1971, p. 3.

29 Martin Popoff, From Dublin To Jailbreak: Thin Lizzy's 1969-76 (Bedford: Wymer, 2011), p. 90.

30 Sounds, December 19, 1970, p. 20.

31 Colin Harper, Review of Back To The Blues, Irish Times, February 23, 2001.

32 Ray Telford, Sounds, December 19, 1970, p. 16.

33 Martin Popoff, From Dublin To Jailbreak: Thin Lizzy's 1969-76 (Bedford: Wymer, 2011), p. 32

34 Martin Popoff, From Dublin To Jailbreak: Thin Lizzy's 1969-76 (Bedford: Wymer, 2011), pp. 4-5.

35 Mat Snow, 'Gary Moore: No Sweat', Q, April 1992, pp. 36-41.

36 Review of Grinding Stone, Billboard, December 14, 1974, p. 64.

37 Martin Popoff, From Dublin To Jailbreak: Thin Lizzy's 1969-76 (Bedford: Wymer, 2011), p. 90.

38 Martin Popoff, From Dublin To Jailbreak: Thin Lizzy's 1969-76 (Bedford: Wymer, 2011), p. 91.

39 Beverley Legge, 'They make me dizzy Thin Lizzy', Disc, 23 February 1974, p. 19.

40 Mat Snow, 'Gary Moore: No Sweat', Q, April 1992, pp. 36-41.

NOTES TO CHAPTER TWO

41 Martin Popoff, From Dublin To Jailbreak: Thin Lizzy's 1969-76 (Bedford: Wymer, 2011), p. 15.

42 Martin Popoff, From Dublin To Jailbreak: Thin Lizzy's 1969-76 (Bedford: Wymer, 2011), p. 81.

43 Paul Weir, 'Thin Lizzy', Record Mirror, July 7, 1973, p. 14.

44 Alan Byrne, Thin Lizzy (London: SAF Publishing, 2006), p. 61.

45 'Thin Lizzy at the Stadium', Irish Times, January 19, 1974, p. 12.

46 Alan Byrne, Thin Lizzy (London: SAF Publishing, 2006), p. 61.

47 Quoted in Martin Popoff, From Dublin To Jailbreak: Thin Lizzy's 1969-76 (Bedford: Wymer, 2011), p. 95.

48 Review of Rocker (1971-1974), Billboard, February 12, 1977, p. 68.

49 Mark Putterford, Phil Lynott: The Rocker (London: Omnibus Press, 2002), p. 82.

50 Ronnie Gurr, 'Snowy White Meets the Black Prince', Record Mirror, April 26, 1980, p. 8-9.

51 Martin Popoff, From Dublin To Jailbreak: Thin Lizzy's 1969-76 (Bedford: Wymer, 2011), p. 119.

52 Beverley Legge, 'They make me dizzy Thin Lizzy', Disc, 23 February 1974, p. 19.

53 Martin Popoff, From Dublin To Jailbreak: Thin Lizzy's 1969-76 (Bedford: Wymer, 2011), p. 90.

54 Martin Popoff, From Dublin To Jailbreak: Thin Lizzy's 1969-76 (Bedford: Wymer, 2011), p. 92.

55 Pete Makowski, 'Thin Lizzy: Buzy Lizzy', Sounds, 27 March 1976.

56 Russell Kyle, 'Why Gary is happy to be a Thin man', Evening Times, March 29, 1979, p. 10.

57 Russell Kyle, 'Why Gary is happy to be a Thin man', Evening Times, March 29, 1979, p. 10.

58 'Thin Lizzy – Rocking Back Again', Music Week, November 2, 1974, p. 55.

59 Harry Doherty, 'The Year Queen Lizzy Shook America', Melody Maker, February 19, 1977.

60 Los Angeles Free Press, Vol. 14, No.14 (664) April 8-14, 1977, p. 18.

61 Martin Popoff, Thin Lizzy: A Visual Biography (Bedford: Wymer, 2020), p. 73.

62 Harry Doherty, 'The Year Queen Lizzy Shook America', Melody Maker, February 19, 1977. Many years later Gorham contradicted himself somewhat, telling Rock Candy magazine that he felt Moore would have been happier if Lizzy was a three-piece so that Moore could have the sole spotlight. See Rock Candy, Interview with Scott Gorham. Issue 33, August 2022, pp. 50-61.

63 Mark Putterford, Phil Lynott: The Rocker (London: Omnibus Press, 2002), p. 157.

64 Harry Doherty, 'The Year Queen Lizzy Shook America', Melody Maker, February 19, 1977.

65 Alan Byrne, Thin Lizzy (London: SAF Publishing, 2006), p. 117.

66 Harry Doherty, 'The Year Queen Lizzy Shook America', Melody Maker, February 19, 1977.

67 Patricia Goldstein, 'In Search of Thin Lizzy', Creem, pp. 38-41 & 76-77.

68 Steve McDonell, 'Rockin at Wendler Arena', The Delta Collegiate, January 27, 1977, p. 5.

69 Harry Doherty, 'The Year Queen Lizzy Shook America', Melody Maker, February 19, 1977.

70 Sally Rayle, 'Queen, Thin Lizzy at the Forum', Los Angeles Free Press, Vol. 14, No. 10 (660), March 11-17, 1977, p. 20.

71 Mark Putterford, Phil Lynott: The Rocker (London: Omnibus Press, 2002), p. 121.

72 David Brown, 'It ain't sham rock it's the story of Thin Lizzy', Record Mirror, June 18, 1977, pp. 8-9, 19.

73 David Brown, 'It ain't sham rock it's the story of Thin Lizzy', Record Mirror, June 18, 1977, pp. 8-9, 19.

74 Don Snowden, 'Thin Lizzy', Los Angeles Times, 1977.

75 Martin Popoff, The Sun Goes Down: Thin Lizzy's Final Years (Bedford: Wymer, 2012), p. 4.

76 Jon Tiven, 'Thin Lizzy: "Fighting" Phil', Circus, November 1975.

77 Mark Putterford, Phil Lynott: The Rocker (London: Omnibus Press, 2002), p. 121.

78 Martin Popoff, The Sun Goes Down: Thin Lizzy's Final Years (Bedford: Wymer, 2012), p. 27.

79 Martin Popoff, The Sun Goes Down: Thin Lizzy's Final Years (Bedford: Wymer, 2012), p. 20.

80 Pete Makowski, 'Thin Lizzy Rule At Reading OK?', Sounds, 27 August 1977.

81 'Thin Lizzy', Record Mirror, September 30, 1978, p. 37.

82 Rosalind Russell, What a way to launch a venue!! The Greedies London Electric Ballroom, Record Mirror, August 5, 1978, p. 27.

83 Martin Popoff, The Sun Goes Down: Thin Lizzy's Final Years (Bedford: Wymer, 2012), p. 51.

84 Alan Byrne, Thin Lizzy (London: SAF Publishing, 2006), p. 127.

85 Accessed Sept 1, 2022. Available online at: https://thinlizzyguide.com/tours/dates/1978/780923.htm

86 Martin Popoff, The Sun Goes Down: Thin Lizzy's Final Years (Bedford: Wymer, 2012), p. 52.

87 Joseph Shapiro, 'Kansas, Thin Lizzy Give Fans Double Treat', Commercial Appeal, Memphis, August 11, 1978.

88 Mark Putterford, Phil Lynott: The Rocker (London: Omnibus Press, 2002), p. 152.

89 Barry Cain, 'Thin Lizzy Hammersmith Odeon', Record Mirror, December 23, 1978, p. 21.

90 Martin Popoff, The Sun Goes Down: Thin Lizzy's Final Years (Bedford: Wymer, 2012), pp. 33-34.

91 Alan Byrne, Thin Lizzy (London: SAF Publishing, 2006), pp. 131-32.

92 Martin Popoff, The Sun Goes Down: Thin Lizzy's Final Years (Bedford: Wymer, 2012), p. 58.

93 Martin Popoff, The Sun Goes Down: Thin Lizzy's Final Years (Bedford: Wymer, 2012), p. 61. See also Mark Putterford, Phil Lynott: The Rocker (London: Omnibus Press, 2002), p. 156.

94 Harry Doherty, Review of Black Rose: A Rock Legend. Melody Maker, April 21, 1979.

95 Michael Davis, Review of Black Rose: A Rock Legend, Creem, August 1979, pp. 54-5.

96 Review of Black Rose: A Rock Legend, Cash Box, May 19, 1979, p. 18

97 Harry Doherty, Review of Black Rose: A Rock Legend. Melody Maker, April 21, 1979.

98 Philip Silverton, Review of Black Rose: A Rock Legend, Sounds, April 28, 1979.

99 Martin Popoff, The Sun Goes Down: Thin Lizzy's Final Years (Bedford: Wymer, 2012), p. 57.

100 Martin Popoff, The Sun Goes Down: Thin Lizzy's Final Years (Bedford: Wymer, 2012), p. 58.

101 Martin Popoff, The Sun Goes Down: Thin Lizzy's Final Years (Bedford: Wymer, 2012), pp. 56-7.

102 Martin Popoff, The Sun Goes Down: Thin Lizzy's Final Years (Bedford: Wymer, 2012), p. 72.

103 Martin Popoff, Thin Lizzy: A Visual Biography (Bedford: Wymer, 2020), p. 119.

104 Harry Doherty, 'Deutschland Liebt Lizzy', Melody Maker, June 16, 1979.

105 Bob Ross, 'Journey, Thin Lizzy Find "New Wave" of Success', St. Petersburg Times, July 20, 1979, p. 30.

106 Neil Jeffries, 'The Boys Are Back', Kerrang! No. 326, February 2, 1991, pp. 28, 37-41.

107 Martin Popoff, The Sun Goes Down: Thin Lizzy's Final Years (Bedford: Wymer, 2012), pp. 53 & 55.

108 Mark Putterford, Phil Lynott: The Rocker (London: Omnibus Press, 2002), pp. 164-65.

109 Cash Box, July 28, 1979, p. 24; Cash Box, August 4, 1979, p. 39.

110 Mark Putterford, Phil Lynott: The Rocker (London: Omnibus Press, 2002), p. 165.

111 Harry Shapiro, 'Feel the Force', Classic Rock, Issue 305, September 2022, pp. 56-62.

112 Martin Popoff, The Sun Goes Down: Thin Lizzy's Final Years (Bedford: Wymer, 2012), p. 55.

113 Harry Shapiro, 'Feel the Force', Classic Rock, Issue 305, September 2022, pp. 56-62.

114 Neil Jeffries, 'Waiting For An Alibi', Kerrang! No.49, August 25-September 7, 1983, pp. 18-21.

115 Paul Elliott, 'No Sleep…', 8-page pull-out article about London's Hammersmith Odeon, in Kerrang! No. 378, February 8, 1992, pp. 29-36.

116 See Gary Moore, Emerald Aisles: Live in Ireland (Virgin Music Video, 1985).

NOTES TO CHAPTER THREE

117 Malcolm Dome/Jon Hiseman, CD booklet notes, Strange New Flesh, remastered, 2-CD edition, Esoteric Recordings, 2012.

118 Chris Welch, 'Jon Hiseman: Why I've Re-formed Colosseum', Melody Maker, July 19, 1975.

119 Mark Putterford, 'The Wild One', Kerrang!, No. 141, March 5-18, 1987, p. 53.

120 Charles Waring, CD booklet notes to Wardance/Electric Savage, Digitally Remastered editions, 2021.

121 Pete Makowski, 'True Stories: boy protege comes good', Sounds, February 1, 1975.

122 Neville Marten, 'Catch Him If You Can!', Guitarist, March 1989 pp. 33-40.

123 Tony Bacon, Interview with Gary Moore, Music UK, No. 13, January 1983, pp. 18-22.

124 Charles Waring, CD booklet notes to Wardance/Electric Savage, Digitally Remastered editions, 2021.

125 Pete Makowski, 'True Stories: boy protege comes good', Sounds, February 1, 1975.

126 Quoted in Martin Popoff, The Sun Goes Down: Thin Lizzy's Final Years (Bedford: Wymer, 2012), p. 27.

127 Pete Makowski, 'True Stories: boy protege comes good', Sounds, February 1, 1975.

128 'London Report', Cash Box, August 16, 1975, p. 46.

129 Pete Makowski, 'True Stories: boy protege comes good', Sounds, February 1, 1975.

130 Billboard, March 20, 1976, p. 56; Record Mirror, Review of Strange New Flesh, April 10, 1976, p. 33.

131 Chris Welch, Review of Strange New Fruit, Melody Maker, June 5, 1976.

132 A bootleg of a gig recorded at the Capitol Cinema Capitol in Basel, Switzerland on May 21, 1976, indicates a set list containing 'Dark Side of The Moog', 'Secret Places', 'Down To You', 'Siren Song', 'The Awakening', the Graham Parker song, 'Walkin' In The Park', and solo performances by Hiseman and Moore. 'Siren Song' and 'The Awakening' were non-album tracks recorded by the band in demo form only.

133 Geoff Barton, 'David Coverdale's Whitesnake: a four-track single', MusicWeek, June 3, 1978, p. 5.

134 Review of Electric Savage, Cash Box, August 20, 1977, p. 26.

135 Review of Electric Savage, Walrus!, July 18, 1977, p. 34.

136 Charles Waring, CD booklet notes to Wardance/Electric Savage, Digitally Remastered editions, 2021.

137 Review of Wardance, Record World, April 22, 1978, p. 24.

138 Review of Wardance, Cash Box, May 6, 1978, p. 20.

139 Music Week, January 21, 1978, p. 3; 'A Webber family affair', Music Week, January 28, 1978, p. 16.

140 Terri Anderson, 'Variations', Music Week, February 11, 1978, p.48.

141 'Variations Premieres in N.Y. & L.A.', Record World, May 13, 1978, p. 20; Chris White, 'Variations', Music Week, July 22, 1978, p. 78.

142 Music Week, March 25, 1978, p. 2.

143 Pete Makowski, 'True Stories: boy protege comes good', Sounds, February 1, 1975.

144 Music Press advertisements from 1977 list the following tour dates: November 10 Warwick University, Coventry; 12 Nottingham Boat Club; 13 Chelmsford Chancellor Halls; 15 Lady Mitchell Hall, Cambridge; 16 Eric's, Liverpool; 17 Town Hall, Loughborough; 19 Norwich University; 20 Victoria Palace, London; 25 Edinburgh University; and 26 Glasgow University.

145 Nick Robertshaw, Review of Colosseum II at Victoria Palace, November 1977, Music Week, December 3, 1977, p. 67.

146 Chris Welch, 'Jon Hiseman: Why I've Re-formed Colosseum', Melody Maker, July 19, 1975.

147 Mick Wall, 'Gary Moore', Classic Rock, Issue 287, May, 2021, pp. 52-61.

148 Richard Walmsley, 'Moore Music', International Musician and Recording World, November 1985, pp. 90-95.

149 Chris Welch, 'Rocking Back to Happiness', Metal Hammer Vol. 3, No. 22, November 7, 1988, pp. 21-23.

150 Chris Welch, 'Jon Hiseman: Why I've Re-reformed Colosseum', Melody Maker, July 19, 1975.

151 Advert for Back On The Streets, New Musical Express, January 20, 1979, p. 13.

152 Advert for Back On The Streets, Cash Box, November 17, 1979, p. 25.

153 On the reverse cover, the songs attributed solely to Moore are instead credited to 'Moore/Campbell', possibly referring to Donna Campbell who was a friend of Moore's at the time.

154 Neville Marten, 'Catch Him If You Can!', Guitarist, March 1989, pp. 33-40.

155 BBC Masters of Rock: Gary Moore. Narrated by Bruce Dickinson. Broadcast February 10, 2011 on BBC 6.

156 Mark Putterford, Phil Lynott: The Rocker (London: Omnibus Press, 2002), p. 157.

157 Quoted in Alan Byrne, Thin Lizzy (London: SAF Publishing, 2006), p. 128.

158 Mike Daly, Review of Back On The Streets, The Age, July 12, 1979, p. 10.

159 Review of Back On The Streets, Walrus! October 28, 1979.

160 Review of Back On The Streets, Cash Box, October 13, 1979, p. 10.

161 Harry Doherty, Review of Back On The Streets, Melody Maker, December 16, 1978.

162 'Heavy Metal Update', Creem, October, 1983, pp. 45-47.

163 Ronnie Gurr, Record Mirror, November 11, 1978, p. 10.

164 'Singles to Watch', Cash Box, December 8, 1979, p. 18.

165 Harry Shapiro, 'Feel the Force', Classic Rock 305, September 2022, pp. 56-61.

166 Moore later revealed that Hughes was fired for making a series of unreasonable demands. See Dante Bonutto, 'Running Free', Kerrang! No. 102, September 5-18, 1985, pp. 19-21, 59.

167 G-Force tour advert. Music Week, May 24, 1980, p. 33.

168 Review of G-Force, Music Week, June 21, 1980, p. 26; Ronnie Gurr, 'Moore or Less', Record Mirror, June 6, 1980, p. 26.

169 Review of 'Hot Gossip', Record Mirror, May 31, 1980, p. 10. Wild Horses was ex-Thin Lizzy guitarist, Brian Robertson's band, so this was a natural comparison upon which to draw.

170 Chris Westwood, 'Making It Count', Record Mirror, June 21, 1980, p. 10.

171 Tour advert. New Music News, Vol. 1, No. 3, 1980, p. 5.

172 Brian Harrigan, 'Metal Fatigue in the Over Thirties', New Music News, Vol. 1, No. 1, p. 12.

173 Mat Snow, 'Gary Moore: No Sweat', Q, April 1992, pp. 36-41.

174 Chas de Whalley, 'Sharon Osbourne: The Power Behind the Throne', Kerrang!, No. 33, January 13-26, 1983, p. 37.

175 Chris Welch, 'Gary Glitters', Kerrang!, No. 21, July 29-August 11, 1982, pp. 26-27.

176 Neil Jeffries, 'Wandering Star', Kerrang!, No. 59, January 12-25, 1984, pp. 8-10.

177 Allan F. Moore, 'Hard rock'. Grove Music Online. Oxford University Press. Accessed January 17, 2023. https://www.oxfordmusiconline.com/grovemusic/view/10.1093/gmo/9781561592630.001.0001/om-o-9781561592630-e-0000046249

178 These lyrical themes continued throughout Moore's career. In a review of Run For Cover (1985), journalist Scott Howlett noted that Moore 'writes about social and political issues in his tunes as opposed to the rancid topics most of the others endear themselves to — cars, women, drinking, sex. Gary Moore writes about love in a spiritual, rather than sexual vein and the political disruption which affects his world.' See 'Gary Moore the fastest and the best', Sydney Morning Herald, October 6, 1985, p. 116.

179 Malcolm Dome, 'Room at the Top', Kerrang! No. 73, July 26-August 12, 1984, pp. 34-37.

180 Chris Welch, Review of Dirty Fingers, Kerrang! No. 70, June 14-27, 1984, p. 10.

181 Neil Jeffries, 'Wandering Star', Kerrang!, No. 59, January 12-25, 1984, pp. 8-10.

182 Chris Welch, Review of Dirty Fingers, Kerrang! No. 70, June 14-27, 1984, p. 10.

NOTES TO CHAPTER FOUR

183 Harry Doherty, Review of Back On The Streets, Melody Maker, December 16, 1978.

184 Mark Putterford, 'The Wild One', Kerrang!, No. 141, March 5-18, 1987, p. 52.

185 Chris Welch, 'Gary Glitters', Kerrang! No. 21, July 29-August 11, 1982, pp. 26-27.

186 In 1993, Moore made a guest appearance on the track 'She Moves Me' from Paul Rodgers' album Muddy Water Blues: A Tribute To Muddy Waters (London/PolyGram). Moore also joined Rodgers on stage at the Royal Albert Hall in 2006. A reviewer wrote of this performance, 'it wasn't until the guitarist Gary Moore emerged from the wings — replacing both of the guitarists in [Rodgers'] group — that Rodgers became truly galvanised, as they sparred like a pair of old bantam cocks'. See David Sinclair, 'Paul Rodgers'. Times (London), October 5, 2006.

187 Review of Corridors Of Power, Billboard, March 19, 1983, p. 59.

188 Review of Corridors Of Power, Record-Journal (Connecticut, USA), June 17, 1983, p. 15.

189 Michael Davis, Review of Corridors Of Power, CREEM, September 1983, p. 59.

190 Chris Welch, Review of Corridors Of Power', Kerrang! No. 27, October 21-November 3, 1982, p. 12.

191 Peter Stockton, Review of Corridors Of Power, Smash Hits, October 28, 1982, p. 23.

192 Sylvie Simmons, 'Gary Moore on Peter Green', Rolling Stone, 1995; Cliff Jones, 'I'm Peter Green', MOJO, September, 1996.

193 Review. of 'Always Gonna Love You', Cash Box, April 30, 1983, p. 10.

194 Chris Welch, 'Shout For Moore', Kerrang! No. 32, 1983, pp. 44-47.

195 Review of 'Falling In Love With You', Cash Box, July 2, 1983, p. 12.

196 Review of 'Falling In Love With You', Kerrang! No. 37, 1983, p. 43.

197 Steven Rosen, 'Gary Moore: Guitar on a Rampage', Guitar World, November 1984.

198 Neil Jeffries, 'Wandering Star', Kerrang!, No. 59, January 12-25, 1984, pp. 8-10.

199 Chris Welch, 'Gary Glitters', Kerrang! No. 21, July 29-August 11, 1982, pp. 26-27.

200 Chris Welch, 'Shout For Moore', Kerrang! No. 32, 1983, pp. 44-47.

201 See 'Reading Report: Gary Moore', Kerrang! No. 25, September 23-October 6, 1982.

202 Chris Welch, live review, Kerrang! No. 32, December 30-January 12, 1983, p. 37.

203 Kerrang! No. 42, May 19-June 2, 1983, p. 11.

204 Neil Jeffries, 'Wandering Star', Kerrang!, No. 59, January 12-25, 1984, pp. 8-10.

205 Chris Welch, live review, Kerrang! No. 32, December 30-January 12, 1983, p. 37.

206 Neil Jeffries, 'Wandering Star', Kerrang!, No. 59, January 12-25, 1984, pp. 8-10.

207 Neville Marten, 'Catch Him If You Can!'. Guitarist, March 1989 pp. 33-40.

208 Steven Rosen, 'Gary Moore: Guitar on a Rampage', Guitar World, November 1984.

209 Dave Shack, 'After the Moore, Metal Forces, March 1989, pp. 32 & 41.

210 Allan F. Moore, 'Hard rock'. Grove Music Online. Oxford University Press. Accessed January 17, 2023. https://www.oxfordmusiconline.com/grovemusic/view/10.1093/gmo/9781561592630.001.0001/om-o-9781561592630-e-0000046249

211 Neil Carter, quoted in Martin Popoff, The Sun Goes Down: Thin Lizzy's Final Years (Bedford: Wymer, 2012), pp. 80-81.

212 Review of Victims of the Future, Cash Box, April 14, 1984, p. 14.

213 Jerry Spangler, Review of Victims Of The Future, Deseret News, June 29, 1984, p. W7.

214 Howard Johnson, Review of Victims Of The Future, Kerrang!, No. 59, January, 1984.

215 Tony Jasper, Music Week, January 14, 1984, p. 12.

216 Smash Hits, January-February, 1984, p. 20.

217 Howard Johnson, Review of 'Hold On To Love', Kerrang!, No. 59, January 12-25, 1984, p. 36.

218 Howard Johnson, Review of Victims Of The Future, Kerrang!, No. 59, January 12-25, 1984, p. 13.

219 Malcolm Dome, 'Room at the Top', Kerrang! No. 73, July 26-August 12, 1984, pp. 34-37.

220 Scott Howlett, 'Gary Moore the fastest and the best', Sydney Morning Herald, October 6, 1985, p. 116.

221 Malcolm Dome, 'Room at the Top', Kerrang! No. 73, July 26-August 12, 1984, pp. 34-37.

222 Neil Jeffries, 'Wandering Star', Kerrang!, No. 59, January 12-25, 1984, pp. 8-10.

223 Derek Oliver, 'Happy Together', Kerrang!, No. 94, May 16-29, 1985, pp. 20 & 25.

224 Richard Walmsley, 'Moore Music', International Musician and Recording World, November 1985, pp. 90-95.

225 Quoted in Martin Popoff, The Sun Goes Down: Thin Lizzy's Final Years (Bedford: Wymer, 2012), p. 170.

226 Mick Wall, Review of 'Out In The Fields', Kerrang! No. 94, May 16-29, 1985, p. 39.

227 Mark Putterford, 'Phoenix Rising: Glenn Hughes', Kerrang! No. 87, February 7-20, 1985, pp. 16-17.

228 Richard Walmsley, 'Moore Music', International Musician and Recording World, November 1985, pp. 90-95.

229 Richard Walmsley, 'Moore Music', Intertnational Musician and Recording World, November 1985, pp. 90-95.

230 Mark Putterford, Review of After the War, Kerrang! No. 102, September 5-18, 1985, p. 11.

231 Richard Walmsley, 'Moore Music', International Musician and Recording World, November 1985, pp. 90-95.

232 Dante Bonutto, 'Gary Moore', Kerrang!, No. 114, February 20-March 5, 1986, pp. 24-25.

233 Richard Walmsley, 'Moore Music', International Musician and Recording World, November 1985, pp. 90-95.

234 Smash Hits, No. 11, September 24, 1985, p. 77.

235 Russell Kyle, Review of Run For Cover, Evening Times (Scotland), September 18, 1985, p. 21.

236 Mark Putterford, Review of After The War, Kerrang! No. 102, September 5-18, 1985, p. 11.

237 Scott Howlett, 'Gary Moore the fastest and the best', Sydney Morning Herald, October 6, 1985, p. 116.

238 B. Clark, Courier-Mail (Australia), November 28, 1985.

239 Hughes claimed at the time that Moore wouldn't allow him to promote his Phenomena project, and pressured him to focus solely on the collaboration with Moore. See Dave Dickson, 'Keep Watching the Skies', Kerrang! No. 98, July 11-24, 1985, pp. 35-37. In response, Moore listed numerous problems Hughes had caused including hiring two friends as roadies without discussing it with Moore and asking to rename the band 'The Gary Moore Band featuring Glenn Hughes'. Moore claimed Hughes had developed a drug habit, had serious personality problems that would require professional help, and was a compulsive eater, weighing in at 17 stone during the recording of the album. See Dante Bonutto, 'Running Free', Kerrang! No. 102, September 5-18, 1985, pp. 19-21, 59. A few years later, Hughes was still blaming Moore for the end of their friendship: 'The whole Gary Moore project was a joke from start to finish', he proclaimed. 'There's no question that Gary is one of the best guitar players ever, but he is almost impossible to work with, and I think that almost everyone who's ever worked with him will agree'. See Mark Putterford, 'Hughes Next?', Metal Hammer Vol. 3, No. 8, April 25, 1988, p. 64.

240 This info is based on the set list for the concert at Festival Hall, Osaka, Japan, on October 9, 1985. The full list of songs was: Run For Cover, Reach For The Sky, Murder In The Skies, Shapes Of Things, Cold Hearted, End Of The World, Nothing To Lose, Empty Rooms, Victims Of The Future, Out In The Fields, All Messed Up, Rockin' Every Night, Back On The Streets, and Parisienne Walkways.

241 Dante Bonutto, 'Gary Moore', Kerrang!, No. 114, February 20-March 5, 1986, pp. 24-25.

242 Friday Morning Quarterback, January 24, 1986, p. 29.

243 Friday Morning Quarterback, February 7, 1986, p. 27.

244 Friday Morning Quarterback, March 21, 1986, p. 26.

245 Review of Run For Cover, Billboard, February 2, 1986, p. 80.

246 Cash Box, Review of Run For Cover, February 1, 1986, p. 10.

247 Mike Abrams, Review of Run For Cover, Ottawa Citizen, May 23, 1986, p. F5.

248 'Out In The Fields' would later feature in the 1989 American film Honor Bound, an espionage thriller set during the Cold War. The song's militaristic themes and its plea for peace made it an apposite addition to the film's soundtrack. See Review of Honor Bound, Sight and Sound, August 1, 1992, p. 56.

249 Jerry Spangler, Deseret News (Utah), April 4, 1986, p. 6W.

250 Music & Media, December 2, 1985, p. 22; Dante Bonutto, 'Gary Moore', Kerrang!, No. 114, February 20 to March 5, 1986, pp. 24-25.

251 Martin Popoff, The Sun Goes Down: Thin Lizzy's Final Years (Bedford: Wymer, 2012), p. 158.

252 Mark Putterford,'The Wild One', Kerrang!, No. 141, March 5-18, 1987.

253 Harold Mac Wonderlea and Christine Rehmann, 'Gary Moore, The Wild Irishmen: The former Thin Lizzy is becoming a fat cat, indeed', Guitar World Sept 1987 pp. 26-? Reprinted on Sept 15, 2011 as 'Gary Moore Discusses His Latest Album, Gear and Phil Lynott in 1987 Guitar World Interview at: https://www.guitarworld.com/gw-archive/gary-moore-discusses-his-latest-album-gear-and-phil-lynott-1987-guitar-world-interview

254 Music & Media, April 4, 1987, p. 19.

255 Mark Putterford, 'The Wild One', Kerrang!, No. 141, March 5-18, 1987.

256 Harold Mac Wonderlea and Christine Rehmann, 'Gary Moore, The Wild Irishmen: The former Thin Lizzy is becoming a fat cat, indeed', Guitar World Sept 1987 pp. 26-? Reprinted on Sept 15, 2011 as 'Gary Moore Discusses His Latest Album, Gear and Phil Lynott in 1987 Guitar World Interview at: https://www.guitarworld.com/gw-archive/gary-moore-discusses-his-latest-album-gear-and-phil-lynott-1987-guitar-world-interview

257 Jon Lewin, 'Moore's Code', Making Music, Issue 12, March 1987, pp. 24-25.

258 Steve Newton, The Georgia Straight (Canada), May 8, 1987.

259 Harold Mac Wonderlea and Christine Rehmann, 'Gary Moore, The Wild Irishmen: The former Thin Lizzy is becoming a fat cat, indeed', Guitar World Sept 1987 pp. 26-? Reprinted on Sept 15, 2011 as 'Gary Moore Discusses His Latest Album, Gear and Phil Lynott in 1987 Guitar World Interview at: https://www.guitarworld.com/gw-archive/gary-moore-discusses-his-latest-album-gear-and-phil-lynott-1987-guitar-world-interview

260 Mark Putterford, 'The Wild One', Kerrang!, No. 141, March 5-18, 1987.

261 Jon Lewin, 'Moore's Code', Making Music, Issue 12, March 1987, pp. 24-25.

262 Tim Goodyer, 'He Ain't Heavy...', [Interview with Neil Carter] Music Technology, September, 1987, p. 40.

263 Jon Lewin, 'Moore's Code', Making Music, Issue 12, March 1987, pp. 24-25.

264 Jon Lewin, 'Moore's Code', Making Music, Issue 12, March 1987, pp. 24-25.

265 Steve Newton, The Georgia Straight (Canada), May 8, 1987.

266 Larry Kilman, 'Record Reviews', Associated Press, July 29, 1987.

267 'Hard Rock/Heavy Metal Music News', Hard Report, September 25, 1987, p. 11.

268 Derek Oliver, Review of Wild Frontier, Kerrang!, No. 141, March 5-18, 1987.

269 Jon Lewin, 'Moore's Code', Making Music, Issue 12, March 1987, pp. 24-25.

270 Mark Putterford, 'The Wild One', Kerrang!, No. 141, March 5-18, 1987.

271 Jon Lewin, 'Moore's Code', Making Music, Issue 12, March 1987, pp. 24-25.

272 Dante Bonutto, 'Celt Hero', Kerrang! No 135, December 11-24, 1986, p. 31.

273 Mark Putterford, 'The Wild One', Kerrang!, No. 141, March 5-18, 1987.

274 Paul Elliott, 'A Bouquet of Black Roses', Kerrang!, No. 141, March 5-18, 1987.

275 Music & Media, No. 51/52, December 27, 1986, p. 30.

276 Review of Wild Frontier, RPM Magazine, May 23, 1987, p. 10.

277 Review of Wild Frontier, Billboard, April 4, 1987, p. 78.

278 Larry Kilman, 'Record Reviews', Associated Press, July 29, 1987.

279 David Sinclair, Review of Gary Moore at Hammersmith Odeon, The Times, May 28, 1987.

280 Hard Report, July 17, 1987, p. 26; Hard Report, August 14, 1987, p. 30.

281 Chris Welch, 'Rocking Back to Happiness', Metal Hammer Vol. 3, No. 22, November 7, 1988, pp. 21-23.

282 Dave Shack, 'After the Moore', Metal Forces, March 1989, pp. 32 & 41.

283 Valerie Potter, 'Soldier of Fortune', Metal Hammer, Vol. 2, No. 2, February 6, 1989, pp. 10-13.

284 Mark Putterford, 'Back on the War Path', RAW No. 10, January 11-24, 1989, pp. 34-6.

285 See Paul Henderson, 'Gary Goes to War', Kerrang! No. 225, February 11, 1989, pp. 28-31.

286 When the digital audio tape cassette medium was introduced in 1987, one if its selling points was that it could produce identical or superior sound quality than vinyl. However, the format never became widely popular.

287 Dante Bonutto, 'Moore the Merrier', RAW No. 1, August 31-September 13, 1988, pp. 6-7.

288 On this album Moore mainly played his famous Peter Green Les Paul, together with a red Hamer Chaparral, and a white Charvel, although the latter was used mainly on stage. See Interview with Graham Lilley by Neville Marten. Guitarist 403, February 2016.

289 Dante Bonutto, 'Moore the Merrier', RAW No. 1, August 31-September 13, 1988, pp. 6-7.

290 Paul Henderson, 'Gary Goes to War', Kerrang! No. 225, February 11, 1989, pp. 28-31.

291 Chris Welch, 'Rocking Back to Happiness', Metal Hammer Vol. 3, No. 22, November 7, 1988, pp. 21-23.

292 Metal Hammer Vol. 5, No. 5, March 20, 1989, p. 17.

293 Mark Putterford, 'Back on the War Path', RAW No. 10, January 11-24, 1989, pp. 34-6.

294 Paul Henderson, 'Gary Goes to War', Kerrang! No. 225, February 11, 1989, pp. 28-31.

295 Dave Shack, 'After the Moore', Metal Forces, March 1989, pp. 32 & 41.

296 Music & Media, January 21, 1989, p. 25.

297 Paul Henderson, 'Gary Goes to War', Kerrang! No. 225, February 11, 1989, pp. 28-31.

298 Chris Welch, 'Rocking Back to Happiness', Metal Hammer Vol. 3, No. 22, November 7, 1988, pp. 21-23.

299 Neville Marten, 'Catch Him If You Can!', Guitarist, March 1989 pp. 33-40.

300 Paul Henderson, 'Gary Goes to War', Kerrang! No. 225, February 11, 1989, pp. 28-31.

301 Music & Media, October 28, 1989, p. 24; RAW No. 30, October 18-31, 1989, p41

302 Neville Marten, 'Catch Him If You Can!', Guitarist, March 1989 pp. 33-40.

303 Malcolm Dome, 'Room at the Top', Kerrang! No. 73, 1984, pp. 34-37.

304 Paul Henderson, 'Gary Goes to War', Kerrang! No. 225, February 11, 1989, pp. 28-31. In fact, Lenny Wolf of Kingdom Come didn't see the humour in the song. In a Metal Hammer interview, he said: 'Gary seems to be so unhappy with his sales figures, that he's trying out the whole Zep routine himself. Maybe they influence him as well, and he's never admitted it... Do you know that Gary sold about a seventh of the amount of records we sold in the States? Just to put things straight.' See Metal Hammer Vol. 5, No. 5, March 20, 1989, p. 105.

305 Valerie Potter, 'Soldier of Fortune', Metal Hammer, Vol. 2, No. 2, February 6, 1989, pp. 10-13.

306 Neville Marten, 'Catch Him If You Can!', Guitarist, March 1989 pp. 33-40.

307 Mark Putterford, 'Back on the War Path', RAW No. 10, January 11-24, 1989, pp. 34-6.

308 Music & Media, March 25, 1989, p. 30.

309 Valerie Potter, Review of 'Ready For Love', Metal Hammer, Vol. 5 No. 4, March 6, 1989, p. 59.

310 RAW No. 14, March 7-20, 1989, p. 27.

311 Mark Putterford, 'Back on the War Path', RAW No. 10, January 11-24, 1989, pp. 34-6.

312 Paul Henderson, 'Gary Goes to War', Kerrang! No. 225, February 11, 1989, pp. 28-31.

313 Valerie Potter, Review of After the War, Metal Hammer, Vol. 2, No. 2, February 6, 1989, p. 65.

314 Review of After the War, Billboard, April 15, 1989, p. 78.

315 Review of After the War, Cash Box, March 11, 1989, p. 25.

316 Review of After the War, CMJ New Music Report, March 10, 1989, p. 34.

317 Review of After the War, Gavin Report, March 3, 1989, p. 64.

318 Lyn Guy, 'Gary Moore Hammersmith Odeon, London', Kerrang!, June 3, 1989.

NOTES TO CHAPTER FIVE

319 Neville Marten, 'Catch Him If You Can!', Guitarist, March 1989, pp. 33-40.

320 Mark Putterford, 'Back on the War Path', RAW No. 10, January 11-24, 1989, pp. 34-6.

321 Valerie Potter, 'Soldier of Fortune', Metal Hammer, Vol. 2, No. 2, February 6, 1989, pp. 10-13.

322 Mark Putterford, 'Back on the War Path', RAW No. 10, January 11-24, 1989, pp. 34-6.

323 Mick Wall, 'Jumping At Shadows', Classic Rock, Issue 202, October, 2014, pp. 56-60.

324 Martin Popoff, The Sun Goes Down: Thin Lizzy's Final Years (Bedford: Wymer, 2012), p. 158.

325 Martin Townsend, Vox, 'The Man Who Would Be King', April 1, 1992, p. 64.

326 BBC Masters of Rock: Gary Moore. Narrated by Bruce Dickinson. Broadcast February 10, 2011 on BBC 6.

327 Mick Wall, 'Jumping At Shadows', Classic Rock, Issue 202, October, 2014, pp. 56-60.

328 Andy Bradshaw, 'From Blues to Infinity', Metal Hammer Vol. 5, No. 7 March 26-April 8, 1990, pp. 16-19.

329 Martin Townsend, Vox, 'The Man Who Would Be King', April 1, 1992, p. 64.

330 Mat Snow, 'Gary Moore: No Sweat', Q, April 1992, pp. 36-41.

331 Andy Bradshaw, 'From Blues to Infinity', Metal Hammer Vol. 5, No. 7 March 26-April 8, 1990, pp. 16-19.

332 'Moore Coming On', Hitmakers, June 29. 1990, p. 7; Music & Media, March 24, 1990, p. 16; David Sinclair, 'From beer-sodden standards to sedate cocktail sounds', The Times, March 30, 1990.

333 Jackie Bodner, Network 40, September 14, 1990, p. 48; Michael Ellis, Hot 100 Singles Spotlight, Billboard, February 16, 1991, p. 76.

334 Martin Popoff, The Sun Goes Down: Thin Lizzy's Final Years (Bedford: Wymer, 2012), p. 159.

335 Harry Shapiro, 'How Gary Moore reignited the British blues scene with the help of a famous guitar', Classic Rock, August 12, 2014. Available online at: https://www.loudersound.com/features/gary-moore-the-story-of-still-got-the-blues

336 Andy Bradshaw, 'From Blues to Infinity', Metal Hammer Vol. 5, No. 7 March 26-April 8, 1990, pp. 16-19.

337 Robin Denselow, 'Sex drugs and rock 'n' roll', The Guardian, March 22, 1990.

338 Paul Sexton, 'No more time for the blues', The Times, June 20, 1997, p. 35

339 Andy Bradshaw, 'From Blues To Infinity', Metal Hammer Vol. 5, No. 7 March 26-April 8, 1990, pp. 16-19.

340 Review of Still Got The Blues Billboard, June 30, 1990, p. 78; & Billboard, July 14, 1990, p. 63.

341 Review of Still Got The Blues. Cash Box. July 28, 1990, p. 28.

342 Review of Still Got The Blues. CMJ New Music Report, June 8, 1990, p. 43.

343 Review of Still Got The Blues. Music & Media, April 21, 1990. p. 21.

344 Review of Still Got The Blues. RPM, June 16,1990, p. 8.

345 Robin Denselow, 'Sex drugs and rock 'n' roll', The Guardian, March 22, 1990.

346 Jerry Ewing, Review of Still Got The Blues, Metal Forces No. 51, June 1990, p. 27.

347 Andy Bradshaw, Review of Still Got The Blues, Metal Hammer Vol. 5, No. 7 March 26-April 8, 1990, p. 35.

348 Andy Gill, 'Wallowing in the puddles', The Independent, March 30, 1990.

349 Mark Putterford, 'Come The Tour...' Metal Forces No. 70, March 1992, pp. 42-43.

350 Advert for Still Got The Blues, Billboard, August, 1990.

351 Joseph Gallivan, 'The Critic's Choice', The Independent, August 12, 1990; Martin Townsend, Vox , 'The Man Who Would Be King', April 1, 1992, p. 64.

352 'Merrier no Moore! Gary's got the blues!', Kerrang!, February 24, 1990; Bob Daisley, Kerrang! No. 253, August 26, 1989, p. 11.

353 W. C. Handy, Father of the Blues: An Autobiography (New York: Macmillan, 1941) pp. 74-75.

354 Bill Wyman and Ray Coleman, Stone Alone (London: Penguin, 1991 [1990]), p. 341.

355 Jones, LeRoi [Amiri Baraka]. Black Music (New York: William Morrow, 1967), pp. 205-6.

356 Keith Richards & James Fox, Life (London: Orion, 2012), p. 122.

357 Keith Richards & James Fox, Life (London: Orion, 2012), p. 105.

358 Paul Oliver, 'The future of the blues: Looking back at looking forward,' in Blues Off The Record: Thirty Years of Blues Commentary (Tunbridge Wells, UK: Baton Press, 1984), pp. 285–289.

359 Paul Tingen, 'Green', Musician, October 1, 1997, p. 28.

360 Mick Wall, 'Gary Moore', Classic Rock, Issue 287, May, 2021, pp. 52-61.

361 Philip Key, 'Gary Moore tells Philip Key that, even for a legend, practice still makes perfect', Daily Post (North Wales), April 20, 2007.

362 Jim O'Neal, 'I Once Was Lost, But Now I'm Found: The Blues Revival of the 1960s', from Nothing but the Blues: the music and the musicians, edited by Lawrence Cohn (NY: Abbeville Press, 1993), pp. 347-387. At p.378.

363 David Sinclair, 'Three-chord wonders from the primal ooze', The Times, December 24, 1990.

364 Andy Coleman, 'Blues double bill marks swan song: B B King & Gary Moore', Birmingham Evening Mail, March 24, 2006.

365 Clarence Page, 'How white fans saved B. B. King's blues', Chicago Tribune May 15, 2015. Available online at: https://www.chicagotribune.com/columns/clarence-page/ct-bb-king-blues-page-perspec-0504-20150515-column.html

366 Robbert Tilli, 'Gary Moore', Music & Media, March 21, 1992, p. 15.

367 Ian Markham-Smith, 'Moore Joins BB On Tour', The Mirror (Eire edition), October 31, 2005, p. 4.

368 John Fordham, 'BB King Hallam FM Arena, Sheffield 4/5', Guardian, March 31, 2006.

369 'Unrivalled bluesman is true great', Birmingham Evening Mail, April 3, 2006; Chris Field, 'Blues King improves with age; BB King and Gary Moore NEC Arena', Birmingham Post, April 4, 2006.

370 David Flaherty, Review of Power of the Blues, Sunday Herald Sun (Australia), July 25, 2004.

371 The Encyclopedia of the Blues says of Collins: 'He was not confident about his vocal talents — he certainly was not a great singer but his acrid voice is not unpleasant.' Gérard Herzhaft, Encyclopedia of the Blues. 2nd edition (University of Arkansas Press, 1992), p. 42.

372 Harry Shapiro, 'How Gary Moore reignited the British blues scene with the help of a famous guitar', Classic Rock, August 12, 2014. Available online at: https://www.loudersound.com/features/gary-moore-the-story-of-still-got-the-blues

373 Bill Greensmith, Mark Camarigg & Mike Rowe (eds.), Blues Unlimited: Essential Interviews from the Original Blues Magazine (University of Illinois Press, 2015), pp. 345-358.

374 Lol Henderson & Lee Stacey (eds.), Encyclopedia of Music in the 20th Century (London & NY: Routledge, 2014), p. 343.

375 Andy Bradshaw, 'From Blues to Infinity', Metal Hammer Vol. 5, No. 7 March 26-April 8, 1990, pp. 16-19.

376 Andy Bradshaw, 'From Blues To Infinity', Metal Hammer Vol. 5, No. 7 March 26-April 8, 1990, pp. 16-19.

377 David Mead, 'Classic interview (1995): Gary Moore', Guitarist, December 23, 2019. Available online at: https://www.musicradar.com/news/classic-interview-gary-moore-talks-blues-for-greeny-jack-bruce-bb-king-albert-collins-and-never-playing-with-clapton

378 Martin Popoff, From Dublin To Jailbreak: Thin Lizzy's 1969-76 (Bedford: Wymer, 2011), p. 6.

379 Moore was also perhaps influenced by the Allman Brothers Band who included many of the aforementioned classic blues songs in their live shows. In 1971, while Moore was in Skid Row, the band toured with the Allman Brothers and likely heard a number of these covers. When Moore quit Skid Row to form his own band, he said he wanted it to be a dual guitar band like the Allman Brothers Band. Yet Moore has never mentioned the Allman Brothers as an influence, nor is Duane Allman and Dickey Betts' particular style of playing reflected in Moore's body of work. See Mat Snow, 'Gary Moore: No Sweat', Q, April 1992, pp. 36-41.

380 Martin Popoff, From Dublin To Jailbreak: Thin Lizzy's 1969-76 (Bedford: Wymer, 2011), pp. 5-6.

381 Paul Sexton, 'No more time for the blues', The Times, June 20, 1997.

382 Philip Key, 'Gary Moore tells Philip Key that, even for a legend, practice still makes perfect', Daily Post (North Wales), April 20, 2007.

383 'Entertainment-WENN - Last Take 2', Broadcast News, June 30, 1995.

384 Don Muret, 'Fleetwood Mac Founder Returns to Music Scene', Amusement Business, Vol. 110, Iss. 33, August 17, 1998, p. 6.

385 WENN: Broadcast News, April 21, 1995.

386 Moore also contributed to a live performance of the song when he made a guest appearance with Lynott's all-star punk band The Greedy Bastards (aka 'The Greedies') at the Electric Ballroom in Camden on July 29, 1978. See Martin Popoff, Thin Lizzy: A Visual Biography (Bedford: Wymer, 2020), p. 91.

387 Interview with Gary Moore in 1994. Available on the Ballads & Blues 2011 re-release.

388 Dave Johnson, Review of Blues For Greeny, Hard Report, March 29, 1996, p. 47.

389 Jim Farber, Review of Blues For Greeny, Daily News, April 14, 1996, p. 35.

390 Lyall Johnson, Review of Blues For Greeny, Sunday Herald Sun, July 23, 1995.

391 Neil Slaven, 'Review of Blues For Greeny', Vox, Jul 1, 1995, p. 92

392 David Sly, 'Review of Blues For Greeny', Advertiser, October 5, 1995; Norman Provencher, Review of Blues For Greeny, Ottawa Citizen, July 8, 1995.

393 David Mead, 'Classic interview (1995): Gary Moore', Guitarist, December 23, 2019. Available online at: https://www.musicradar.com/news/classic-interview-gary-moore-talks-blues-for-greeny-jack-bruce-bb-king-albert-collins-and-never-playing-with-clapton

394 Charles Shaar Murray, 'Cryin' the Blues', Observer Music Monthly, 16 November 2003.

395 From the Buddy Guy album, Slippin' In (Silvertone, 1994).

396 Mike McClellan, 'Bland cliches fail to hook new fans', Sunday Herald Sun (Melbourne), April 26, 1992.

397 Shane Sutton, 'The metamorphosis continues', The Advertiser, September 2, 1993.

398 Tony Green, 'Lucky Streak', St. Petersburg Times (Florida), June 3, 1994.

399 Norman Provencher, Review of Blues For Greeny, Ottawa Citizen, July 8, 1995.

400 David Sinclair, The Times, August 10, 1990, p.17

401 David Sinclair, 'From beer-sodden standards to sedate cocktail sounds', The Times, March 30, 1990.

402 Nick Hasted, 'End of an era as the King of blues kicks off his final UK tour: B B King Halam Arena, Sheffield', The Independent, March 30, 2006.

403 P. Speelman, 'A Deft Hand At The Blues , Sunday Herald, May 20, 1990.

404 Richard Dooley, Review of Close As You Get, Halifax Daily News (Nov Scotia), June 7, 2007.

405 Max Bell, Review of Blues Alive, Vox, June 1, 1993, p. 91.

406 David Mead, 'Classic interview (1995): Gary Moore', Guitarist, December 23, 2019. Available online at: https://www.musicradar.com/news/classic-interview-gary-moore-talks-blues-for-greeny-jack-bruce-bb-king-albert-collins-and-never-playing-with-clapton

407 Alan Paul, 'Interview with Albert King', Guitar World, July 1991.

408 'Moore & Collins: Together Again', World Music, August 30, 1991, p. 33.

409 Review of Collins Mix, Vox, January 1, 1994, p. 61. See also Neil Slaven's review of the album. Slaven also makes the point that King's playing overshadowed all the guest musicians, apart from Moore. Vox, December 1, 1993, p. 10

410 Matthew Magee, 'Different Shades of Blue', Sunday Tribune (Ireland), May 11, 2003.

411 Ulrich Adelt, Blues Music in the Sixties A Story in Black and White (Rutgers University Press, 2010), pp. 135-36.

412 J. D. Considine,'Eric Clapton Is Not GOD And He Knows It', Musician 97, Nov 1, 1986, pp. 86-99.

413 Robert Sandall, 'Fast forward , Sunday Times, July 5, 1992.

414 Neil Slaven, Vox, December 1, 1994, p. 126.

415 Tony Clayton-Lea, 'Gary Moore Olympia Theatre, Dublin', Irish Times, Sept 12, 2011, p. 16. Clayton-Lea wasn't a total fan of Moore's work: he called the guitarist a gracious, earnest and honourable man who provided 'silver-winged approximations' of Clapton, Green and Mick Taylor, but despite 'great moments' he thought the end result was a 'pastiche with knobs on'.

416 Robert Sandall, 'Fast forward', Sunday Times, July 26, 1992.

417 Roger Trapp, 'Rebirth of the blues', The Independent, November 29, 1992.

418 Robbert Tilli, 'Sympathy For The Blues Is Still Alive', Music & Media, July 3, 1993, pp. 13-16.

419 Robbert Tilli, 'Sympathy For The Blues Is Still Alive', Music & Media, July 3, 1993, pp. 13-16.

420 Gérard Herzhaft, Encyclopedia of the Blues. 2nd edition (University of Arkansas Press, 1997), p. 108.

421 Mark Putterford, 'Come The Tour...' Metal Forces No. 70, March 1992, pp. 42-43.

422 BBC Masters of Rock: Gary Moore. Narrated by Bruce Dickinson. Broadcast February 10, 2011 on BBC 6.

423 Michael Heatley, Review of Peter Green: The Biography by Martin Celmins, Vox, September 1, 1995, p. 110.

424 Norman Provencher, 'Jimmy Rogers unique among bluesmen', The Ottawa Citizen, March 23, 1995; Colin Harper, 'Jimmy Rogers, Belfast', The Independent, March 16, 1996.

425 Sian Llewellyn, 'I jumped on the Blues bandwagon? I was the bandwagon!', Louder, March 23, 2007. Available online at: https://www.loudersound.com/features/gary-moore-i-jumped-on-the-blues-bandwagon-i-was-the-bandwagon

426 Martin Popoff, From Dublin To Jailbreak: Thin Lizzy's 1969-76 (Bedford: Wymer, 2011), p. 6.

427 Robert Johnson, The Complete Recordings (Columbia, 1990), sleeve notes by Eric Clapton, p. 22.

428 Eric Clapton, Clapton: The Autobiography (New York: Broadway, 2007), p. 40.

429 Pete Welding, "Hell Hound on his Trail: Robert Johnson", Downbeat Music '66 (Chicago: Maher, 1966.), pp. 73-74, 76, 103. At p. 76.

430 'In Touch With The Blues: Back From the Crossroads', Vox, May 1, 1993, p. 78.

431 Keith Richards & James Fox, Life (London: Orion, 2012), p. 163.

432 John Scanlon, Easy Riders, Rolling Stones: In the Road in America from Delta Blues to '70s Rock (London: Reaktion, 2015), p. 30.

433 Craig Werner, A Change is Gonna Come: Music, Race and the Soul of America (Edinburgh: Canobgate, 2002), p. 65.

434 'It's a Long Way to the Top (If You Wanna Rock 'N' Roll)', Young, Young & Scott, performed by AC/DC on their album T.N.T. (Albert Productions, 1975).

435 Moore said of Still Got The Blues that it was blues 'very much being played in a rock style which is probably why it was so accessible to all those people, let's face it, it was almost like a pop-blues album.' See Matthew Magee, 'Different Shades of Blue', Sunday Tribune (Ireland), May 11, 2003. In contrast, Moore said Blues For Greeny was 'much more a pure blues record... There's a lot less of the more aggressive, busy sort of playing on the record. It's a more straightforward, clean sound'. See David Mead, 'Classic interview (1995): Gary Moore', Guitarist, December 23, 2019. Available online at: https://www.musicradar.com/news/classic-interview-gary-moore-talks-blues-for-greeny-jack-bruce-bb-king-albert-collins-and-never-playing-with-clapton

NOTES TO CHAPTER SIX

436 Tony Bacon, Interview with Gary Moore. Music UK, No. 13, January 1983, pp. 18-22.

437 Chris Welch, 'Gary Glitters', Kerrang! No. 21, July 29-August 11, 1982, pp. 26-27.

438 Mick Wall, 'Jumping At Shadows', Classic Rock, Issue 202, October, 2014, pp. 56-60.

439 Steven Rosen, 'Gary Moore: Guitar on a Rampage', Guitar World, November 1984.

440 Dave Shack, 'After the Moore', Metal Forces, March 1989, pp. 32 & 41.

441 Jon Lewin, 'Moore's Code', Making Music, Issue 12, March 1987, pp. 24-25.

442 Paul Colvert, Interview with Jeff Beck and Gary Moore, Vox 33, June 1, 1993, pp. 36-38

443 Mark Putterford, 'Back on the War Path', RAW No. 10, January 11-24, 1989, pp. 34-6.

444 Mark Putterford, 'Back on the War Path', RAW No. 10, January 11-24, 1989, pp. 34-6.

445 Valerie Potter, 'Soldier of Fortune', Metal Hammer, Vol. 2, No. 2, February 6, 1989, pp. 10-13.

446 Paul Henderson, 'Gary Goes to War', Kerrang! No. 225, February 11, 1989, pp. 28-31.

447 Dave Shack, 'After the Moore', Metal Forces, March 1989, pp. 32 & 41.

448 Steven Rosen, 'Gary Moore: Guitar on a Rampage', Guitar World, November 1984.

449 Steven Rosen, 'Gary Moore: Guitar on a Rampage', Guitar World, November 1984. Some of the most successful live album releases are rumoured to have substantial studio overdubs. These include Kiss's Alive, Thin Lizzy's Live and Dangerous, Paul McCartney's Wings Over America, Queen's Live Killers, Peter Frampton's Frampton Comes Alive!, and Judas Priest's Unleashed in the East, which some fans refer to jokingly as Unleashed in the Studio.

450 Gary Moore: Live At Monsters Of Rock (Sanctuary Visual Entertainment, 2003). Moore's remarks about Blues Alive are on the interview bonus material on this DVD.

451 Dave Roberts, Review of Rockin' Every Night – Live in Japan, Sounds, July 2, 1983, p. 29.

452 Neil Jeffries, Review of Rockin' Every Night – Live in Japan, Kerrang! No.45, July 1-13, 1983, pp. 14-15.

453 Mark Putterford, Review of Rockin' Every Night, Kerrang! No. 124, July 10-23, 1986, p. 14.

454 Malcolm Dome, Kerrang! No. 71, June 28-July 11, 1984, p. 40.

455 Malcolm Dome, 'Room at the Top', Kerrang! No. 73, 1984, pp. 34-37.

456 Mick Wall, Derek Oliver, et al, 'Fields of Fire', Kerrang! No. 76, September 6-19, 1984, pp. 41-45.

457 'The Metal Decade', Metal Hammer Vol. 4, No. 24, December 11-26, 1989, p. 64.

458 Derek Oliver, 'Sounding Off!', Kerrang! No. 77 September 20-October 3, 1984, pp. 42-43

459 Steven Rosen, 'Gary Moore: Guitar on a Rampage', Guitar World, November 1984.

460 P. J. O'Rourke, 'The Piece of Ireland that Passeth all Understanding', Holidays in Hell (London: Picador, 1989), pp. 276-288.

461 Paul O'Mahony, Kerrang! No 86, January 24-February 6, 1985, pp. 41 & 43.

462 Andy Bradshaw, 'From Blues To Infinity', Metal Hammer Vol. 5, No. 7 March 26-April 8, 1990, pp. 16-19.

463 Or 10 out of 12 tracks if considering the CD release, which also featured 'That Kind of Woman', 'All Your Love' and 'Stop Messin' Around', with the latter two appearing on An Evening Of The Blues.

464 Harry Shapiro, 'How Gary Moore reignited the British blues scene with the help of a famous guitar', Classic Rock, August 12, 2014. Available online at: https://www.loudersound.com/features/gary-moore-the-story-of-still-got-the-blues

465 Martin Townsend, Vox, 'The Man Who Would Be King', April 1, 1992, p. 64.

466 Andy Bradshaw, Review of Gary Moore at the Hammersmith Odeon, Metal Hammer Vol. 5, No. 12, June 4-17, 1990, p. 88.

467 Melinda Newman, Review of An Evening of the Blues, Billboard, February 2, 1991, p. 59.

468 Review of An Evening of the Blues, Sounds, March 30, 1991, p. 32.

469 These tracks are: 'The Stumble', 'All Your Love', 'You Don't Love Me', 'Cold Cold Feeling' (featuring Albert Collins), 'Farther Up the Road' (featuring Albert Collins), 'Stop Messin' Around', 'The Blues is Alright' (with Albert Collins), and 'The Messiah Will Come Again'.

470 Harry Shapiro, 'How Gary Moore reignited the British blues scene with the help of a famous guitar', Classic Rock, August 12, 2014. Available online at: https://www.loudersound.com/features/gary-moore-the-story-of-still-got-the-blues

471 Andy Gill, 'Wallowing in the puddles', The Independent, March 30, 1990; Lynden Barber, Review of After Hours, Sydney Morning Herald (Australia), April 28, 1992.

472 Review of After Hours, Billboard, March 21, 1992, p. 115.

473 Review of After Hours, Hit Parader 334, July 1992, p. 95.

474 Max Bell, Review of Blues Alive, Vox, June 1, 1993, p. 91.

475 Troy J. Agusto, Review of Blues Alive, Cash Box, July 24, 1992.

476 Review of Blues Alive, Music & Media, June 12, 1993, p.11.

477 Nick Krewen, Review of Blues Alive, Hamilton Spectator (Ontario, Canada), July 22, 1993.

478 Tony Green, Review of Blues Alive, St. Petersburg Times, July 23, 1993.

479 Shane Sutton, Review of Blues Alive, The Advertiser, September 2, 1993.

480 Later that year, Moore played seven Peter Green tracks during his performance at the Montreux festival. This performance was recorded and released over a decade later as part of the Gary Moore Essential Montreux 5-CD boxset (Eagle Records, 2009). An edited visual record was released as Gary Moore: The Definitive Montreux Collection (Eagle Vision, 2-DVD, 2007).

481 Sylvie Simmons, 'Gary Moore on Peter Green', Rolling Stone, 1995.

482 Harry Shapiro, 'Peter Green: The End of The Game', Record Collector, August 1993.

483 Cliff Jones, 'I'm Peter Green', Mojo, September 1996.

484 Harry Shapiro, 'The Impossible Dream', Classic Rock 243, December 2017 pp. 44-46.

485 BBC Masters of Rock: Gary Moore. Narrated by Bruce Dickinson. Broadcast February 10, 2011 on BBC 6; Chris Morris, 'As The Cream Turns: Bruce, Baker Reunite; Gary Moore Is 3rd Member Of New Virgin Trio BBM', Billboard, July 2, 1994.

486 Review of Around the Next Dream, Billboard, August 27, 1994, p. 102; Andy Robson, review of Around the Next Dream, Vox, August 1, 1994, p. 94; Charles Shaar Murray, review of Around the Next Dream, Guitar World, 1994; Bill Bengle, review of Around the Next Dream, In-Tune (South Jersey, USA), September 1994, p. 18; and Steve Baltin, review of Around the Next Dream, Cash Box, August 20, 1994, p. 9.

487 Matthew Magee, 'Different Shades of Blue', Sunday Tribune (Ireland), May 11, 2003.

488 Gordon Barr, 'Moore to Give', Evening Chronicle (Newcastle), October 26, 1999.

489 Mick Meikleham, review of A Different Beat, Uncut 31, December 1, 1999, p. 94.

490 BBC Masters of Rock: Gary Moore. Narrated by Bruce Dickinson. Broadcast February 10, 2011 on BBC 6.

491 Paul Sexton, 'Moore gets more rhythm', Music & Media, June 21, 1997, p. 16.

492 Paul Sexton, 'No more time for the blues', The Times, June 20, 1997, p. 35; Paul Sexton, 'Moore gets more rhythm', Music & Media, June 21, 1997, p. 16.

493 Steve McCarty, 'Moore of the modern side', South China Morning Post (Hong Kong), August 22, 1997.

494 Steve McCarty, 'Moore of the modern side', South China Morning Post (Hong Kong), August 22, 1997.

495 'Getting a lot Moore of Gary', Gloucester Citizen, November 15, 2002.

496 Tim Brannigan, 'Some Moore, Please!', Irish News, September 28, 2002.

497 Alan Poole, Review of Scars, Coventry Evening Telegraph, September 27, 2002.

498 Review of Scars, Southland Times (New Zealand), September 7, 2002.

499 Keith Clark, 'We Want Three Moore', Bristol Post, November 21, 2002.

500 Moore also used the Hendrix chord on the track 'Walking By Myself' from Still Got The Blues.

501 Alan Poole, Review of Monsters of Rock, Coventry Evening Telegraph, September 5, 2003.

502 'Moore's Almanac', Belfast Telegraph, May 24, 2007.

NOTES TO IN MEMORIAM

503 Harry Doherty, Review of Back On The Streets, Melody Maker, December 16, 1978.

504 Nick Bowcott, Circus 315, May 31, 1986, p. 71.

505 Review of Still Got The Blues, CMJ New Music Report, June 8, 1990, p. 43.

506 Harry Shapiro, 'Feel the Force', Classic Rock 305, September 2022, pp. 56-61.

507 Glenn Hughes, Rock Candy Magazine no. 17, Dec 2019-Jan 2020.

508 Kerrang!, No. 30, December 2-15, 1982, p. 37.

509 Malcolm Dome/Jon Hiseman, CD booklet notes, Strange New Flesh, remastered, 2-CD edition, Esoteric Recordings, 2012.

510 Quoted in Martin Popoff, The Sun Goes Down: Thin Lizzy's Final Years (Bedford: Wymer, 2012), p. 2.

511 Quoted in Martin Popoff, The Sun Goes Down: Thin Lizzy's Final Years (Bedford: Wymer, 2012), p. 71.

512 Jon Sutherland, 'A Fan's Tribute To Phil Lynott', Cash Box, January 25, 1986, p. 34.

513 New Sunday Times (Malaysia), April 27, 1986, p. 10.

514 Quoted in Martin Popoff, The Sun Goes Down: Thin Lizzy's Final Years (Bedford: Wymer, 2012), p. 74.

515 Ozzy Osbourne, quoted in Mick Wall, 'Jumping At Shadows', Classic Rock, Issue 202, October, 2014, pp. 56-60.

516 Colin Harper, Review of Back to the Blues, Irish Times, February 23, 2001.

517 Greg Lake, quoted in Peter Bishop, 'Greg Lake Goes Solo: 3 Concerts On Tap, Pittsburgh Press, November 19, 1981, p. D7.

518 Harry Shapiro, 'How Gary Moore reignited the British blues scene with the help of a famous guitar', Classic Rock, August 12, 2014. Available online at: https://www.loudersound.com/features/gary-moore-the-story-of-still-got-the-blues

519 Paddy Moloney, The Late Late Show, RTE, 1987.

520 Review of Back to the Blues, Irish Times, February 23, 2001.

521 Kerrang! No. 253, August 26, 1989, p. 11.

522 Quoted in Scott Howlett, 'Gary Moore the fastest and the best', Sydney Morning Herald, October 6, 1985, p. 116.

523 Quoted in Scott Howlett, 'Gary Moore the fastest and the best', Sydney Morning Herald, October 6, 1985, p. 116.

524 Quoted in Scott Howlett, 'Gary Moore the fastest and the best', Sydney Morning Herald, October 6, 1985, p. 116.

525 'Metallica's Kirk Hammett remembers one of his top guitar heroes', Rolling Stone 1125, March 3, 2011, p. 24.

526 'Thin Lizzy's Vivian Campbell Pays Homage to the Late Gary Moore'. AOL Music, April 6, 2011.

527 Obituary, The Daily Telegraph, February 8, 2011.

528 Pierre Perrone, Obituary, The Independent, February 8, 2011.

529 Anna Roberts, 'Friends pay tribute to Thin Lizzy's Gary Moore', The Argus, February 8, 2011.

530 Dave Simpson, 'Gary Moore: the guitarist as gunslinger', The Guardian, February 7, 2011.

531 Obituary, Sunday Times, February 13, 2011.

532 Obituary, The Guardian, February 8, 2011.

533 Bryan Alexander and Shirley Halperin, 'Musicians Pay Tribute to Thin Lizzy Guitarist' Hollywood Reporter, February 6, 2011.

534 Ronan McGreevy, 'Former Thin Lizzy guitarist Gary Moore (58) dies in Spain', Irish Times, February 11, 2011.

535 'Legendary guitarist Gary Moore laid to rest in moving ceremony', Irish Independent, February 24, 2011.

536 Padraic Coffey, 'Gary Moore', Sunday Independent (Ireland), February 13, 2011.

Gary Moore: A Selected Discography

Back On The Streets 1978

G-Force 1980

Corridors Of Power 1982

Rockin' Every Night -
Live In Japan 1983

Live 1983

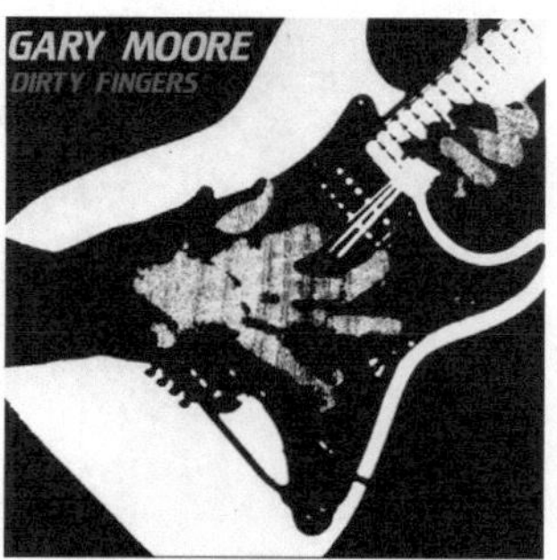

Dirty Fingers 1984

Victims Of The Future 1984

We Want Moore! 1984

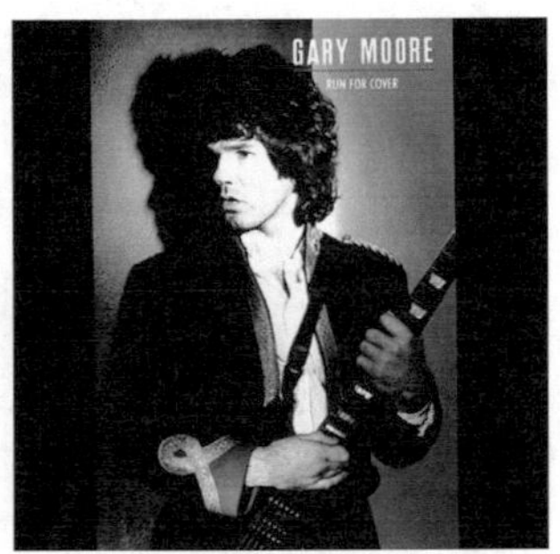

Run For Cover 1985

Wild Frontier 1987

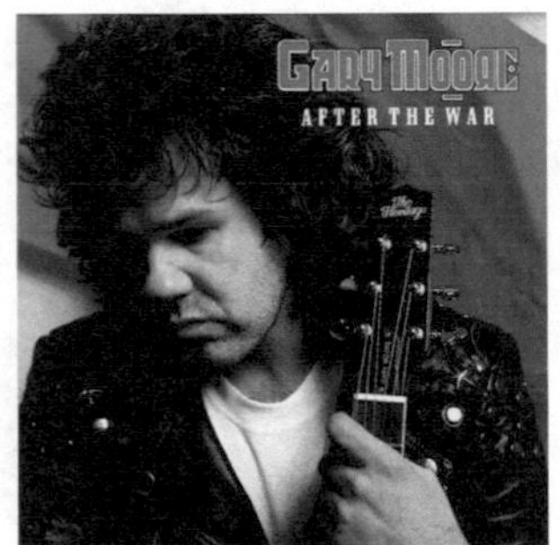

After The War 1988

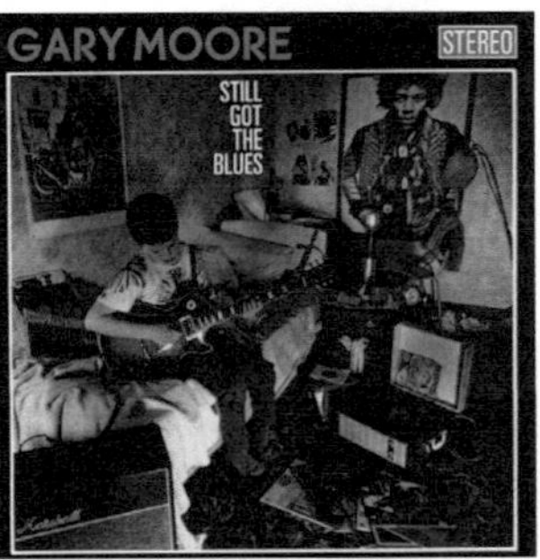

Still Got The Blues 1990

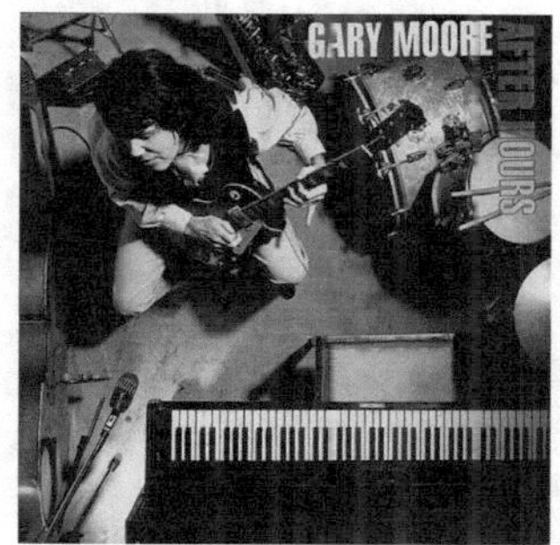

After Hours 1992

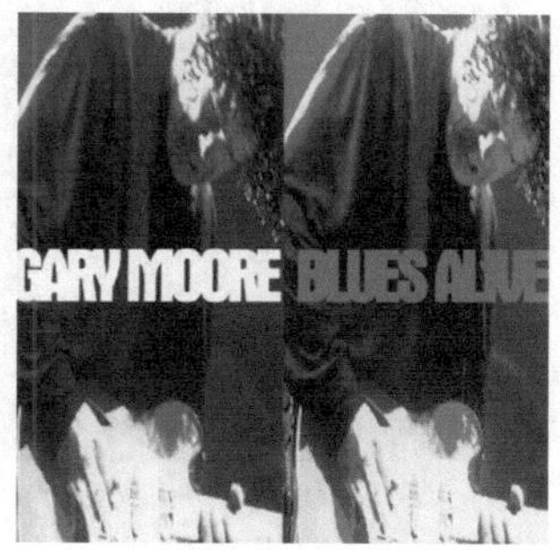

Blues Alive 1993

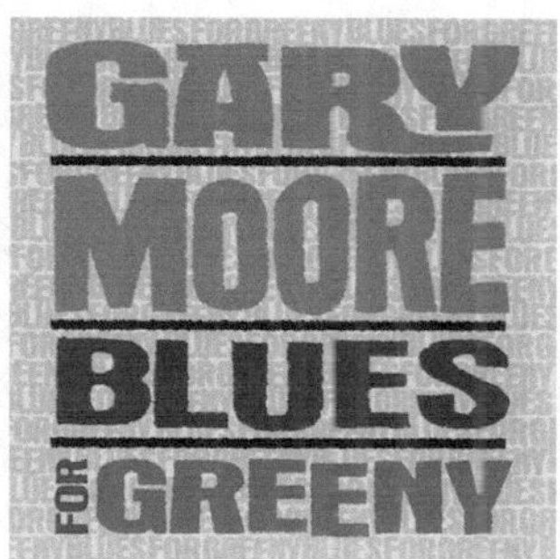

Blues For Greeny 1995

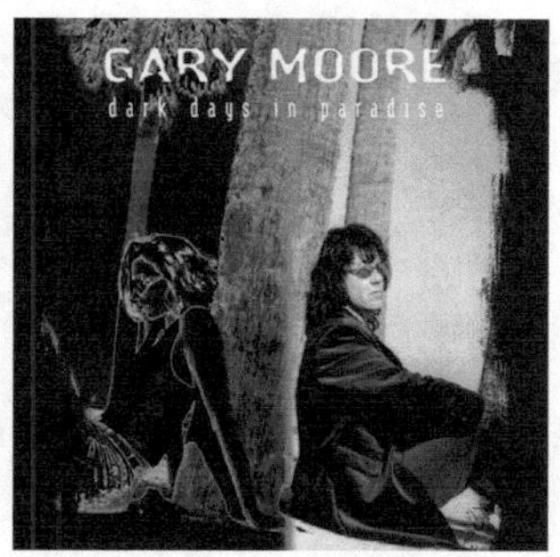

Dark Days In Paradise 1997

A Different Beat 1999

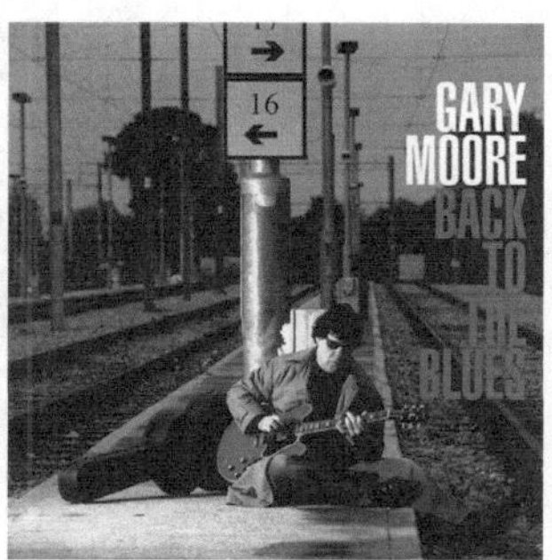

Back To The Blues 2001

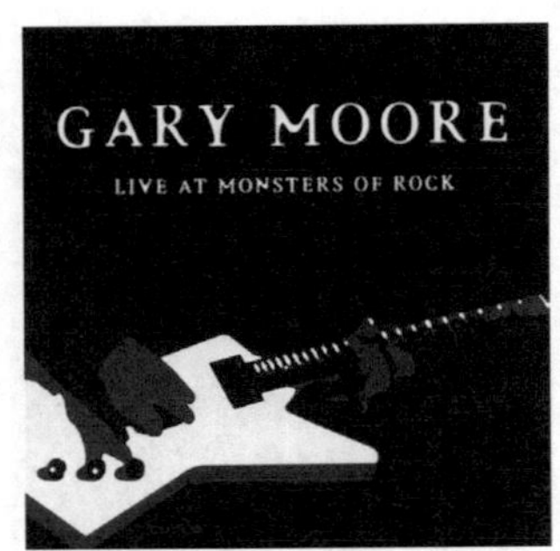

Live At Monsters Of Rock 2003

Power Of The Blues 2004

Old New Ballads Blues 2006

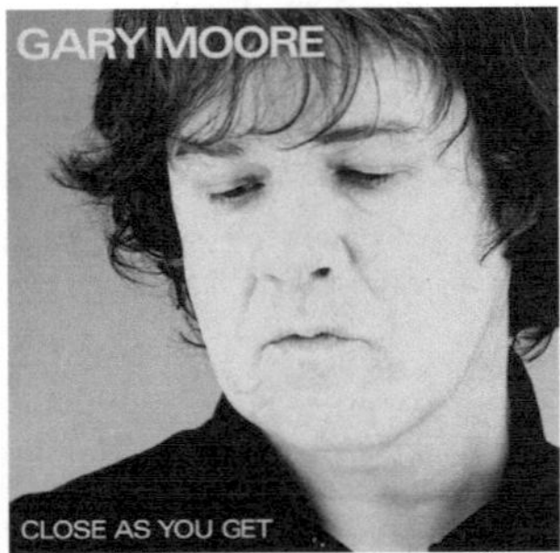

Close As You Get 2007

Bad For You Baby 2008